Your Finances
GOD'S WAY

Scott LaPierre

HARVEST HOUSE PUBLISHERS
EUGENE, OREGON

Cover design by Kyler Dougherty

Cover photo © AndreyPopov / Getty Images

Interior design by KUHN Design Group

Italics in quoted Scripture indicate emphasis by the author.

Published in association with The Blythe Daniel Agency, Inc., P.O. Box 64197, Colorado Springs, CO 80962-4197, www.theblythedanielagency.com.

For bulk, special sales, or ministry purchases, please call 1-800-547-8979. Email: Customerservice@hhpbooks.com

Ⓜ is a federally registered trademark of the Hawkins Children's LLC. Harvest House Publishers, Inc., is the exclusive licensee of the trademark.

Your Finances God's Way
Copyright © 2022 by Scott LaPierre
Published by Harvest House Publishers
Eugene, Oregon 97408
www.harvesthousepublishers.com

ISBN 978-0-7369-8400-3 (pbk)
ISBN 978-0-7369-8401-0 (eBook)

Library of Congress Control Number: 2021949967

Printed in the United States of America

22 23 24 25 26 27 28 29 30 / BP / 10 9 8 7 6 5 4 3 2 1

Your Finances God's Way is dedicated to my children.
I pray this book and accompanying workbook will help
you to steward your finances in ways that please God.

Contents

One of Our Most Important Stewardships

was driving home feeling terribly discouraged. I don't think it would be too much to say this was one of the lowest points of my life. I had to tell my wife, Katie, who was pregnant with our first child, that I had just been laid off. With the loss of my job as an elementary schoolteacher also came the loss of our medical insurance.

You see, about two years earlier, I learned of a teaching position available on a local naval base that would give me credit for my military service. This resulted in a considerable raise, but the one drawback was that I lost my secure, tenured position at the district where I taught. The Great Recession hit, and schools began cutting new teachers. So even though I'd been teaching almost ten years, I was included in the terminations. I knew it was going to be difficult to find a position anywhere because every district was facing the same financial crunch.

You might be thinking, *So, a book about finances God's way. Did you just think that God would somehow provide you a job?* Actually, I did! Years earlier, I became a Christian in my early twenties during my first year of teaching elementary school. Soon after, my passion for ministry increased. So you can probably imagine my excitement when a local church, Grace Baptist in Lemoore, California, was looking for a part-time youth pastor. I applied, they hired me, and my elementary school schedule—which granted me summers and holidays off—worked wonderfully with my church position.

After losing the teaching position on the naval base, I was still a part-time youth pastor, but the pay wasn't enough to support my family. I told my senior pastor I would have to look for a teaching position elsewhere, and more than likely, that would mean no longer serving as their youth pastor. Grace Baptist's leadership team stepped out in faith and brought me on full-time. I knew this was a huge financial strain on the church, but because I felt called to ministry and trusted God to provide, I gratefully accepted the job. Within a few months, as I made the transition to full-time youth pastor, my income dropped by nearly two-thirds. My medical insurance and retirement were gone as well. I had to support my growing family on a fraction of the salary I had received earlier.

Believe it or not, we didn't feel the financial pinch. We had already been living frugally, so we didn't have to make any lifestyle changes. The major difference was that we couldn't put as much extra money toward our mortgage. This book is the genesis of how all of us, regardless of our financial situation, can use what God has provided even when we find ourselves with less to spend because of commitments, payments, a crisis, or job change. I'll give you Tip One right now: Live off less money than you make, and you'll be prepared if you ever *really* must live off less money than you make! In the pages ahead, I'll share more tips to put in your financial-planning pocket. But first, I'd like to share why finances God's way matters so much to me and why I want it to count for you too.

SOME CREDIBILITY AND ENCOURAGEMENT

There are many finance books already available, so why another one? What makes this one different? Is there any reason you should trust what I have to say?

Of greatest importance is that I'm not asking you to trust me, but rather, God. This book is not a collection of my opinions about money, but God's words as revealed in Scripture. You'll see in the following chapters I do my best to unpack the Bible's key verses related to money. God is the One "who gives you power to get wealth" (Deuteronomy 8:18), and He "makes poor and makes rich" (1 Samuel 2:7). That means God knows what you should and shouldn't do with your finances, and He has provided you with the needed instructions in His Word. My desire is to present these instructions in a clear, engaging, and biblical manner.

I've taught extensively on money to the church I serve. The most common type of counseling that I give is for marriages, with many of the sessions revolving around finances. The time I've spent with people in counseling—whether couples or individuals—has made me familiar with the most common problems in marriage, and many of them relate to finances. I have seen people struggle, and the time I've spent studying the Bible has equipped me to help them find solutions. I've been blessed to watch the truths of God's Word resolve their problems, restore their relationships, and strengthen their financial situations. *Your Finances God's Way* is the culmination of hundreds of hours of Bible study and counseling. I wrote this book because I am passionate about this area of Scripture and life.

As a pastor and counselor, I have witnessed the blessings that come from obeying God and the negative consequences that result from disobedience. As a husband and father, I have experienced firsthand these blessings and consequences myself. As of 2021, our oldest child of nine, Rhea Grace, is 14. Perhaps God will bless us with more. We have always been a single-income family. I was a schoolteacher when Katie and I married; then I became a full-time youth pastor. And in 2010, I moved from that role to become the senior pastor at Woodland Christian Church in Woodland, Washington.

At no time have we ever lived off anything more than modest salaries, but God still enabled us to pay off all our debt, including our mortgage. Some months we put a few hundred dollars toward debt, while other months we allocated a few thousand. When Katie inherited $10,000, we didn't think twice before putting it toward the mortgage, and every tax return went toward the mortgage. The year I worked part-time as a youth pastor and full-time as an elementary schoolteacher provided the most money we ever made. More than half of each paycheck went toward the mortgage.

Whether you make a lot of money or a little, you're in the prime of your career or just starting out, you already have a family or look to start one, these principles work because they're rooted in God's Word.

I share my story for three reasons. First, to give you confidence in the biblical principles presented in this book. Second, I don't want you wondering, *Has Scott "walked the talk," or is he a hypocrite?* When I talk about debt, I want you to know we don't have any. When I talk about paying off a mortgage, I want you to know that's what we've done. Third, I don't want you thinking, *That's easy for you to say, Scott; you've probably made more than I make.* Whether you make a lot of money or a little, you're in the prime of your career or just starting out, you already have a family or look to start one, these principles work because they're rooted in God's Word.

In the following chapters, I'll talk more about how my family handles finances without causing us to feel like we are going without, and how managing finances God's way brings freedom, not lack. For now, I'll simply share that our financial situation reminds me of what Jesus did with the fish and loaves (Matthew 14:13-21) and what Elisha did with the widow's oil (2 Kings 4:1-7). In both accounts, there was not much available—a few fish, loaves, and vessels—but God stretched the resources dramatically. He can do the same with our money if we seek to honor Him. The opposite is also true: If we do not honor the Lord with our finances, He can keep even considerable wealth from stretching very far. As God says, "Those who honor Me I will honor, and those who despise Me shall be lightly esteemed" (1 Samuel 2:30).

THE PROBLEM WITH MONEY PROBLEMS

Some years ago, I was at the gym, and a man approached me about his financial problems. Although we hardly knew each other, he was experiencing so much anxiety he felt compelled to talk to someone, and I happened to be the one. I could tell when he walked away that he was as stressed as when we started talking. Who knows how long he continued feeling that way, but I hope he sought some help because financial problems don't go away on their own. That he would speak with someone he hardly knew reveals how heavily financial burdens can weigh on us.

Aside from health issues and rebellious children, few things cause as much anxiety as finances. When people lie awake at night agonizing over something, it's often related to money: *Why did I buy that? We should've started saving earlier. What are we going to do about this bill?* Even secular research reveals the prevalence of financial worry. According to a study released by the American Psychological Association, almost three out of four Americans experience anxiety from finances part of the time, and nearly one out of four Americans experience extreme financial anxiety.[1] In a poll conducted by the Harvard School of Public Health, more than half of the people who experienced a great deal of stress in the last month identified financial problems as a factor.[2] If statistics are any indication, you're probably in the first category, and maybe even in the second.

Financial problems are devastating because they negatively affect other areas of our lives, such as our marriages, friends, jobs, and churches. Sixty-one percent of couples admit that financial discussions turn into arguments.[3] Money problems are the number-one cause of divorce in America.[4] When people are in danger of losing their jobs, homes, cars, savings, or insurance because of financial hardships, extreme stress is produced.

Unemployed fathers feel like failures if they're unable to provide. Young adults who have established themselves can be forced to return to live with their parents until they are able to get back on their feet. Stay-at-home moms find themselves needing to return to work. Families have trouble being just that—a family. A study of households with school-aged children revealed they were able to spend only 45 minutes together on typical workdays.[5] How much worse is this situation when fathers must work excessive overtime or even take on two jobs to stay on top of bills and expenses?

Is there any good news? Yes! As much as money problems can hurt multiple areas of our lives, strong finances can help strengthen the same areas. My prayer is this book will make that true for you and help you enjoy the blessings of living more comfortably, spending more time with your family, preparing for your earthly and heavenly future, and having more money for giving, saving, and retiring. The biblical principles outlined in the following chapters have worked in my family, my church, and the lives of people I've counseled. They can work for you too! Be encouraged that we'll go through this together. I will share what you need to know each step of the way, helping you learn what to do and not do with your money.

"ARE YOU GOING TO HELP ME BECOME RICH?"

You should know up front that my primary desire is not to help you live extravagantly! Instead, my goal is to help you be a good steward of the money God has given you. Let me provide a simple picture from the Bible of what I want *Your Finances God's Way* to accomplish for you. After Elisha helped the Shunammite woman in 2 Kings 4, her needs were met. She had enough to be comfortable, but she wasn't wealthy. Elijah said, "Go, sell the oil and pay your debt; and you and your sons live on the rest" (verse 7). This book will enable you to pay your debts and live comfortably on the rest.

How will we accomplish this goal? Primarily we will use the biblical practice of "putting off and putting on" (Ephesians 4:22-32 and Colossians 3:5-14). You want to better manage your finances or you wouldn't be reading these words; therefore, it's important to understand the single greatest reason we fail to change and make improvements: We "put off" without "putting on." For example, we put off doing the wrong things (such as wasting money and increasing debt), but we fail to put on the right things (such as paying off debt and being patient before making purchases). If we want to stop a certain behavior, there's a corresponding behavior we must also start. This principle can be applied to multiple areas of the Christian life, including the stewardship of our finances.

As you learn what to put off and put on, this will dramatically increase the likelihood that you'll manage your finances God's way. When you finish the last chapter, you will know what it takes to be free from financial anxiety, prepared for the future, experience contentment, and give charitably.

In that list of blessings, you'll notice I didn't include becoming rich. Though you will gain more spending ability, my intent isn't to make you wealthy. Why? Before Jesus taught the parable of the rich fool, He warned, "Beware of covetousness" (Luke 12:15). In 1 Timothy 6:10, Paul warned against the love of money. Coveting and the love of money can be destructive, so I wouldn't want to steer you in that direction.

HOW WEALTHY ARE WE?

If you're like me, you probably read verses about riches and covetousness and think they apply to others, but not you. Yet if you live in America, measured by the living standards of the rest of the world, and especially those throughout history, you live in the wealthiest nation that has ever existed. America enjoys staggering material prosperity.

Take, for instance, the average household wealth, which is the money available to invest, save, or spend after income taxes. This is less than $17,000 per household in Russia, $60,000 in France, $83,000 in the United Kingdom, and $86,000 in Canada. The nation in second place is Switzerland with $128,000. The United States is first with $176,000, or 40 percent more than the second-place finisher.[6] Now, many of us don't see nearly that amount of money in our household, but on average, you can see where we stand globally with our wealth.

There are 7.85 billion people in the world. China is the world's most populous nation with 1.44 billion people, which is 18.6 percent. It has 10.5 percent of the world's wealth. The United States has 333 million people, which is a little more than 4 percent of the world's population, but we have 41.6 percent of the world's wealth.[7]

The US poverty threshold for a family of five is $30,500, which means if a family makes less than this, they're considered living in poverty.[8] The official poverty rate in the United States is 12.3 percent (approximately 39.7 million people).[9] The average global income for a family of five is about $10,500, which means Americans in poverty still make about three times more than the average for the rest of the world.[10] Even the "poor" in the US are, on average, three times wealthier than people in the rest of the world.

You might be saying, "But things are more expensive in the United States!" True, but even after adjusting for cost-of-living differences, the average American still earns an income that is ten times higher than the average income earned in the rest of the world. In the United States, an annual income of $32,400 doesn't seem very high, but it's a salary that puts those earners among the top 1 percent of the world's earners.[11]

Why am I sharing these statistics? You might have started reading this book thinking, *My biggest financial problem is I don't have enough money!* I don't want to sound presumptuous, but as you work through this book, you might discover that's not the case. Frequently what people perceive to be an income problem may be a spending or budgeting problem. If you're in need of answers now, the key is to figure out how to live on the money you already have.

And if it turns out that you do find a way to make more money—whether through a raise, gift, tax return, or investment—the best goal is for your spending to remain the same, and your giving and saving to increase. This financial principle is straightforward in that it's easy to see what to do (increase giving and saving) and not do (increase spending). Because we all have different financial obligations, ultimately, the one thing we need most for handling our finances well is wisdom.

FINANCES REQUIRE WISDOM

More wisdom is required with finances than most parts of the Christian life; therefore, managing money involves more than mere self-control and discipline. Yes, we're going to "put off" and "put on," but some topics are not as simple as "Do this, but don't do that," or "This is good, but this is bad." Wisdom is required to find the right balance in these areas.

For example, we're to save money, but not hoard it for ourselves. We must spend money on bills, food, clothing, and other necessities, but we must use discretion to avoid trivial purchases. We must make large purchases, such as homes and vehicles, while pursuing Christian modesty and avoiding extravagance. We're commanded to give, but not at every opportunity that presents itself. We need wisdom to know when and how to spend, give, and save.

Solomon was the richest man ever to live. First Kings 10:21 says, "All King Solomon's drinking vessels were gold…Not one was silver, for this was accounted as nothing in the days of Solomon." He had such an obsession with money that he accumulated enough gold to cause silver to become worthless. Yet he still recognized wisdom's greater value: "How much better to get wisdom than gold!" (Proverbs 16:16). Solomon also wrote,

> Blessed is the one who finds wisdom, and the one who gets understanding, for the gain from her is better than gain from silver and her profit better than gold. She is more precious than jewels, and nothing you desire can compare with her (Proverbs 3:13-15 NIV; see also Proverbs 2:1-5 and 8:10-21).

This book is primarily about money, but it's important to keep wisdom's greater value in mind because "a foolish man devours [precious treasure]" (Proverbs 21:20 NIV). This verse is often loosely quoted as, "A fool and his money are soon parted." Unwise people waste money and spend it so carelessly that they soon find themselves penniless. To put it simply: Those who lack wisdom will lack money no matter how much they make. No amount of money is enough for foolish people who don't know how to manage it well because they will soon be separated from it. The best helps you can give people who don't know how to manage their finances are wisdom, a budget, and possibly a rebuke, because it is sinful to waste what God has given us. Giving poor stewards the wisdom to be good stewards is more valuable than any amount of money.

The wisdom we need is found in God's Word. Second Timothy 3:17 says Scripture allows us to "be complete, thoroughly equipped for every good work," and this includes managing our finances. The following chapters will provide an abundance of guidance from Bible verses because if we are going to do things God's way, we need to know (and obey) what God's Word says!

THE APPROACH TAKEN IN THE FOLLOWING CHAPTERS

The early chapters don't have as much direct financial application, so as you read them, you might be tempted to ask, "When are you going to start telling me what to do with my money?" The opening chapters of this book are designed to establish the foundation that you will need for getting through the rest of the book.

Think about the way the epistles are written in the New Testament. Typically, they begin with theology followed by application. For example:

- Romans is theology in chapters 1–11, followed by application in chapters 12–16.

- Galatians is theology in chapters 1–4, followed by application in chapters 5–6.

- Ephesians is theology in chapters 1–3, followed by application in chapters 4–6.

These books are written this way because it is not enough to simply tell people what to do. They must know *why* they are doing what they are told to do; otherwise, their hearts won't be in it. What good is there in learning what to do without a heart to obey?

Typically, when people's hearts aren't committed, they simply go through the motions. They begin well, but when sacrifice and self-denial are involved (both of which are needed to manage finances God's way), they give up. We have nine children. We know we can tell them what to do and they will comply, but if their hearts aren't involved, their obedience will not last. They will conform for a little while, perhaps as long as they live in our home, but as soon as they are on their own, they will disregard our instruction.

That's the reason for the way I've set up *Your Finances God's Way*. Many financial books deal with the physical aspect of finances, which is to say they talk about practical ways to manage money. This book does as well, but the early chapters take us beyond the physical (our bank accounts) to the spiritual (our hearts). While money is amoral (or nonspiritual), our relationship to it is moral and spiritual. We handle money the way we do because of our hearts. By focusing on the heart, we are directing our saving, spending, and giving. When people don't understand that heart issues—such as covetousness, contentment, generosity, patience, self-control, and stewardship—determine what they do with their money, they rarely manage their finances in ways that please God.

For us to have committed hearts that handle money well, we must be shaped by the truth. Because of our sinful flesh, which tempts us to disobey, we are not naturally inclined to do what is right. Instead, obedience is the byproduct of changed hearts. Proverbs 4:23 says, "Keep your heart with all vigilance, for from it flow the springs of life" (ESV). Simply put, we do what we do because of our hearts—our hearts determine our actions. The truth (theology, parables, and passages dealing with stewardship and faithfulness) in the earlier chapters will prepare our hearts to obey the later chapters that are filled with application.

THE *YOUR FINANCES GOD'S WAY* WORKBOOK

I have written an accompanying workbook to help you apply the teachings that follow and plant them in your heart. James 1:22 says, "Be doers of the word, and not hearers only, *deceiving yourselves.*" This verse reveals a common mistake we make with God's Word: We believe we have done enough by learning without obeying.

As believers, our responsibility goes much further than simply obtaining information. We must also apply it, or none of the knowledge gained will benefit us. Answering the questions in the workbook will help reinforce the teachings from the book so you can be not just a hearer (or reader), but a doer (or obey-er).

OUR RELATIONSHIP WITH MONEY REFLECTS OUR RELATIONSHIP WITH CHRIST

Consider this: Jesus talked about money more than He talked about anything else except the kingdom of God. He talked about money more than He talked about heaven and hell—combined. There are 39 parables, and almost one-third of them (11) are about money. In the Gospels, one out of every ten verses (288 total) are about money. [12]

Some people hear a sermon about money and think, *Shouldn't he be preaching about something important and spiritual, such as prayer, forgiveness, love, or Jesus?* Because the Bible has so much to say about money, money is important and spiritual. Jesus said the Bible is about Him (Luke 24:27, 44; John 5:39, 46; Hebrews 10:7), so what we do with money says much about our relationship with Him. What we do with money reveals our obedience (or disobedience) to Jesus, who said, "If you love me, you will keep my commandments" (John 14:15 ESV).

Please keep this in mind as you read the following chapters: Our financial decisions are outpourings of our faith. It wouldn't be too much to say that financial maturity often parallels spiritual maturity. Rare is the Christian who is spiritually mature but financially immature. We should handle our finances well not because we want to be rich, but because we want to please our Lord and Savior. This should be our highest motivation. The obvious question, then, is this: How can we do so? I'm glad you asked! Let's get started.

CHAPTER 1

Stewardship and Faithfulness

Everything belongs to God. Deuteronomy 10:14 says, "Indeed heaven and the highest heavens *belong to the Lord your God*, also the earth with all that is in it." God said, "Every beast of the forest *is mine*, the cattle on a thousand hills. I know all the birds of the hills, and all that moves in the field *is mine*" (Psalm 50:10-11 ESV). Psalm 89:11 says, "The heavens *are Yours*; the earth also *is Yours*; the world and all its fullness, You have founded them." First Corinthians 10:26 quotes Psalm 24:1: "The earth *is the Lord's*, and all its fullness."

Of course, God's possessions include all the wealth throughout history. This means your money isn't your money! It's God's money. In Haggai 2:8, God said, "The silver *is Mine*, and the gold *is Mine*." David wanted to build a house (or temple) for God. When he was told he couldn't, he did everything he could to help his son Solomon make this happen, only stopping short of doing the building himself. David collected the materials, including the silver and gold. After the people gave even more than was needed, David prayed in 1 Chronicles 29:14, 16:

> Who am I, and who are my people, that we should be able to offer so willingly as this? For *all things come from You, and of Your hand we have given You*...O Lord our God, all this abundance that we have prepared to build You a house for Your holy name is *from Your hand, and is all Your own*.

David understood they were simply giving back to God what He had given them. John 3:27 says, "A man can receive nothing unless it has been given to him from heaven." When we understand that all wealth belongs to God, our entire perspective of money changes. We come to view our finances correctly as one big stewardship.

If we understand money is a stewardship, we will be wiser with the money God has given us. We will be less likely to waste it because we understand it is God's money, versus our own. We will even find it easier to be generous and give it away because we know it is God's money, versus our own.

ENCOURAGED BY THE PARABLE OF THE TALENTS

The apostle Paul said, "It is required in stewards that one be found faithful" (1 Corinthians 4:2). If you've ever put someone in charge of something that belongs to you, you know the one thing you value more than anything else is faithfulness. The parable of the talents gives us the encouragement we need to be faithful.

A talent was the largest denomination of money in the Greco-Roman world, estimated to be worth as much as 6,000 denarii. Because a denarius was one day's wage, this was approximately 20 years' worth of work. Although the talents in the parable can represent any of the stewardships in our lives—time, marriage, children, abilities, possessions, positions in life—because Jesus chose a unit of money, this makes the parable particularly applicable to the stewardship of finances.

John MacArthur said this parable "illustrates the tragedy of wasted opportunity."[1] Second only to time, there aren't many things we waste more than money. This parable should inspire us to act otherwise and be faithful stewards:

> The kingdom of heaven is like a man traveling to a far country, who called his own servants and delivered his goods to them. And to one he gave five talents, to another two, and to another one, to each according to his own ability; and immediately he went on a journey. Then he who had received the five talents went and traded with them, and made another five talents. And likewise he who had received two gained two more also. But he who had received one went and dug in the ground, and hid his lord's money. After a long time the lord of those servants came and settled accounts with them.
>
> So he who had received five talents came and brought five other

talents, saying, "Lord, you delivered to me five talents; look, I have gained five more talents besides them." His lord said to him, "Well done, good and faithful servant; you were faithful over a few things, I will make you ruler over many things. Enter into the joy of your lord." He also who had received two talents came and said, "Lord, you delivered to me two talents; look, I have gained two more talents besides them." His lord said to him, "Well done, good and faithful servant; you have been faithful over a few things, I will make you ruler over many things. Enter into the joy of your lord" (Matthew 25:14-23).

The "man" or "lord" in this parable is Jesus, and the trip "to a far country" is His return to heaven. So far, "a long time" has been 2,000 years. The master expects the servants to carry on the work he started; therefore, he gave them talents. The servants are professing believers. I must say "professing" because it's clear the third servant is unsaved. The words "delivered his goods to them" reveal this pictures a stewardship—God entrusts us with His goods that He expects us to use for His service.

The master returned from his journey and wanted to know what the servants did with the talents he gave to them. The first man said, "Lord, you delivered to me," showing he understood the talents were entrusted to him rather than earned by him.

GOD JUDGES CHRISTIANS' STEWARDSHIPS VERSUS THEIR SINS

The master returns and judges the servants, introducing one of the more common questions I receive as a pastor: Will Christians be judged? Yes and no. No, our sins are not judged because they were paid for at the cross. If you're in Christ, you will never stand before the Great White Throne, which is the terrifying judgment at which unbelievers will learn they will pay for their sins by spending eternity in the lake of fire (Revelation 20:11-15). But even though we won't find ourselves before the Great White Throne, we will stand before the Judgment Seat of Christ to give an account of our stewardship:

- "Why do you pass judgment on your brother? Or you, why do you despise your brother? For *we will all stand before the judgment seat of God*" (Romans 14:10 ESV).

- "*We must all appear before the judgment seat of Christ*, so that each one may receive what is due for what he has done in the body, whether good or evil" (2 Corinthians 5:10 ESV).

Paul's use of the word "we" shows he's talking about himself and other believers. The "evil" we have done is mentioned because even though we won't be punished for our sins, they can result in loss of rewards: "If anyone's work is burned, *he will suffer loss*; but he himself will be saved" (1 Corinthians 3:15). To put it simply, at the end of our lives, our sins will not be judged, but our stewardships will. If we've been faithful, we will be rewarded. Keeping this in mind encourages us to be faithful stewards of our finances.

Going back to the parable, because God distributes the talents, we might expect Him to give each person the same amount. Instead, one received five, another two, and the third only one. Likewise, each of us does not receive the same amount of money. This might seem unfair, but there are three ways God creates equity.

First, God Gives What We Can Handle

The first way God creates equity is evident in the words "according to his ability." The Lord "[knows] all people and [needs] no one to bear witness about man [to Him]" (John 2:24-25 ESV). He knows how much to give each person. God does not overestimate or underestimate our abilities:

- The man with much ability was given five talents.

- The man with average ability was given two talents.

- The man with minimal ability was given one talent.

If the man with minimal ability had been given five talents, he would've been overwhelmed by the responsibility. Conversely, if the man with much ability had been given only one talent, his potential would've been wasted. Instead, God gives everyone exactly what he or she should have because He knows what we can (and can't) handle.

This is both encouraging and challenging. It's encouraging in that God does not give us more wealth than we can faithfully steward. It is challenging in that if we are unfaithful, we can't make the excuse that we would have done better if we had received a different amount.

If nobody receives more than they can handle, this begs some questions:

Why do people use the wealth God has given them in ungodly ways? Why do people act like the third servant and squander what God has given them? When people are poor stewards, does that mean God was unwise in the amounts He gave them? Not at all. We are free moral agents who choose to be faithful or unfaithful. This is the main point of the parable. When we are bad stewards, it's not a reflection of God's wisdom in distribution. Instead, it is a reflection of our unfaithfulness. When we squander what the Lord has entrusted to us, the blame rests squarely on us. The third servant demonstrated this when he tried to blame God for his results and was rebuked.

Second, God Judges Our Proportion Versus Our Portion

The second way God is equitable is shown in the second servant's reward. He heard the same words as the first servant: "Well done, good and faithful servant; you have been faithful over a few things, I will make you ruler over many things. Enter into the joy of your lord" (Matthew 25:23; cf. 25:21). Considering the second servant produced only two talents—less than half of what the first servant produced—we might expect the master to say something different to him, such as, "Fair job, mediocre servant. You have been mediocre over few things; I will set you over few things. Enter into the partial joy of your master."

Why would two servants receive the same reward when one servant produced more than twice as much (five versus two) as the other? Our rewards are not based on how much we produce (the portion). Instead, they're based on our faithfulness (the proportion). Although the first servant's portion was larger, their proportions were the same. They both doubled what they were given, which means they were equally faithful. The lesson: We're only responsible for being faithful with the money entrusted to us. No more. No less.

We see this principle in the Old Testament when God commanded giving a tithe (proportion), versus a certain amount (portion), which we will discuss in chapter 7. The application is that God might expect us to give more or less than others (portion). Someone with five talents of wealth might give many times more than someone with two talents or one, but if they're equally faithful (proportion), they will receive equal rewards.

Jesus communicated the same principle: "For everyone to whom much is given, from him much will be required; and to whom much has been committed, of him they will ask the more" (Luke 12:48). The Lord expects more from those who have been given more, a fact that should sober people living in first-world countries. The Lord expects less from those who have been given less, which should encourage impoverished people.

Third, God Does Not Compare Us with Others

Again, we encounter encouragement and challenge. The encouragement is we *don't need to* compare ourselves. For lack of a better word, we don't have to worry about being as "good" as others. The challenge is that we *can't* compare ourselves with others. In other words, we can't say, "Well, I'm doing better than him, so I must be doing okay." Should we compare ourselves with others there are only two possible outcomes. Let's briefly discuss each of them.

The First Danger of Comparing: Discouragement

I'll use myself as an example. A few of my stewardships are pastor, author, and speaker. The parable challenges me to serve the Lord with the "talents" He's given me. At the same time, I'm encouraged regarding God's expectations. I know that God doesn't expect me to produce as much as other pastors, authors, and speakers. If I thought I had to be like John MacArthur, Tim Keller, or Paul Tripp, I would be discouraged and feel like a failure. Instead, I'm comforted knowing that even though my ministry doesn't compare with theirs, I can still equally please the Lord if I am equally faithful.

The standard is faithfulness to what God expects of us, not what others are doing.

The Second Danger of Comparing: Pride

Second Corinthians 10:12 says, "We dare not class[ify] ourselves or compare ourselves with those who *commend themselves*. But they, measuring themselves by themselves, and comparing themselves among themselves, *are not wise*." Paul said we are unwise to compare ourselves with others because it can lead to pride ("commend themselves"). We might say things like, "I do so much for the Lord—if only others did as much as me." But the standard is faithfulness to what God expects of us, not what others are doing.

THE SAME REWARD FOR GOING TO BATTLE AND
GUARDING THE SUPPLIES

There's an account in the Old Testament that provides a good illustration of the way God views and rewards faithfulness. Let me fill you in on the background of the story.

God commanded Saul to exterminate the Amalekites, but Saul ended up sparing many of them, including their king, Agag (1 Samuel 15:9). There's a principle Jesus stated that applies to this situation: "Wisdom is justified by her children" (Matthew 11:19; see also Luke 7:35). "Justified" means "declared right," so Jesus meant the wisdom of decisions is justified, or declared right, by what is produced (the children) from them. God's wisdom in commanding Saul to exterminate the Amalekites was justified, or declared right, when those he let live later captured David and his men's wives and children (1 Samuel 30:1-5). As David and his men headed off after the Amalekites to rescue their wives and children, 1 Samuel 30:9-10 tells us what happened:

> David went, he and the six hundred men who were with him, and came to the Brook Besor, where those stayed who were left behind. But David pursued, he and four hundred men; for two hundred stayed behind, who were so weary that they could not cross the Brook Besor.

Two hundred of the 600 men were too exhausted to continue ("could not cross"). This doesn't mean they didn't want to; instead, they were physically unable to do so. David continued with the 400 men. They found the Amalekites, rescued their wives and children, and on the way back, they encountered the 200 men who stayed behind:

> David came to the two hundred men who had been so weary that they could not follow David, whom they also had made to stay at the Brook Besor. So they went out to meet David and to meet the people who were with him. And when David came near the people, he greeted them (1 Samuel 30:21).

The 200 men who stayed behind must have been overjoyed at seeing their families again, but they were also probably embarrassed that they weren't able to go further, and that other men had to rescue their wives and children for them. David was probably aware of this, so he "came near the people [and] greeted them" to alleviate any shame they were experiencing. This should have been a moment of great joy—among the more beautiful such moments in the Old Testament—but some men tried to ruin it:

> Then all the wicked and worthless men of those who went with David answered and said, "Because they did not go with us, we will not give them any of the spoil that we have recovered, except for every man's wife and children, that they may lead them away and depart" (verse 22).

Ironically, some of the men who went with David thought the 200 men were worthless, but Scripture says they were the "wicked and worthless" ones, or literally, "men of Belial," a New Testament title for the devil. They were described with some of the worst language in Scripture because of two things they said. First, they implied the 200 men could have gone onward but chose otherwise with the words, "They did not go with us." Second, they found an Egyptian in their path who led them to the Amalekites in the middle of the night when they were getting drunk and couldn't have been less prepared for battle (verses 11-19). God's fingerprints were all over the victory, but these men took the credit with the words, "We have recovered." David responded:

> My brethren, you shall not do so with what the LORD has given us, who has preserved us and delivered into our hand the troop that came against us. For who will heed you in this matter? But *as his part is who goes down to the battle, so shall his part be who stays by the supplies; they shall share alike* (verses 23-24).

Unlike the wicked and worthless men, David gave God the credit and defended the 200 men. He could have said they were too tired to go on, which would have excused them but also acknowledged their weakness. Instead, he said they "[stayed] by the supplies" to commend their actions.

David was a man after God's own heart, and his actions illustrated the way God views stewardship and rewards faithfulness: Those who fought the enemy received the same share as those who protected the supplies. The men who went the extra miles and rescued the women and children looked like they did more than those who had stayed behind; therefore, they looked like they deserved more. Similarly, the first servant who produced five talents looked like he did more than the second servant who produced two talents; therefore, he looked like he deserved more. But the way David rewarded his men is similar to the way the master rewarded his servants. Just as David rewarded the 600 men equally because they were equally faithful (they did all they physically could), the master rewarded the two servants equally because they were equally faithful.

ARE YOU THE 400, 200, FIRST SERVANT, OR SECOND SERVANT?

Maybe as you read this, you are thinking, *So God doesn't expect me to give as much as others?* Perhaps. Financially speaking, you might be like the 200 men and God only expects you to guard the supplies, or you're like the second servant and God only expects you to produce two talents. The other possibility is you're like the 400 men and God expects you to travel farther and fight the enemy, or you're like the first servant and God expects you to produce five talents.

What I can tell you is this is an especially important question that each of us must answer. Finances are one of our most important stewardships. Are you being faithful with what God has entrusted to you? The following chapters will give you the biblical information you need to make this determination, but the responsibility is still yours to be faithful. As William Hendriksen said, "The Lord grants us opportunities for service in accordance with the ability He's given us. In the day of judgment, the only question that will matter is, "Have we been faithful with the ability God's given us?"[2]

What if you are the third servant, who didn't produce anything? Great question! That is what we are going to discuss in the next chapter. We will see that whether God expects you to give much or little, He still expects you to give something. People who give nothing, which is to say they do nothing for the Lord, are revealing that they are unbelievers. It is not that our works (including what we do with our finances) save us; rather, our works are evidence that we are saved. For those like the third servant, who had nothing to show, they demonstrate that God was never their Master.

CHAPTER 2

God's Kindness and Severity

———

Before I became a Christian, I believed in God. I wasn't an atheist, but I hadn't heard the gospel, repented of my sins, and put my faith in Jesus Christ. At that time, if you had asked me about God, I would've told you how good, gracious, loving, and kind He is. But I would not have told you how severe, holy, just, and righteous He is. When we describe God with some of His attributes but leave out others, we create a false god, or idol.

Instead, we must do what Romans 11:22 commands and "note then *the kindness and the severity of God*: severity toward those who have fallen, but God's kindness to you." We see God's kindness and severity on full display in the parable of the talents as He deals with the three servants. Let's consider the first two servants, who were recipients of God's kindness, and then the third servant, who was a recipient of His severity.

THE MASTER'S KINDNESS TO THE FAITHFUL SERVANTS

Because the first two servants had been "faithful over a few things," it would make sense for the master to make them rulers over few things. Instead, he said he would "make [them] ruler over many things." God is gracious. We will receive more from Him than we've done for Him.

It should encourage us that the master was pleased with the servants even though they had been "faithful [only] over a few things." If we thought we had to be faithful over many things to please the Lord, we might feel like failures. Instead, God is pleased with faithfulness over only a few things if that's all He's given us.

In addition, the "few things" needn't be big things. In Matthew 10:42,

Jesus said, "Whoever gives one of these little ones only a cup of cold water in the name of a disciple, assuredly, I say to you, he shall by no means lose his reward." Talk about being faithful over little! What's littler than giving someone a cup of water? With God, even the smallest acts will be rewarded.

When the master said, "I will make you ruler over many things," he promoted those men. They went from being servants to rulers. The reward for serving the Lord is greater service in the future.

Bringing God Joy

I'm sure when we have marriages that reflect Christ and the church, when we raise children in the fear and admonition of the Lord, and when children obey their parents, it brings God joy. Although there's one thing in Scripture that seems to bring God more joy than anything else, and that's people being saved. In Luke 15 are three well-known parables about salvation, and joy is the theme of each. In the parables of the lost sheep and the lost coin, Jesus said,

> When he has found [the lost sheep], he lays it on his shoulders, *rejoicing*. And when he comes home, he calls together his friends and neighbors, saying to them, "*Rejoice* with me, for I have found my sheep which was lost!" I say to you that likewise there will be *more joy in heaven over one sinner* who repents than over ninety-nine just persons who need no repentance…When she has found [the lost coin], she calls her friends and neighbors together, saying, "*Rejoice* with me, for I have found the piece which I lost!" Likewise, I say to you, there is *joy in the presence of the angels* of God *over one sinner* who repents (verses 5-7, 9-10).

There's joy in heaven not just over the salvation of hundreds or thousands, but "over one sinner." And though the joy is in heaven, it's "in the presence of the angels." Who is in the presence of the angels? God! This is His joy. The parable of the prodigal son takes a different approach. Instead of using the words *joy* or *rejoicing*, it *shows* the Father's joy at the lost son's repentance:

> The father said to his servants, "Bring out the best robe and put it on him, and put a ring on his hand and sandals on his feet. And bring the fatted calf here and kill it, and let us eat and *be merry*; for this my son was dead and is alive again; he was lost and is found."

And they began to *be merry.* Now his older son was in the field.
And as he came and drew near to the house, he *heard music and
dancing* (verses 22-25).

This is great joy! We should keep in mind how our salvation makes the
Lord feel. If ever we start to feel as though we're just one of many Christians
and, therefore, we're insignificant to the Lord, we should turn to Luke 15
and read these parables.

Experiencing God's Joy

Not only does our salvation bring the Master joy, we also get to share this
joy with Him. In the parable of the talents, we might expect the master to say
to the first and second servants, "Enter into heaven," or "Enter into the joy
of heaven," but they were invited to "enter into the joy of your lord" (Matthew 25:21 and 23). He invited the faithful servants to share in his joy with
him. His joy is part of their reward, and God's joy will be part of our reward.

The Bible mentions five crowns that are available to us as rewards: the
imperishable crown (1 Corinthians 9:24-25), the crown of rejoicing (1 Thessalonians 2:19), the crown of righteousness (2 Timothy 4:8), the crown of
glory (1 Peter 5:4), and the crown of life (Revelation 2:10). In the Sermon
on the Mount, Jesus repeatedly talked about rewards; the word occurs nine
times between Matthew 5:11 and 7:17.[1] As a pastor, one of the more common
questions I've been asked is, "What do these rewards look like?" The parable of the talents reveals at least part of our reward is sharing in the Lord's
joy with Him.

THE MASTER'S SEVERITY TO THE UNFAITHFUL SERVANT

In the same way the first two servants reveal the master's goodness, the
third servant reveals his severity. We might not like to think about God's
severity. Some people even criticize it, saying something like, "What kind of
God would...?" and then they list things they believe make God look bad:
"...keep people out of heaven," "...send people to hell," "...punish them."
The answer to the question is, "The kind of God you should fear and serve!"
Few places in Scripture demonstrate the need to do so more than the master's dealing with the third servant.

The master was on a hot streak with the first two servants, but with the
third servant we see the truth of Proverbs 20:6: "Most men will proclaim

each his own goodness, but who can find a faithful man?" This verse makes two points: First, it is easy to talk about being faithful. Second, it is hard to find faithful people.

In the previous chapter, I mentioned the Great White Throne Judgment that unbelievers will face. It is a sentencing more than a trial, but if an unbeliever could defend himself, imagine if he said something like, "I didn't serve You because I knew You were a God who judges people." This is an absurd defense, because if he knew God judged people, then he had more reason to obey. But this is close to the excuse given by the third servant:

> He who had received the one talent came and said, "Lord, I knew you to be a hard man, reaping where you have not sown, and gathering where you have not scattered seed. And I was afraid, and went and hid your talent in the ground. Look, there you have what is yours."
>
> But his lord answered and said to him, "You wicked and lazy servant, you knew that I reap where I have not sown, and gather where I have not scattered seed. So you ought to have deposited my money with the bankers, and at my coming I would have received back my own with interest" (Matthew 25:24-29).

The master put a hole in the servant's logic. If he knew the master was "a hard man," he should've taken his stewardship more seriously. The servant's words backfired and sealed his fate. While the master's joy was evident with the previous two servants, the third servant witnessed the opposite: indignation. Why? Part of the reason is contained in the words "you knew." The servant *knew* the master was severe but was unfaithful anyway.

The servant made two strong accusations. First, he said the master was cruel and expected more from his servants than he should: He was "a hard man." Second, he said the master took what didn't belong to him, reaping where he hadn't sown, and gathering where he hadn't scattered. In response, the master repeated the words that were true of him ("I reap where I have not sown, and gather where I have not scattered seed"), but left out the words that weren't true—"a hard man." Up to this point, the master's behavior showed him to be gracious and fair. He had given the servants the amounts they could handle, and he rewarded their efforts. But he did expect a return on his investment, and the application for us is that God gives us money and expects us to be faithful stewards who produce a return on His investment, which means using it for His glory.

We have the same expectation when we invest our own money. Imagine giving money to an investment manager. Your hope is that you will receive more than you gave him. It would be ridiculous if the investment manager said to you, "You're such a difficult investor; I didn't invest your money for you. Here—take back what you gave me." You would be frustrated, and you might even say something like the master said: "You could have at least invested it in a savings account so that I would receive some interest!"

People Can Be Wicked Because of What They Don't Do

What might we call an investment manager who acted like the third servant? Lazy! Although I doubt we would call him wicked. Typically, we think people are wicked because of sins they commit, such as murder, adultery, or theft. Surprisingly, the third servant was wicked—not because of what he did (commission), but because of what he didn't do (omission). James 4:17 says, "To him who knows to do good and does not do it, to him it is sin." The sin of failing to do what God wants can be as serious as committing sins we think are wicked.

None of us do all the good God wants us to do, but if our lives are characterized by failing to do the good God wants, then we can be wicked in His eyes. Some people haven't committed the sins that we think make them wicked, but if they've been unfaithful stewards throughout their lives, they'll stand as condemned as those who have committed the most grievous sins.

Could our finances be one of the more common ways that we fail to do what God wants? Do we spend our money in ways that dishonor God? We'll talk about spending in chapter 11, and spending money in immoral ways is a sin of commission. Do we fail to give in ways that would honor God? We'll talk about giving in chapters 6 through 9, and failing to give when we should is a sin of omission.

The Master Expects Something

There are two sides to the master's expectation that his money earn interest: one encouraging and the other sobering. Because the first two servants doubled their investment, it's easy to think the master had high expectations and he would be pleased only if we produced a considerable amount. But when the third servant was judged, we discover the master would've been satisfied with interest alone—a low bar to reach. That's encouraging.

Now for the sobering part: The third servant only received one talent. If anyone looked as though he could have gotten away without producing anything, it is him, yet God still expected something from him. This reveals that nobody can ever say, "I'm not talented. God hasn't blessed me with any gifts to serve Him. If He gave me more, I'd be able to do more for Him, but because I have been given so little, I won't even bother." This excuse won't work. The master doesn't have high expectations, but he still has expectations.

This helps us understand why the master was and wasn't upset. He wasn't upset that the servant had only one talent. The master wouldn't condemn him for having only what had been given to him; however, he was upset that the servant didn't produce anything with the little he was given. The financial application for us is that God will never be upset at how little we have. But even when we have little, we have the opportunity to be faithful or unfaithful.

Are We Saved by Works?

In Matthew 25:30, the master said, "Cast the unprofitable servant into the outer darkness. There will be weeping and gnashing of teeth." The "outer darkness" is the farthest place away from the light. Because 1 John 1:5 says, "God is light and in Him is no darkness at all," we know the "outer darkness" is the farthest we can get from God. "Weeping and gnashing of teeth" speaks of the unending torment of hell. The worst suffering becomes more bearable when we know it will come to an end. But that's not the case here. Hopelessness is the hell within hell because the inhabitants know their suffering will never end.

The two faithful servants had works and were invited into heaven. The unfaithful servant had no works and was cast into hell. This makes it look as though the first two servants were saved by works, and the third servant was unsaved because he had no works. How do we explain this when Ephesians 2:8-9 says, "By grace you have been saved through faith. And this is *not your own doing*; it is the gift of God, *not a result of works*, so that no one may boast"? (ESV). The solution is we aren't saved by works, but works are one of the evidences of being saved. James 2:17 and 20 state that faith without works is dead. A dead faith doesn't produce works. Living faith, on the other hand, is a saving faith that produces works.

Christians use what God has given them to serve Him (produce works), even if only in small ways. If people believe they're Christians but produce no works, they're deceived about their salvation. The absence of works reveals their faith is dead and they are unsaved.

We're wrong if we think Ephesians 2:8-9 teaches that we don't need to have works. These might be the two most well-known verses in the Bible about salvation being by grace through faith apart from works, but the next verse says, "We are His workmanship, created in Christ Jesus *for good works*, which God prepared beforehand that we should walk in them" (Ephesians 2:10). Works are the evidence of salvation because they reveal we are "His workmanship." Conversely, the lack of good works reveals we are not "His workmanship" and will be cast into hell. The third servant reveals this truth.

Faithful Versus Unfaithful Servants

Matthew's Gospel contains many contrasting pairs, such as

- sheep versus wolves in sheep's clothing (Matthew 7:15-20)
- a house built on the rock versus a house built on sand (Matthew 7:24-27)
- wheat versus tares (Matthew 13:24-30)
- a forgiven servant versus an unforgiving servant (Matthew 23:18-35)
- a wise servant versus an evil servant (Matthew 24:45-51)
- foolish virgins versus wise virgins (Matthew 25:1-13)

The parable of the talents features another pair: faithful servants versus an unfaithful servant. In each of these pairs, the counterfeit looks like the genuine—that is, wolves in sheep's clothing look like sheep, the house on the sand looks like the house on the rock, tares look like wheat.

First John 2:19 says, "They went out from us, but they were not of us; for if they had been of us, they would have continued with us; but they went out that they might be made manifest, that none of them were of us." These people looked saved—they looked like genuine Christians until "they went out." It was only going out that revealed "they were not of us." If they had not gone out—perhaps they remained in the church until they died—they would've looked like Christians until they stood before the Lord and heard the words of Matthew 25:30. Just as the storms revealed the one house to be built on sand, and just as the virgins were revealed to be foolish when the door was shut, the third servant's unfaithfulness was revealed when he was judged and found to have no works.

Use or Possibly Lose What God's Given You

The master said, "So take the talent from [the unfaithful servant], and give it to him who has ten talents. For to everyone who has, more will be given, and he will have abundance; but from him who does not have, even what he has will be taken away" (Matthew 25:28-29). Jesus said something similar earlier: "For whoever has, to him more will be given, and he will have abundance; but whoever does not have, even what he has will be taken away from him" (Matthew 13:12). God does not waste words in Scripture. If He's going to take up precious space saying the same thing more than once, it's for a reason. He does not use highlighting, italics, underlining, or bold for emphasis, but He does repeat Himself to ensure we don't miss a point He wants to make.

God doesn't want us to miss the principle that we must use what He has given us or it might be taken away. That is what happened with the unfaithful servant: He didn't use what God gave him, and it was taken from him.

When I was an elementary schoolteacher, at the beginning of each year I distributed a responsibility to each of my students: passing out papers, collecting papers, line leaders, opening the door, taking the lunch money to the office. As the year progressed, some students showed themselves to be unfaithful. No matter how many warnings they were given, the situation didn't improve. Finally, I had to take away their responsibility and give it to a faithful student who already had a responsibility. By the end of the year, I had two extremes in the classroom: some students had an "abundance" of responsibilities, and others ended up with no responsibilities because they had been taken away. Whatever talent God has given us might be taken away if we don't use it.

Thinking of all God has done for us, and all He has in store for us, what more reason could we have to be good stewards of our finances?

BELIEVERS AND UNBELIEVERS EXPERIENCE THE EXTREMES OF GOD'S KINDNESS AND SEVERITY

Unfaithful servants (unbelievers) and faithful servants (believers) also experience extremes as shown by the parable. Take your mind back to the verse that began the chapter: "Note then *the kindness and the severity of God*: severity toward those who have fallen, but God's kindness to you" (Romans 11:22 ESV). This verse was played out with the three servants:

- The unfaithful servant lost everything. His talent was taken from him, and then he was cast into hell, where he would suffer for eternity. For unbelievers, it is punishment upon punishment as they experience the extremes of God's severity.

- The faithful servants gained everything. They were commended by the master, invited to experience his joy with him, promoted from servants over little to rulers over much, and recipients of the unfaithful servant's talent. More was given to them until they "[had] an abundance." For believers, it is blessing upon blessing as we experience the extremes of God's kindness.

As Christians, we inherit eternal life. This alone is tremendous, but we also receive other immeasurable blessings. Romans 8:32 says, "He who did not spare His own Son, but delivered Him up for us all, how shall He not with Him also freely give us all things?"

Thinking of all God has done for us, and all He has in store for us, what more reason could we have to be good stewards of our finances? As you read the upcoming chapters, let this be your motivation. We are faithful with our money not because *we must be* to be saved, but because *we want to be* because we are saved. We manage our finances well not out of obligation, but out of appreciation; not out of indebtedness, but out of gratefulness.

CHAPTER 3

Money Is the Foundation of Faithfulness

---

n the introduction, I said I wanted you to have the motivation to be a good steward of your finances. What could accomplish this better than a parable Jesus taught about financial stewardship? The parable of the unjust steward is one of Jesus's most controversial and confusing teachings because it seems to commend immorality; therefore, please bear with me through the groundwork that explains why this is not the case. Luke 16:1-2 opens the parable:

> [Jesus] said to the disciples, "There was a rich man who had a manager, and charges were brought to him that this man was wasting his possessions. And he called him and said to him, "What is this that I hear about you? Turn in the account of your management, for you can no longer be manager" (ESV).

The manager here is a steward, which is how it's translated in many Bibles. Stewards don't own anything. Instead, they're responsible for someone else's possessions, which is why this person is called a manager. Stewards were trusted servants because they had full authority over their master's possessions and could conduct business transactions in the master's name.

The master thinks the steward is incompetent ("wasting his possessions") versus dishonest, so he told the steward he would fire him in the future, versus immediately. This was a mistake because it allowed the steward to keep control of the master's assets and rip him off. Luke 16:3-8 records the steward's thoughts and actions after learning of his termination:

> The manager said to himself, "What shall I do, since my master is taking the management away from me? I am not strong enough to dig, and I am ashamed to beg. I have decided what to do, so that when I am removed from management, people may receive me into their houses." So, summoning his master's debtors one by one, he said to the first, "How much do you owe my master?" He said, "A hundred measures of oil." He said to him, "Take your bill, and sit down quickly and write fifty." Then he said to another, "And how much do you owe?" He said, "A hundred measures of wheat." He said to him, "Take your bill, and write eighty." The master commended the dishonest manager for his shrewdness (ESV).

If you ever learned you would lose your job, you would probably immediately start thinking about what you would do next. That's what the steward did, but he found his options unattractive. He was "not strong enough to dig," perhaps because he was old or disabled, and he was too "ashamed to beg," perhaps because doing so was beneath him after having held such a prestigious position.

More than likely, the steward lived in his rich master's house. When he was fired, not only would he lose his job, he would also lose his nice living situation. So he decided to win people's favor so they would "receive [him] into their houses," and he accomplishes this by meeting with the master's debtors and decreasing their bills.

If you owed money and someone offered to take 20 to 50 percent off your bill, you would likely jump at the opportunity, but hopefully only if it was done morally. The words "sit down quickly" reveal this was a secret transaction, unauthorized by the master. So why did the master commend the steward's ingenuity? Everyone in the parable is immoral: the steward, who ripped off his master; the debtors, who went along with the plan; and the master, who admired the steward's actions.

WAS JESUS APPLAUDING DISHONESTY OR DOING SOMETHING ELSE?

The confusing part is obvious: Jesus seemed to commend the steward's dishonesty, right? Wrong. The master did, but Jesus called him dishonest (Luke 16:8).

If Jesus wasn't commending the steward, what was He doing? This point clarifies the entire parable: Jesus was contrasting two groups—unbelievers and believers. He was saying unbelievers do some things better than believers. The rest of Luke 16:8 makes this clear: "The sons of this world [unbelievers] are more shrewd in dealing with their own generation than the sons of light [believers]" (ESV).

"Their own generation" refers to the time unbelievers live in, or this life. Unbelievers are shrewder when they deal with the affairs of this life than believers are when they deal with the affairs of the next life. This is another confusing part of the parable because it sounds like Jesus is commending unbelievers and criticizing believers. Is that what He's doing? Yes! Verse 1 says Jesus was speaking "to the disciples," which means this parable is intended as a rebuke to people who claim to follow Him. Some unbelievers are shrewder (more zealous and passionate) with their physical affairs than some believers are with their spiritual affairs. Let's consider these ways.

The Steward Took Seriously that He Would Give an Account

The steward learned he was going to have to stand before his master and "give an account of his management," or stewardship, and he took that seriously. Some unbelievers take more seriously that they'll stand before an earthly, human master—whether a boss or employer—and give an account, than believers take seriously that they'll stand before their Master, the God of heaven and earth, and give an account.

Following college, I've done four things professionally. First, I was an officer in the Army. Second, I was a supervisor at a distribution center for a major box store. Third, I was an elementary schoolteacher. Now I'm a pastor. In each of these professions, I received evaluations. While I wasn't afraid—just like we don't need to be afraid when we go before the Judgment Seat of Christ—I did want to do well. I took my evaluations seriously and tried to please whomever I worked for at the time.

How much more seriously should you and I take standing before Christ? Considering all He's done for us, how much more should we want to please Him? If we strive to be faithful for an earthly, human master, how much more should we strive to be faithful for our Lord and Savior? And when it comes to faithfulness, few stewardships are more important than that of our finances.

The Steward Prepared for the Future

Again, Jesus isn't commending the sinful way the steward prepared for the future, but He is telling us to learn from his planning and foresight. The steward said, "When I am removed from management, people may receive me into their houses." He used his present circumstances to prepare the best future for himself.

It's sad when unbelievers prepare for their temporary futures better than believers prepare for their eternal futures. How tragic is it when unbelievers work harder for their earthly lives than believers work for their heavenly lives?

The Steward Knew He Had a Narrow Window of Time to Use His Master's Resources

The steward learned he had a little time before he would lose his job, and he took advantage of this window. We too have a narrow window of time. Our lives are short:

- Job 7:7—"Remember that my life is a breath!"

- Psalm 102:3—"My days are consumed like smoke."

- Psalm 144:4—"Man is like a breath; his days are like a passing shadow."

- James 4:14—"What is your life? It is even a vapor that appears for a little time and then vanishes away."

We should use the little time we have before "losing our jobs," which is to say before our lives come to an end. As Jesus said, "We must work the works of Him who sent Me while it is day; the night is coming when no one can work" (John 9:4). We must take advantage of the narrow window we have.

The steward used what he had at his disposal, which happened to be the resources the master entrusted to him. Similarly, what do we have at our disposal? Because we're stewards, we have the resources the Master has entrusted to us. Not only our finances, but also our time, relationships, possessions, money, talents, abilities, and gifts. Are we using these resources to the best of our ability? Are we using to the fullest what the Master has entrusted to us for His glory and honor?

The Steward Worked Hard

Consider these statistics. American employees work 137 more hours per year than Japanese workers, 260 more hours per year than British workers, and

499 more hours per year than French workers.[1] Americans average 47-hour work weeks.[2] Twenty-five million Americans (21 percent of the workforce) work at least 49 hours per week, and 11 million Americans (9 percent of the workforce) work more than 59 hours per week.[3] Four out of five Americans spend their lunch break at their desk so they can keep working.[4] Americans receive 15 vacation days per year, while workers in Asia receive 19 and workers in Europe receive 28.[5] You might be quick to say, "We should get more vacation!" The problem is 51 percent of Americans don't use all the vacation time they have. When Americans take vacation, 61 percent admit to doing some work during that time.[6] Many Americans spend part of the year working for nothing, donating on average the equivalent of $561 to their employers.[7]

Think of how hard unbelievers work to make money and get ahead. All the overtime—early mornings, late evenings, and 60-, 70-, even 80-hour work weeks. All the sacrifices—sleep, relationships, health, enjoyment, pleasure, and hobbies. Jesus's point can be summarized this way: What if Christians worked as hard for God's kingdom as unbelievers work for their earthly kingdom?

We should ask ourselves: How much effort do we invest in our relationship with Christ? We go to church on Sunday, but what about Monday through Saturday? How much time do we spend serving Him? What have we sacrificed for the Lord, such as enjoyment, pleasure, or hobbies? Are there early mornings or late evenings we've given Him in prayer and Bible reading?

The Steward Used Money to Make Friends

At the end of the parable, Jesus said, "I tell you, make friends for yourselves by means of unrighteous wealth, so that when it fails they may receive you into the eternal dwellings" (Luke 16:9 ESV). "Unrighteous wealth" refers to earthly wealth. It's called unrighteous not because it's evil, but because it belongs to the world. Unfortunately, when some teach this parable, they say it's about giving of your time, energy, or expertise. There are verses in the Bible that tell us to give of our time, energy, and expertise, but in this parable, Jesus is talking specifically about money. The problem with applying this parable to things other than money is that people would rather give anything but money, so when they come away thinking they can substitute money with something else, they use this parable as their justification for doing so. But Jesus has money in view here. So no matter how much we give of something else, if we're not giving money, we're not obeying the Lord.

The steward used the money he had at his disposal (his master's money) to make friends for himself that would receive him into their houses. Spiritually speaking, we should do the same. Every believer is a brother or sister in Christ, but Jesus says people who come to salvation because of our giving are friends we have made for ourselves "by means of unrighteous wealth." In other words, we should use our earthly wealth to help spread the gospel so others can become Christians.

The phrase "eternal dwellings" refers to heaven; that's where our everlasting homes are located. We should use our Master's money to make friends who will "receive [us] into eternal dwellings," or welcome us into heaven when we arrive. Imagine the beauty of this: We make friends for eternity when we invest in the gospel and people are saved!

Earlier we read that God expresses joy when a person comes to salvation: "There is *joy in the presence of the angels* of God over one sinner who repents" (Luke 15:10). Knowing this should also encourage us to give to the spread of the gospel, because anyone who loves the Lord wants to bring Him joy. To emphasize the importance of this, Jesus taught two financial principles.

Principle One: If We Can't Be Faithful with Money, We Can't Be Faithful with Much Else

In the parable of the talents (Matthew 25:14-30) and the parable of the minas (Luke 19:11-27), Jesus said something like, "Because you have been faithful in little, I will give you responsibility over much." In the parable of the unjust steward, Jesus said something similar, but with a specific focus on money:

> One who is faithful in a very little is also faithful in much, and one who is dishonest in a very little is also dishonest in much. If then you have not been faithful in the unrighteous wealth, who will entrust to you the true riches? And if you have not been faithful in that which is another's, who will give you that which is your own? (Luke 16:10-12 ESV).

This is straightforward: If we're faithful with a little we can be faithful with much, but if we can't be faithful with little, we won't suddenly become faithful with much. When we give our children small stewardships, if they don't handle those well, we don't give them bigger stewardships and expect them to do a better job. But in these verses, Jesus doesn't refer to other stewardships—such as time, relationships, and talents—as He does in the parables of the talents and minas. Instead, He focuses on money, and we know this because of His second use of the phrase "unrighteous wealth."

While Jesus is saying people who aren't faithful with small amounts of money won't be faithful with larger amounts of money, that's not the point He's making. He didn't say, "If you have not been faithful with the unrighteous wealth, who will entrust to you *more wealth*?" Instead, He said, "Who will entrust to you *true riches*?" True riches are not physical, earthly riches. They are spiritual, heavenly riches.

The words "very little," which occur twice, refer to the "unrighteous wealth" or earthly riches. The words "in much," which also occur twice, refer to the "true riches" or heavenly riches. Jesus says earthly riches are "very little" because money is the foundation, or are the training wheels, of faithfulness. If we can't be faithful with earthly wealth, we can't get rid of our training wheels and be faithful with heavenly wealth. If we haven't been trustworthy handling physical riches, God will not let us handle spiritual riches, or the true riches of the kingdom.

"That which is another's" is God's, because as stewards, "our" money is God's money. If we're unfaithful with His money, He won't "give [us] that which is [our] own," referring to eternal rewards, in that we keep them forever. This doesn't mean that if we're bad with money we're not Christians or we lose our salvation. But it does mean it's going to hurt our treasure in heaven. Poor financial stewardship reveals hearts that are focused on earth instead of heaven, preparing for earthly futures instead of heavenly homes, and God takes notice. There are few eternal rewards for people who have been poor financial stewards because they haven't invested much in eternity (heaven).

Principle Two: Serving God or Money

Let's make sure we understand imperatives and indicatives so that we interpret the second principle correctly. Imperatives are commands, such as, "Love your neighbor as yourself," "Pray without ceasing," and "Forgive as you've been forgiven." Indicatives are statements—they indicate something, such as, "You are an heir with Christ," "You have been forgiven," and "You are justified by faith."

Sometimes we confuse imperatives and indicatives. For example, Jesus said, "You are the salt of the earth...You are the light of the world...He who abides in Me, and I in him, bears much fruit" (Matthew 5:13-14; John 15:5). These are indicatives, not imperatives. Jesus isn't telling us *to do* something, such as, "*Try hard to* be salt, light, and produce fruit." Instead, He's telling us *we are* something: "You are salt, light, and fruit producers."

If we're devoted to money, we're not devoted to Christ. If we're devoted to Christ, we're not devoted to money. It's one or the other.

The second principle in Luke 16:13 is also an indicative rather than an imperative: "No servant can serve two masters; for either he will hate the one and love the other, or else he will be loyal to the one and despise the other. You cannot serve God and mammon [money]." Wouldn't we expect Jesus to say, "You cannot serve God *and another master*"? Instead, He said, "You cannot serve God *and money*." Money can become our master and make us its slave. When that happens, God is no longer the Lord—or Master—of our life. Because this is an indicative (versus an imperative), He is not commanding us not to "serve God and money" or be more devoted to Him than money. Instead, He's indicating we "*cannot* serve Him and money." If we're devoted to money, we're not devoted to Christ. If we're devoted to Christ, we're not devoted to money. It's one or the other.

Saying we can serve both God and money is like saying we can walk in two different directions. We *can* have two masters if they want the same things. For example, children have two masters—their mother and father—and it works because (hopefully) both parents want the same things. But God and money want different things:

- If money is our master, we'll waste our lives living only for the present. We won't use our resources for the next life. When we make it to heaven, we'll find ourselves without eternal rewards or friends to welcome us.

- If God is our master, we'll serve Him by making money serve us. Instead of being mastered by money, we will master money. When we make it to heaven, we will receive our eternal rewards and be welcomed by our friends because we have used our money to invest in the next life.

WE MUST CHOOSE

Two accounts in the Old Testament help illustrate the decision we face. After Joshua led the nation of Israel into the Promised Land, they encountered the false gods of the Canaanites. Years later, the people never forsook the Lord, but sadly, some engaged in idolatry. They probably thought they could add the worship of idols to the worship of God. Joshua knew otherwise. He brought the people together and told them these famous words:

> Fear the LORD and *serve him* in sincerity and *in faithfulness*. Put away the gods that your fathers served beyond the River and in Egypt, and *serve the LORD*. And if it is evil in your eyes to *serve the LORD, choose this day whom you will serve*, whether the gods your fathers served in the region beyond the River, or the gods of the Amorites in whose land you dwell. But as for me and my house, *we will serve the LORD* (Joshua 24:14-15 ESV).

Joshua knew it was impossible for the Israelites to serve the Lord and the false gods in the Promised Land. It was an issue of service and faithfulness. To serve the gods of the Canaanites was to be unfaithful to God. To be faithful to God meant putting away the false gods. The same is true for us: to serve money is to be unfaithful to God, and to be faithful to God means refusing to serve money.

Perhaps you're thinking, *This is a little dramatic. Joshua was dealing with idols, but we are only dealing with money.* But twice, Paul associated covetousness with idolatry:

- "Put to death your members which are on the earth: fornication, uncleanness, passion, evil desire, and covetousness, which is idolatry" (Colossians 3:5).

- "This you know, that no fornicator, unclean person, nor covetous man, who is an idolater, has any inheritance in the kingdom of Christ and God" (Ephesians 5:5).

Covetousness is idolatry because when we covet, we desire something more than we desire God. Because the first commandment forbids idolatry, and the tenth commandment forbids covetousness, the Ten Commandments begin and end with the same commandments. When we covet money, it becomes an idol that is comparable with any of the ones Joshua was confronting. We can serve money as much as the Israelites could serve the false gods of Canaan, and we would be making the same choice they had made when they served the false gods of Canaan: the choice to not serve God.

Fast-forward seven centuries and consider a similar situation. Ahab was the king of the northern kingdom of Israel. He and his wife, Jezebel, led the nation to worship Baal. God raised up the prophet Elijah to bring the people back to Himself. In the dramatic showdown on Mount Carmel, Elijah said, "How long will you falter between two different opinions? *If the* LORD *is God, follow Him; but if Baal, follow him.* But the people answered him not a word" (1 Kings 18:21). Again, the people had to choose, but sadly, their silence showed the choice they had already made.

Do you have any trouble choosing between God and money? If so, before beginning the next chapter, please repent. Put off a love of money and put on a love of God. Choose not to serve money and instead, choose to serve God.

Let me encourage you by concluding this chapter with Joshua and Elijah's words rephrased to apply directly to our situation with money:

> Fear the Lord and serve Him in sincerity and in faithfulness. Put away serving money and serve the Lord. If it is evil in your eyes to serve the Lord, choose this day whom you will serve, whether God or money. But as for me and my house, we will serve the Lord. How long will you go faltering between two different opinions? If the Lord is God, follow Him; but if money, then follow it.

CHAPTER 4

The Dangers of Loving Money

During college, I took a world religions class. A Buddhist monk was brought in as a guest speaker. He had no modern-day luxuries, such as a vehicle, computer, or refrigerator, because he thought these were sinful (immoral). He thought it was good (moral) to allow himself only what was necessary for survival, such as food, water, and shelter.

But this is not what Jesus meant when He said, "If anyone desires to come after Me, let him deny himself, and take up his cross daily, and follow Me" (Luke 9:23). There, Jesus referred to denying ourselves immoral pleasures, but the monk was abstaining from things that are amoral (non-sinful, or spiritually neutral). Colossians 2:20-23 records:

> If you died with Christ from the basic principles of the world, why, as though living in the world, do you subject yourselves to regulations—"Do not touch, do not taste, do not handle," which all concern things which perish with the using—according to the commandments and doctrines of men? *These things indeed have an appearance of wisdom in self-imposed religion, false humility, and neglect of the body, but are of no value against the indulgence of the flesh.*

When people rigorously neglect the amoral and follow legalistic, man-made commands, there's "an appearance of wisdom," but there's "no value against [indulging] the flesh," which is to say there's no spiritual benefit. It's heartbreaking when people spend years rigorously denying themselves in ways that have no moral or spiritual benefit.

The Bible teaches that drunkenness and homosexuality are immoral

(1 Corinthians 6:9-10). It's tragic when people spend years getting drunk or participating in homosexual relationships because they're convinced their immoral actions are amoral.

We must understand morality because if we don't, we might find ourselves in one of the above situations and fail to see the goodness (morality) of certain behaviors and the sinfulness (immorality) of others. These are the two mistakes we typically make with morality. Let's consider them in more detail so we'll be prepared to view our money correctly.

MISTAKE 1: THINKING SOMETHING IS AMORAL WHEN IT IS MORAL OR IMMORAL

Many verses discuss the morality of our words. For example:

- Matthew 12:37— Jesus said, "For by your words you will be justified, and by your words you will be condemned."

- 1 Peter 3:10—"He who would love life and see good days, let him refrain his tongue from evil, and his lips from speaking deceit."

Most people know their speech is moral, but they might not know that *the amount they speak* (and listen) is also moral (versus amoral). James 1:19 says, "My beloved brethren, let every man be swift to hear, slow to speak, slow to wrath." This verse contains three commands, which means we're dealing with morality: it is moral to be quick to hear, slow to speak, and slow to anger; and it is immoral to be slow to hear, quick to speak, and quick to anger. Anger and listening might be mentioned together because they're closely related. As a pastor, when I'm counseling couples, sometimes it's obvious early on who's more at fault when problems arise because they're slow to hear and quick to get angry.

Ecclesiastes teaches that one way to identify fools is they talk too much: "A fool's voice is known by his many words...a fool also multiplies words" (Ecclesiastes 5:3; 10:14). David took so seriously how much he spoke that he prayed God would protect his mouth: "Set a guard, O LORD, over my mouth; keep watch over the door of my lips" (Psalm 141:3).

Proverbs is filled with contrasts between wise and foolish people. One of the contrasts is wise people listen, but foolish people babble on: "The wise in heart will receive commands, but a prating fool will fall" (Proverbs 10:8).[1]

MISTAKE 2: THINKING SOMETHING IS IMMORAL WHEN IT IS AMORAL

Food, guns, and knowledge are amoral, which means people are not spiritually better or worse if they do or don't eat certain foods, have or don't have guns, or have more or less knowledge than others. But *what we do* with food, guns, and knowledge is moral.

Certain foods are healthier or unhealthier than others, but spiritually they're not better or worse than other foods. First Corinthians 8:8 says, "Food does not commend us to God; for neither if we eat are we the better, nor if we do not eat are we the worse."[2] Food is amoral, but our relationship to it is moral. We can commit the sin of gluttony, or, on the other side of the spectrum, the sins of anorexia and bulimia. God doesn't care what we eat, but He cares how much we eat.

Guns are also amoral, but they can be used in moral and immoral ways. The same is true of knowledge, which is information, but it can be used in moral and immoral ways. Some people have used their knowledge morally to benefit humanity:

- Jacob Perkins used his knowledge of mechanical engineering to invent refrigeration.

- The Wright brothers used their knowledge of aviation to develop human flight.

- Tim Berners-Lee used his knowledge of computer programming to develop the World Wide Web.

- Isaac Newton used his knowledge of astronomy to promote creationism.

Other people used their knowledge immorally in detrimental ways to humanity:

- Genghis Khan used his knowledge of politics and war to lead a Mongol horde that killed millions of people.

- Karl Marx used his knowledge of law and philosophy to try to destroy capitalism and create a classless, communist society.

- Margaret Sanger used her knowledge of reproduction to establish organizations that evolved into Planned Parenthood.

- Richard Dawkins uses his knowledge of biology to promote atheism and the theory of evolution.

What does all of this have to do with our finances? Good question! People make these same mistakes with money. First, they think the way they spend money is amoral when, in fact, every purchase is either moral or immoral. Second, they think money is immoral when it is amoral.

THE AMORAL NATURE OF MONEY

Because money is amoral, having more or less of it is not good or bad. The rich and poor are made in God's image, and therefore they have equal value: "The rich and the poor have this in common, the LORD is the maker of them all" (Proverbs 22:2).

Many of the greatest people in Scripture were wealthy. In the Old Testament, there were Abraham, Job, and Solomon. In the New Testament, there were Joseph of Arimathea, Lydia, and those who hosted church in their homes because they were wealthy enough to have homes that accommodated large groups.

You could look at this list of wealthy people and say, "They're rich, but we don't know that God wanted them to be rich. Maybe God wanted them to be poor, but they disobeyed Him!" The problem is we're told God gave them riches, which we wouldn't read if riches were immoral. Genesis 13:2 says, "[Abraham] was *very rich in livestock, in silver, and in gold.*" In the Abrahamic Covenant in the previous chapter, God said, "I will make you a great nation; *I will bless you* and make your name great, and you shall be a blessing" (12:2). Part of the blessing was wealth. Proverbs 10:22 says, "The blessing of the LORD makes one rich, and He adds no sorrow with it." Sometimes God blesses people with riches, and when He does, nothing negative accompanies it.

When Solomon replied that he wanted an understanding mind so he could better govern the people of Israel, God said, "Because...you have not asked for possessions, wealth, honor, or the life of those who hate you, and have not even asked for long life...wisdom and knowledge are granted to you. *I will also give you riches, possessions*, and honor, such as none of the kings had who were before you, and none after you shall have the like" (2 Chronicles 1:11-12 ESV). After Job's suffering ended, "The LORD blessed the latter days of Job more than his beginning. And he had 14,000 sheep, 6,000 camels, 1,000 yoke of oxen, and 1,000 female donkeys" (Job 42:12). This is rich, whether in the ancient world or ours.

Solomon, Hannah, and David saw wealth coming from God: "Every man to whom *God has given riches and wealth*…a man to whom *God has given riches and wealth* and honor, so that he lacks nothing for himself of all he desires" (Ecclesiastes 5:19; 6:2); "The LORD *makes poor and makes rich*" (1 Samuel 2:7); and "*Both riches and honor come from You*, and You reign over all" (1 Chronicles 29:12). God also gives the ability to obtain riches: "You shall remember the LORD your God, for it is He who *gives you power to get wealth*" (Deuteronomy 8:18). Would God do this if money was immoral?

Although, before you start thinking that being rich is good, or moral, consider that some of the greatest men in Scripture were also poor, including our Lord: "Though He was rich, yet for your sakes *He became poor,* that you *by His poverty* might become rich" (2 Corinthians 8:9). Jesus said, "Foxes have holes, and birds of the air have nests, but *the Son of Man has nowhere to lay His head*" (Matthew 8:20). Jesus lived in such poverty during His earthly ministry He didn't even have a bed. The apostles followed His example: "Peter said, 'See, *we have left all* and followed You'" (Matthew 19:27).

Clearly, being rich or poor is not moral or immoral, righteous or sinful, because money is amoral. But what we do with money, and the way we feel toward it is moral. Let's consider these two important truths in detail.

How We Spend Money Is Moral

Money, like other possessions, such as homes or vehicles, is a resource we can use honorably or dishonorably. Regardless of how much or little money we have, every cent we spend is moral or immoral.

We can spend money morally by caring for our families, blessing others, and giving to the church. We can spend money immorally if we buy something ungodly, support something sinful, or satisfy our covetousness.

James Moffatt said, "A man's treatment of money is the most decisive test of his character—how he makes it and how he spends it."[3] We can tell what our priorities are by looking at our checkbook and calendar. They reveal what we do with two of our most valuable assets: our money and time. The way we spend these reveals much about our morality.

How We Feel About Money Is Moral

Our relationship with money, which is to say the way we feel about it, is also moral. Consider how many verses condemn loving money:

- Luke 16:14 criticizes the Pharisees for being lovers of money.

- First Timothy 3:3 says one of the qualifications for elders is they don't love money.

- Second Timothy 3:2 says one of the behaviors characterizing the wickedness of the last days will be love for money.

- Hebrews 13:5 commands us to keep our lives free from the love of money.

Why so many verses warning against loving money? The answer is in 1 Timothy 6:9-10:

> Those who desire to be rich fall into temptation, a snare, into many senseless and harmful desires that plunge people into ruin and destruction. For *the love of money is a root of all kinds of evils.* It is through this craving that some have wandered away from the faith and pierced themselves with many pangs (ESV).

Let's unpack these powerful verses over the rest of the chapter.

THE LOVE OF MONEY, VERSUS MONEY, IS THE PROBLEM

Consider the way the Amplified Bible translates parts of 1 Timothy 6:9-10: "Those who...crave to get rich [with a compulsive, greedy longing for wealth]...the love of money [that is, the greedy desire for it and the willingness to gain it unethically]..." These verses are not about people who say, "It would be nice to be rich." Instead, they are about people so fixated on riches it controls their lives, and this is the danger.

You have probably heard the well-known maxim, "Money is the root of all evil." This sounds similar to what 1 Timothy 6:10 says, but there are two differences, which, although subtle, are significant.[4]

First, the maxim says money is the cause of all evil in the world, but we've already discussed that money itself is amoral. There is plenty of evil that has nothing to do with money. It's not right to think money is immoral or responsible for evil because that puts the blame in the wrong place. Jesus blamed our hearts: "Out of the heart proceed evil thoughts, murder, adulteries, fornications, thefts, false witness, blasphemies" (Matthew 15:19), and James blamed our flesh: "Each one is tempted when he is drawn away by his own desires and enticed. Then, when desire has conceived, it gives birth to sin; and sin, when it is full-grown, brings forth death" (James 1:14-15). Evil is not birthed from money, but it is birthed from us giving in to temptation.

Second, the maxim makes money the problem, but Paul said, "The *love* of money is the root of all kinds of evils" (ESV). We should blame our relationships to money, not money itself. We get into trouble when we love money, regardless of how much wealth we have. People can love money whether they're rich or poor. The poor would love to be rich, and the rich would love to be richer. This should cause us to examine how we feel about money: Do we covet it, dream about it, and obsess over it? These are important questions because the love of money can be, as Paul said, "a snare."

TRAPPED BY THE LOVE OF MONEY

I once watched a fascinating video of a man trapping a monkey.[5] He hollowed out a space on the side of a mound and put food in it. The opening was large enough only for a monkey to insert his hand to get the food. Then the man stood behind a tree a little distance away and waited. A monkey went to the opening, put in his hand, and grabbed the food. The opening wasn't big enough for the monkey to remove its hand with the food, and because it wouldn't let go, it was trapped. While the monkey tried to free itself, the man came up from behind and captured it.

While it's easy to mock the monkey because it was caught by its own foolishness, the same can happen to us. Paul said those who love money "fall… into a snare" (1 Timothy 6:9 ESV). The Greek word translated snare is *pagis*, and it refers to a trap in which animals are entangled and caught unexpectedly, like the monkey. Let's consider the ways loving money can snare us so we can avoid being trapped.

Loving Money Leads to Sin

Murder, adultery, and lying are clearly evil, but it is the desire to be rich really that bad? It is, because of the sin it produces.

We would expect Paul to say desiring to be rich *is* the temptation, but instead, he said if we "desire to be rich [we] *fall into* temptation" (ESV). In other words, loving money causes us to be tempted. The Greek word translated "desire" is *boulomai,* and it means "to will deliberately." This speaks of people who have decided they will be rich, versus allowing God to make them rich (assuming that is His will for their lives). The desire to be rich leads to temptation because this leads people to be willing to do almost anything to reach their goal. Nothing—including resisting sin—will stand between them and the money they're committed to obtaining.

Once the love of money has taken root in people's hearts, rare is the evil that can't be perpetrated. Many crimes are motivated by greed, jealousy, covetousness, or all the above. People will lie, cheat, steal, and even murder to become rich. So instead of saying money is the root of all evil, because the problem is actually the love of money, a fitting statement would be that the *lack of money* is the root of *their* evil.

A few verses earlier, 1 Timothy 6:6 says, "Godliness with contentment is great gain." People who love money lack contentment. If they were content, they wouldn't desire to be rich. Instead of being filled with godliness, they're filled with ungodliness, which leads to their sinful behavior. Here are some examples from Scripture:

- Achan was willing to steal and then deceive to get what he wanted (Joshua 7:10-26).

- Balaam was willing to go against the expressed will of God to get what he wanted (Numbers 22:4-41).

- Gehazi coveted the money Naaman offered, and he was willing to engage in numerous sins to get it (2 Kings 5:15-27).

- Judas was willing to betray the Lord for thirty pieces of silver (Matthew 26:14-16).

People who love money have broken the first of the Ten Commandments because they have made money their god, and they have broken the second commandment because they have made money their idol. Then, it is only slightly more compromising to break the other commandments, which forbid lying, stealing, adultery, taking God's name in vain, and murder. J.C. Ryle said,

> Let us all be on our guard against the love of money. The world is
> full of it in our days. The plague is abroad. Thousands who would

hate the idea of worshiping [an idol] are not ashamed to make an idol of gold. We are all liable to the infection, from the least to the greatest. We may love money without having it, just as we may have money without loving it. It is an evil that works very deceitfully. It carries us captives before we are aware of our chains. Once it becomes master, it will harden, paralyze, scorch, freeze, blight, and wither our souls. It overthrew an apostle of Christ: Judas. Let us take heed that it does not overthrow us.[6]

Loving Money Hurts Others

We might think loving money only affects the sinner but, as is the case with all sin, there are far-reaching consequences that affect everyone around the sinner, such as family, friends, neighbors, and coworkers. These people must

- experience the sinner's obsession and discontentment
- suffer through the compromise and deceit
- shoulder the financial and legal problems caused

Achan is a perfect example. Think of the cost to his family! Proverbs 15:27 says, "Whoever is greedy for unjust gain troubles his own household" (ESV). Could there be a better example than Achan? The "greedy for unjust gain [trouble their] household" as they

- neglect their families—how many people have sacrificed marriages for jobs, or put the next promotion ahead of their children?
- fight over money—how many families have been destroyed after someone died and the relatives quarreled over the inheritance? These people love money more than their family members. As a lawyer will tell you, "Where there's a will, there are relatives."

Loving Money Ruins and Destroys

Loving money is also a trap because it will "plunge people into ruin and destruction" (1 Timothy 6:9 ESV). Here, the words "ruin" and "destruction" are synonymous. God repeats Himself to drive home the devastating consequences.

The Greek word translated "plunge" is *bythizō*, and it means "to sink into the deep, or drown." The only other place it occurs in Scripture is when the disciples experienced the miraculous catch of fish: "They signaled to their partners in the other boat to come and help them. And they came and filled both the boats, so that they began to sink [*bythizō*]" (Luke 5:7). Just as the disciples began to sink and inevitably would've drowned, people's love of money—figuratively speaking—causes them to sink and drown. The form of *bythizō* presents a continual action, which means that as long as people love money, they will keep sinking, drowning, and heading toward ruin and destruction.

We know there are negative consequences to loving money in this life, but what about the next life? In other words, are we talking only about temporary ruin and destruction, or are we talking about eternal ruin and destruction? There are eternal consequences too!

The following verse, 1 Timothy 6:10, says, "It is through this craving that some have *wandered away from the faith* and pierced themselves with many pangs" (ESV). We are saved by faith, so when people have "wandered away from the faith," they have wandered away from salvation. This isn't to say they have lost their salvation, but that they have abandoned the way to be saved. The imagery is of people straying off a path and finding themselves in thorn bushes where they "pierce themselves with many pangs."

Other verses also communicate the eternal consequences. First Corinthians 6:10 says, "[The] greedy...will [not] inherit the kingdom of God" (1 Corinthians 6:10 ESV). The rich man who ignored Lazarus loved money and went to hell (Luke 16:23). The rich young ruler serves as a sobering example of "[wandering] away from the faith" (1 Timothy 6:10 ESV). Let's examine his account so as not to miss the warning it provides.

Loving Money Requires Repentance

Nobody wants to think they would walk away from the Lord, but when people do, what would you imagine causes them to do so? Would it be the loss of a child, an unfaithful spouse, a terminal disease, or a Christian friend's betrayal? The rich young ruler did because he loved money:

> As [Jesus] was going out on the road, one came running, knelt before Him, and asked Him, "Good Teacher, what shall I do that I may inherit eternal life?"

So Jesus said to him, "Why do you call Me good? No one is good but One, that is, God. You know the commandments: 'Do not commit adultery,' 'Do not murder,' 'Do not steal,' 'Do not bear false witness,' 'Do not defraud,' 'Honor your father and your mother'" (Mark 10:17-19).

There's much to appreciate about the ruler. He looks humble and genuine. He thinks highly of Jesus and is interested in spiritual matters. He believes in God and wants to go to heaven. Jesus's response to him shouldn't be interpreted as though He is not good or not God. Instead, He is saying the opposite: There is only One who is good, and that is God—so if the ruler calls Jesus good, he must also recognize Jesus is God.

Jesus answered the ruler's question by telling him he could inherit eternal life if he kept God's commandments (obeyed the law) perfectly. Because none of us can do that, God graciously provided a way for us to be righteous by faith apart from the law: "The *righteousness of God* has been manifested *apart from the law*...The *righteousness of God through faith* in Jesus Christ for all who believe...For we hold that one is justified *by faith apart from works of the law*" (Romans 3:21-22, 28 ESV).

If we can't be righteous by the law, what purpose does it serve? It reveals our unrighteousness: "By the law is the *knowledge of sin*" (Romans 3:20). Paul said, "If it had not been for the law, I would not have known sin" (Romans 7:7 ESV). Recognizing our sin reveals our need for the Savior; therefore, Jesus shared the Ten Commandments with the ruler so he would see his need for Christ:

> You know the commandments: "Do not commit adultery," "Do not murder," "Do not steal," "Do not bear false witness," "Do not defraud," "Honor your father and mother."
>
> And he answered and said to Him, "Teacher, all these things I have kept from my youth."
>
> Then Jesus, looking at him, loved him, and said to him, "One thing you lack: Go your way, sell whatever you have and give to the poor, and you will have treasure in heaven; and come, take up the cross, and follow Me." But he was sad at this word, and went away sorrowful, for he had great possessions (Mark 10:19-22).

In a truly remarkable demonstration of pride, self-deception, or both, the ruler said he had kept all the commandments. Because the ruler didn't recognize his sin, Jesus told him to sell his possessions. This ended up revealing the ruler's sin of covetousness.

Part of Jesus's dealing with the ruler is descriptive (describing what happened), and part is prescriptive (prescribing, or instructing, us to do the same). Jesus told him to sell everything he had and give it to the poor. This is descriptive of what happened, but it is not prescriptive for us—we don't need to sell everything we have and give it to the poor. John 2:24 says Jesus "knew all people" (ESV), and Hebrews 4:12 says He "is a discerner of the thoughts and intents of the heart." Because Jesus knew the ruler and what was in his heart, He knew what he needed to repent of: covetousness and idolatry.

While we might not need to repent of the same as the ruler, the part that is prescriptive is the need to repent. The ruler needed to repent of loving money, and we might need to repent of bitterness, lying, pornography, or theft. Because each of us struggle with different sins, repentance looks different for each person. But the commonality is we must all repent.

CHOKING CHRIST OUT OF OUR LIVES

In the parable of the sower, Jesus said, "He who received seed among the thorns is he who hears the word, and the cares of this world and the *deceitfulness of riches choke the word*, and he becomes unfruitful" (Matthew 13:22). The love of money chokes the spiritual out of our lives, and the ruler is a good example of what it looks like when this happens.

We can have only so many things occupying space in our hearts. To let one thing in is to keep out something else. This is good if we let in Christ, but bad if we let in loving money.

Jesus told him to choose between his possessions and the Lord. Sadly, he chose his possessions. Regardless of how sincere he was and how much he wanted to inherit eternal life, he was not willing to part with his wealth. Jesus told him, "You will have treasure in heaven," but earthly treasure was more important to him. He might be the best example in Scripture of disobeying

Jesus's words in Matthew 6:19-20: "Do not lay up for yourselves treasures on earth...but lay up for yourselves treasures in heaven." In response:

> Jesus looked around and said to His disciples, "How hard it is for those who have riches to enter the kingdom of God!" And the disciples were astonished at His words. But Jesus answered again and said to them, "Children, how hard it is for those who trust in riches to enter the kingdom of God! It is easier for a camel to go through the eye of a needle than for a rich person to enter the kingdom of God" (Mark 10:23-25).

There are different opinions about what it means "for a camel to go through the eye of a needle," but the main point is obvious: It's hard for rich people to enter heaven. Their riches are an obstacle to salvation. Whatever "the eye of a needle" is, a camel can't fit through it. Similarly, people who love money can't "fit" into the kingdom of God. Their wealth doesn't leave room for Christ.

The issue is competition. We can have only so many things occupying space in our hearts. To let one thing in is to keep out something else. This is good if we let in Christ, but bad if we let in loving money. As we discussed earlier, money can become an idol, and we don't have room for two gods in our hearts. We can have Christ, or the love of money, but not both. Let's make sure we choose wisely.

While the ruler thought about the next life, another wealthy man in Scripture thought only about this life, and that's the rich fool. Before we start learning what *to do* with our wealth, the parable about the rich fool will show us what *not to do* with our wealth. In the next chapter, we will learn important ways to avoid being foolish with money.

CHAPTER 5

Learning from a Rich Fool

Malcom Forbes was an American entrepreneur who is most well-known as the publisher of *Forbes* magazine. He's also remembered for several sayings, and one that he said repeatedly is "He who has the most toys wins." Just as you would expect from someone who said this, he lived an extravagant, flamboyant lifestyle. He spent millions (or perhaps billions) on parties, traveling, his collection of yachts, aircraft, art, motorcycles, castles, hot-air balloons, and Fabergé eggs, some of which cost over one million dollars each.

When I was growing up, there was a popular line of clothing called No Fear. They had one shirt that corrected Malcom's quote: "He who dies with the most toys still dies." The people working for the secular clothing company were considerably more biblical than Mr. Forbes. They recognized that regardless of how much a man has, he can't "add a single hour to his span of life," as Jesus said (Matthew 6:27 ESV). The No Fear clothing company also recognized we can't take any of our toys, or possessions, with us, because if we could, then the one who died with the most toys would be the winner.

The rich fool in Jesus's parable seems like the Malcolm Forbes of the Bible. He lived only for this life:

> The land of a rich man produced plentifully, and he thought to himself, "What shall I do, for I have nowhere to store my crops?" And he said, "I will do this: I will tear down my barns and build larger ones, and there I will store all my grain and my goods. And I will say to my soul, 'Soul, you have ample goods laid up for many years; relax, eat, drink, be merry.'" But God said to him, "Fool!

This night your soul is required of you, and the things you have prepared, whose will they be?" So is the one who lays up treasure for himself and is not rich toward God (Luke 12:16-21 ESV).

The rich fool's harvest was so great he ran out of room to store it. As a farmer, because his crops are basically money, it's like he has more money than he knows what to do with. How would you like to have this problem? Believe it or not, it ended up being a big problem for him! He didn't understand the concept of stewardship that we discussed in some earlier chapters, and that anything he had ultimately belongs to God and was meant to be used for His glory.

EVERYTHING COMES FROM GOD

Some things are harder to be viewed as coming from God. For example, if you study for a degree, it's hard to say, "God gave this to me" because you feel like you earned it. The same can be said if you're faithful at work and get promoted, or practice an instrument and became an accomplished musician, or train for a race and win. But with some other things, it is easier to see God's hand in them. For example, we have nothing to do with where and when we are born. While I was working on this book we had our ninth child, and we see God's hand in this child's birth because we can't create life. Only God can do that.

One more thing we should view as coming from God is a good harvest, or "land [producing] plentifully." Although I haven't been a farmer, I know it's a profession that greatly depends on circumstances outside of our control. My father-in-law, Rick, is a farmer. Katie says she remembers growing up watching her father stand at the window looking at the clouds with concern after he just cut the alfalfa because rain would ruin his crop. One of the elders I serve with is a farmer. Over the years he has asked people to pray for his crops because he knew that ultimately, the crops were in God's hands—He must provide and withhold the rain at the right times, as well as warm the earth and make the seed grow: "God gave the growth. So neither he who plants nor he who waters is anything, but only God who gives the growth" (1 Corinthians 3:7 ESV). Farmers can do all the right things, but if God doesn't bless their efforts, then the land won't produce plentifully.

The farmer asked, "What shall I do, for I have nowhere to store my crops?" This is a good question, and there are lots of good answers, such as, "Because

God gave me such a great crop, I'll give back to Him! I'll donate to the temple, the synagogue, the poor, widows, or orphans." But he didn't come up with any good answers. Instead, he thought only about one person: himself.

WISE IN THE WORLD'S EYES, BUT FOOLS TO GOD

Let's be honest: does the rich man look like a fool? Not at all. He was an astute farmer and successful businessman who was able to accumulate considerable wealth. If you took this man's story, made it into a present-day example, and published it in a business magazine—such as *Forbes* or *Bloomberg Businessweek*—what would people say? He's wise! He demonstrated many of the financial principles we will discuss in the following chapters, such as

- not being wasteful—he said, "What shall I do, since I have nowhere to store my crops?"

- planning—he said, "I will do this: I will pull down my barns and build larger ones."

- saving—he said, "There I will store all my grains and my goods."

- preparing for the future—he said, "I will say to [myself]…you have ample goods laid up for many years."

You would be hard-pressed to find someone who seemed to handle money better than this man. He looks like he could have written this book. But did God say to him, "You have been a tremendous steward. What a great job you have done financially." Nope. God called him a fool. It's ironic that a man could look so wise and be called a fool.

Let me make one point from this parable absolutely clear: People can look wise and successful in the world's eyes, but they can be fools and failures in God's eyes. Conversely, people can look wise and successful in God's eyes, but they can look like fools and failures in the world's eyes. Consider Paul's words with added thoughts from me: "Let no one deceive himself. If anyone among you seems to be wise in this age [as the rich fool did], let him become a fool [do what the world says is foolish, such as serve the Lord, give away some of what you have, and avoid debt] that he may become wise [in God's eyes]. For the wisdom of this world is foolishness with God. For it is written, 'He catches the wise in their own craftiness'" (1 Corinthians 3:18-19).

The rich fool is a good example of this. He said, "I will do this and this and this," but God caught him in his craftiness.

Because we want to look good and be wise in God's eyes versus the world's eyes, let's consider why God said this man was a fool. After all, we wouldn't want God to say the same of us.

The Rich Man Was a Fool Because He Didn't Give

As we will see in chapter 14, there are many verses encouraging saving and preparing for the future; therefore, what was wrong with the rich man's plans? In three verses, he said "I" six times and "my" five times. He failed to think about anyone else. There's no mention of a wife, kids, employees (perhaps giving them a bonus), friends, neighbors, or God.

Let me illustrate the rich fool's selfishness by providing a simple economics lesson from the Old Testament. Second Kings 6:25 says, "There was a great famine in Samaria; and indeed [Syria] besieged it until a donkey's head was sold for eighty shekels of silver, and one-fourth of a [quart] of dove droppings for five shekels of silver." They ran out of food, and this was an issue of supply and demand: no supply and high demand, so the prices of everything skyrocketed. You know things are bad when dung is selling for five shekels.

God was going to provide the city with a huge amount of food, so the prophet Elisha said, "Tomorrow about this time [six quarts] of fine flour shall be sold for a shekel, and [twelve quarts] of barley for a shekel, at the gate of Samaria" (2 Kings 7:1). The supply skyrocketed and prices plummeted.

The rich fool wanted to avoid this kind of situation. He knew if he flooded the market with his crop, there would be high supply, low demand, and prices would plummet. Selfishly, he decided to build barns to store his crops so he could control the supply and keep prices high.

During droughts and famines, farmers with grain could hike up their prices and become rich at the expense of their needy neighbors. For example, in Nehemiah's day, the people said,

> With our sons and our daughters, we are many. So let us get grain,
> that we may eat and keep alive…We are mortgaging our fields,
> our vineyards, and our houses to get grain because of the famine…
> We have borrowed money for the king's tax on our fields and our
> vineyards…Yet we are forcing our sons and our daughters to be
> slaves, and some of our daughters have already been enslaved, but

it is not in our power to help it, for other men have our fields and our vineyards (Nehemiah 5:2-5 ESV).

Nehemiah "became very angry" and said they were showing no fear of God (Nehemiah 5:6, 9). The rich fool similarly showed no fear of God. We can imagine how godly leaders would be angry with him because of his selfishness.

To prepare us for the upcoming chapters on giving, the lesson here is that God does not bless us so we can spend our fortunes on ourselves. He blesses us so we can be a blessing to others. Whether we're rich or poor, God expects us to serve Him by serving people. This parable should cause us to look at our wealth and consider how we're using it to benefit others. Are we generous? Do we use what God has blessed us with to be a blessing?

The Rich Man Was a Fool Because He Didn't Plan for Eternity

In Scripture, many people's lives contain ironies. For example, Abraham was the father of faith, but at times he lacked faith and was fearful, such as when he told his wife to say she was his sister because he was afraid for his life. He did this twice (Genesis 12:13; 20:2). Samson was the strongest man to ever live, but he was so weak with Delilah she overcame him (Judges 16:6-17). Solomon was the wisest man to ever live, but he was so foolish later in life he married 700 women who "turned away his heart" from the Lord (1 Kings 11:3).

The rich man's life contains an irony too. He thinks he's a great long-term planner, but he was completely unprepared for the future. He had an earthly, temporal view that ignored the spiritual and eternal. He said he had "goods laid up for *many years*," but God said, "*This night* your soul will be required of you." He didn't have years, months, weeks, or even days. He had hours.

The rich fool got life and death wrong. He got life wrong because he thought life consisted in the abundance of his possessions, but immediately before the parable, Jesus said, "One's life *does not consist in the abundance of the things he possesses*" (Luke 12:15). He got death wrong because he thought his death was far away, but he wouldn't live to see another day. He might be the best example in Scripture of failing to observe James 1:9-11: "Let the… [rich boast] in his humiliation, because as a flower of the field he will pass away. For no sooner has the sun risen with a burning heat than it withers the grass; its flower falls, and its beautiful appearance perishes. So *the rich man also will fade away in his pursuits."* This happened with the rich fool, and it can happen to us too.

How many people have thought they had years, or even decades, ahead of them only to receive the news that they have months or even weeks? These are the fortunate people, because they learned their lives were coming to an end so they could prepare for eternity. What about unbelievers whose lives end unexpectedly, perhaps because of an accident? They have no time to prepare for eternity.

If you ask most people how they want to go, they'll say, "Quietly in my sleep when I'm old." But this is a good way to go only if they know the Lord. If they don't know the Lord, it's a terrible way to go because they won't have any more time to repent. When people are not living for the Lord, the best scenario for them is to receive the news that they don't have much time left so they can be shaken from their spiritual slumber and consider their eternal destiny.

The rich fool should cause us to ask, "Are we thinking about eternity and living in light of it? Do we believe our soul could be required of us tonight, or do we believe—perhaps wrongly—that we have decades left?" And speaking of our souls…

The Rich Man Was a Fool Because He Didn't Know to Whom His Soul Belonged

What did the rich fool lose? You could say all his wealth and possessions, which is true, but he also lost something infinitely more important, and that's his soul. He said, "I will say to my soul, 'Soul, you have many goods laid up for many years'" (Luke 12:19). He thought his soul belonged to him, but God said, "Fool! This night your soul will be required of you." His soul was taken from him because it belonged to God.

In Matthew 16:26, Jesus asked, "What profit is it to a man if he gains the whole world, and loses his own soul? Or what will a man give in exchange for his soul?" Hopefully, you don't have an answer other than "Nothing!" There is nothing worth trading for our soul. The rich man is a great picture of the opposite of Jesus's words—he seemed to gain the whole world but lose his soul.

The rich fool should cause us to ask: "Do I recognize God owns me, including my soul? Do I understand I'm going to be called to give an account for what I've done with the life God has given me? Would I trade the whole world for my soul?"

The Rich Man Was a Fool Because He Wasn't Rich Toward God

People can be physically rich and spiritually poor, or spiritually rich and physically poor. This is illustrated by two churches mentioned in the book of Revelation:

- Smyrna, the persecuted church, was physically poor and spiritually rich. Jesus told them, "I know your tribulation and *your poverty* (but *you are rich*)" (Revelation 2:9 ESV).

- Laodicea, the lukewarm church, was physically rich and spiritually poor. Jesus told them, "You say, '*I am rich*, I have become wealthy, and I have need of nothing'—and do not know that you are wretched, *poor*, blind, and naked" (Revelation 3:17).

The rich fool was also financially rich, but spiritually—and therefore eternally—poor. There's no record of him lying, cheating, or stealing. He seemed to be a diligent, hardworking man who obtained his wealth in an honest, moral way. Although we aren't told he went to hell, it is implied. God's judgment seems surprisingly strong for a man who doesn't look that bad, or some might even say looked moral. What was so bad about him? Jesus gave the answer: "[He was] not rich toward God" (Luke 12:21). No matter how much wealth we accumulate in this life, if we aren't rich toward God, we are poor fools.

The rich fool is like the third servant in the parable of the talents. There's no record of the third servant doing anything evil, but there's also no record of him doing anything good; therefore, he's called a "wicked and lazy servant" (Matthew 25:26). The rich fool is different in that he wasn't lazy—he was hard-working—but he's similar in that he also did nothing for God.

People might look at the rich fool and say, "What a tragedy that he died just when he had everything going for him." This isn't the tragedy. The tragedy is that he entered a Christless eternity. He lived without God throughout his earthly life, and he would do the same throughout his eternal life.

There was no mention of God in the account until He appeared and called the rich man a fool. Can you imagine never thinking about God (or at least never taking Him seriously), and then the first time you do is when you stand before Him on the day of judgment? God gave the rich man many blessings, such as wisdom, strength, wealth, success, business, health, and even creation itself: "He makes his sun rise on the evil and on the good, and sends rain on the just and on the unjust" (Matthew 5:45). The rich fool enjoyed these blessings, including the sunlight and rain on his fields that made him rich. But he gave no thought to the God who gave them to him.

This is a parable, which means I can't say that what happened with the rich fool is exactly what's going to happen to every unbeliever, but there could be similarities. Unbelievers enjoy blessings, such as relationships, jobs, food, wealth, homes, possessions, health, and creation. Every breath they take is from God, yet they don't thank Him, worship Him, or look to the Savior He provided. The first time they'll take Him seriously is when they hear something like, "Fool! This night your soul will be required of you" (Luke 12:20), or "I never knew you; depart from Me" (Matthew 7:23), or "Cast the unprofitable servant into the outer darkness. There will be weeping and gnashing of teeth" (Matthew 25:30). Yes, this is a parable, but it makes important points, and one of the most important is that if we are spiritually bankrupt, we are foolish.

WHAT MONEY CAN'T DO

The world leads us to believe if we are rich enough we can have whatever we want, which makes it tempting to be like the rich fool. But Scripture reveals those with little can be far richer than those with much if they have—and do not have—certain things. For example:

- Proverbs 15:16 says, "Better is a little with the fear of the LORD, than great treasure with trouble." The poorest people with a healthy reverence for God are far richer than people with great treasure and the trouble that might come with it.

- Proverbs 15:17 says, "Better is a dinner of herbs where love is, than a fatted calf with hatred." The simplest meal with healthy relationships is better than the greatest feast with fighting.

- Proverbs 16:8 says, "Better is a little with righteousness, than vast revenues without justice." Right standing with God makes people far richer than the wealthiest, who are unjust.

- Proverbs 17:1 says, "Better is a dry morsel with quietness, than a house full of feasting with strife." Having peace and harmony with little food is better than a house filled with food but accompanied by conflict.

- Psalm 37:16 says, "Better is the little that the righteous has than the abundance of many wicked" (ESV). The poorest godly people are wealthier than the richest ungodly people.

Money can buy a vehicle, house, or even a person's loyalty for a while, but there are also many things even the richest people can't buy. Money can buy beds but not sleep, books but not intellect, food but not an appetite, expensive clothes but not beauty, medicine but not health, pleasures but not peace, luxuries but not culture, amusements but not joy. Scripture provides similar examples:

- Proverbs 19:6 says, "Many entreat the favor of the nobility, and every man is a friend to one who gives gifts." We use the language of finances when talking about relationships. We say we "value" a friend and "invest in" someone, but money can't buy genuine relationships.
- Proverbs 22:1 says, "A good name is to be chosen rather than great riches, loving favor rather than silver and gold." Money can't buy a respected reputation.

The parable of the rich fool reveals other things riches can't buy:

- Money couldn't buy the rich fool longer life when the time came for him to die.
- Money couldn't buy back the opportunities he missed while he was selfish and thought only about himself.
- Money couldn't buy him spiritual riches toward God after ignoring Him throughout his life.

When Simon the sorcerer saw demons being cast out of people, he thought it was the power of magic versus the power of the gospel. He wanted it for himself, so he said, "Give me this power also, that anyone on whom I lay my hands may receive the Holy Spirit." But Peter responded, "Your money perish with you, because you thought that *the gift of God could be purchased with money!*" (Acts 8:19-20). Simon didn't understand the gifts of God cannot be bought. Wealth can be useful for certain ends, such as supporting the spread of the gospel, but it can't purchase spiritual power.

Along those lines, most seriously of all, the parable of the rich fool reveals money can't buy salvation. Only the gospel can!

WHAT THE GOSPEL CAN DO

It's easy to feel good about ourselves when reading about the rich fool because his selfishness is so clear and his condemnation is so strong. But let's be honest: We're selfish too! He focused only on this life, and we often focus only on this life. He didn't plan for eternity, and we often don't plan for eternity. He didn't send anything ahead, but we often don't send anything ahead. He didn't think about God, and we often don't think about God.

At this point you might expect me to tell you, "So stop being selfish, focus on the next life, plan for eternity, send stuff ahead, and think about God." But that's not the gospel! We'll never be completely free from our selfishness; we'll never perfectly plan for eternity; we'll never send everything ahead; and there won't be a day that we always think about God.

God's grace has the glorious effect
of producing obedience in every area of life,
including the handling of our finances.

We need to be saved as much as the rich fool needed to be saved, but that salvation doesn't come through human effort: "He saved us, *not because of works done by us* in righteousness, but according to his own mercy" (Titus 3:5 ESV). The gospel is that if we repent of our sins and put our faith in Christ, He saves us.

Besides revealing that we can't buy salvation, which is to say we can't purchase a right standing with God, what else does this have to do with money? After we are saved, the gospel works in our hearts and empowers us to manage our finances well. If we had to be good stewards of our finances in our own strength, we would end up feeling discouraged and defeated. But if we remember that God's grace allows us to obey and do what's right, we can be encouraged: "God is able to make all grace abound toward you, that you, always having all sufficiency in all things, may have an abundance for every good work" (2 Corinthians 9:8). God doesn't command us without giving us the necessary grace. As has been said before: God does not call the equipped. He equips the called. He is with us, providing for us, and enabling us. His grace has the glorious effect of producing obedience in every area of life, including the handling of our finances.

CHAPTER 6

How to Avoid Being a Rich Fool

People don't become doctors the day they decide they want to pursue a medical career. The decision must be made years earlier, and they must make many sacrifices to endure through an internship and residency. Similarly, if people want to be lawyers, they don't wake up one day and say, "I'm going to be a lawyer," and then start trying cases. The decision to become a lawyer must be made well before, and it involves years of commitment before taking on clients.

You might already have an IRA because you are planning for the golden years. You don't wake up when you're older and say, "Let me start a retirement plan." The decision is made years earlier so you are prepared when you reach retirement. Perhaps you are saving for your children's education. You don't attend their high school graduation and say, "I'd better put something aside to pay for their college." The decision must be made long in advance.

The lesson is that knowledge of the future determines our behavior in the present. When we know what we desire in the future, we will make decisions to reach those goals in the present.

This has great application for us as stewards. If we want to hear "Well done, good and faithful servant," we don't wait until the end of our lives to start being faithful. We make the decision to be faithful starting now. Today! The verses we will examine next can help put us on the right path.

THE RICH HAVE GREATER ACCOUNTABILITY

First Timothy 6 addresses two groups. The first group, "who desire to be rich" and have a "love of money," are in verses 9 and 10, and we talked about them in chapter 4. The second group is "those who are rich in this present age" in verses 17 through 19, whom we will discuss in this chapter.

For now, it is important to notice Paul doesn't criticize the second group, who is rich, but as we know from chapter 4, he criticizes the first group, who desires to be rich. This seems backward! We would expect Paul to criticize the first group, who is rich, while pitying the second group, who is not rich. Why is it this way? Because, as we also discussed, money is amoral. The problem is not being rich. The problem is a love of money, or a strong desire to be rich.

But even though being rich isn't bad, it does mean having a greater accountability before God. Stewardship is more difficult with more money because there is more to steward. So, Paul has special instructions for rich people:

> As for the rich in this present age, charge them not to be haughty, nor to set their hopes on the uncertainty of riches, but on God, who richly provides us with everything to enjoy. They are to do good, to be rich in good works, to be generous and ready to share, thus storing up treasure for themselves as a good foundation for the future, so that they may take hold of that which is truly life (1 Timothy 6:17-19 ESV).

If the parable of the rich fool (which we looked at in the previous chapter) tells rich people what *not to do*, these verses tell rich people what *to do*. Now, maybe you are thinking something like, *Oh, I'm not rich, so these verses don't apply to me.* As I shared earlier, measured by the living standards of the rest of the world, and especially those throughout history, Americans are rich. We must be careful not to read verses about riches and think they apply to others but not us.

With that in mind, the above verses include four instructions to the rich. Let's look carefully at each of them for our spiritual and financial benefit.

First, the Rich Should Be Humble (Versus Proud)

Paul first commands the rich "not to be haughty" (verse 17), because pride is one of the most common temptations they face. Riches and pride (or haughtiness) often go together. The Greek word translated "haughty" means "to have an exalted opinion of oneself." Those with large amounts of money can be tempted to feel superior and look down on those with less money;

therefore, God says, "Don't be high-minded. You are not better than those with less because you have more."

Riches are not an indication of how great we are; instead, they are an indication of how gracious God has been to us.

Proverbs 18:23 says, "The poor man uses entreaties, but the rich answers roughly." Wealthy people might ignore the pleading of the poor, but pride would cause the rich to respond harshly because they think they're better than the poor. Proverbs 28:11 says, "The rich man is wise in his own eyes, but a poor man who has understanding searches him out." Pride causes rich people to think highly of themselves, but poor people with discernment can see right through it because they know they're equal.

If we're rich, how do we avoid haughtiness and looking down on others? Part of the answer is in the words that follow: "God, who richly provides us with everything to enjoy." Keeping in mind that we have what we do only because God provided it leaves no room for haughtiness. Riches are not an indication of how great we are; instead, they are an indication of how gracious God has been to us. In 1 Corinthians 4:7, Paul asked three questions: "Who makes you differ from another? And what do you have that you did not receive? Now if you did indeed receive it, why do you boast as if you had not received it?" The answers are (1) God, (2) nothing, (3) we shouldn't. Recognizing that God gave us all we have, including riches, prevents pride, keeps us humble, and leaves no reason for boasting.

Second, the Rich Should Trust God (Versus Their Riches)

Paul revealed another temptation the rich must resist: "[setting] their hopes on the uncertainty of riches, [instead of] God." One of the dangers with money is it can provide a false sense of security. Think back to the rich fool, who said, "I will say to my soul, 'Soul, you have many goods laid up for many years; take your ease; eat, drink, and be merry'" (Luke 12:19). He was confident about the future not because he trusted in God, but because he trusted in his wealth. We must avoid this by following the advice of the psalmist: "If riches increase, do not set your heart on them" (Psalm 62:10).

In our country, it's an especially strong temptation to trust in riches because we are literally encouraged to do so. Our national retirement plan is called Social Security because it's supposed to make us feel secure about our future. Our investments are called securities and trusts because they're supposed to make us feel secure, and we're supposed to put our trust in them.

Money can take the place of God when we

- view money the way we should view God

- put our faith in money like we should put our faith in God

- make money an idol by calling it "the almighty dollar," as though it's sovereign and able to give us whatever we want

- treat money like a god by living for it, worshipping it, sacrificing to it, and filling our minds with thoughts about it

- let our lives be controlled by having more of it

What's ironic about all this is our money is imprinted with the motto "In God We Trust." This phrase first appeared on coins in 1864 and was adopted as the official motto of the United States in 1956. One year later, in 1957, the words appeared on our paper currency. The words themselves are associated with a number of verses in the Bible:

- "[I] will trust in the LORD" (Psalm 40:3).

- "I have put my trust in the Lord GOD" (Psalm 73:28).

- "It is better to trust in the LORD than to put confidence in man" (Psalm 118:8).

- "Whoever trusts in the LORD shall be safe" (Proverbs 29:25).

If we put our trust in money, there are only two possible outcomes, and both are bad. First, it lets us down. In the parable of the unjust steward, Jesus said, "Make friends for yourselves by means of unrighteous wealth, so that *when it fails* they may receive you into the eternal dwellings" (Luke 16:9 ESV). As already discussed, unrighteous wealth is earthly money, and "it fails" us. Proverbs 11:28 says, "*He who trusts in his riches will fall*, but the righteous will flourish like foliage." Many people will tell you that putting confidence in their bank accounts left them terribly disappointed. Proverbs

18:11 says, "The rich man's wealth is his strong city, and like a high wall *in his own esteem*." Wealthy people think their money makes them invincible, but it's all in their mind.

The other possibility, which is even worse than money failing us, is it *doesn't seem* to fail us. Riches allow us to get what we want, so we think we don't need God. Proverbs 30:8-9 warns of the danger: "Give me [not] riches...lest I be full and deny You, and say, 'Who is the LORD?'" Rich people can stop desiring anything, including God. One of the worst things to happen to rich people is they allow their riches to pull them away from the very God who gave them the riches in the first place. This is why money only *seems* to not fail them. In separating them from God, it fails them in an unimaginable way.

Third, the Rich Should Do Good Works (Versus Only Give)

The rich shouldn't only be rich in money. They "are to do good, to be *rich in good works*" (1 Timothy 6:18 ESV). Rich people have greater potential for acts of service—their wealth provides them with the ability to do things people with less money might not be able to do.

Why stress this to rich people? They might see giving as a substitute for doing. It might be easier for them to give money, instead of time, effort, or energy. It's easier to pay for a mover than to help people move, pay for someone to clean the house than to help people clean their house, pay for groceries than to bring people a meal. For the rich husband, it's easier to buy his wife something expensive than to spend time with her. For the rich mother, it's easier to spend money on her kids than to do things with them. So, Paul says the rich must *do* good works too.

Fourth, the Rich Should Give Generously (Versus Stingily)

The rich should also "be generous and ready to share" (1 Timothy 6:18 ESV). This probably doesn't come as any surprise, as it is the main command we would expect God to give to rich people. We know from the parable of the talents in chapter 1 that some are given more talents (wealth) than others, and God expects more from them. As we will see in future chapters, everyone should give, but rich people should be

- "generous," which refers to the amount given.

- "ready to share," which refers to the attitude toward

giving—anxious to share their wealth to bless others and meet their needs.

If rich people give generously, they will be "thus storing up treasure for themselves as a good foundation for the future, so that they may take hold of that which is truly life" (1 Timothy 6:19 ESV). This means preparing for eternity, because "that which is truly life" refers to the next life—that's the real or true life. Some translations, such as the KJV and NKJV, read "lay hold on eternal life." Paul said something similar a few verses earlier: "*Take hold of the eternal life* to which you were called" (1 Timothy 6:12 ESV).

The words "take hold" or "lay hold" of the next life don't mean we can obtain salvation in our own effort. Only Christ can do that for us. Instead, we must "get a grip" on eternal matters by living with a heavenly, spiritual perspective. The rich should "[store] up treasure for themselves" (1 Timothy 6:19 ESV), similar to Jesus's counsel: "Do not lay not up for yourselves treasures on earth, where moth and rust destroy and where thieves break in and steal, *but lay up for yourselves treasures in heaven*, where neither moth nor rust destroys and where thieves do not break in and steal" (Matthew 6:19-20).

Think back to the rich fool. He did the opposite of what Paul and Jesus said and laid up treasures on earth. The rich fool also disobeyed James 5:1-3, which mirrors Jesus's words: "Come now, you rich, weep and howl for your miseries that are coming upon you! Your riches are corrupted, and your garments are moth-eaten. Your gold and silver are corroded, and their corrosion will be a witness against you...*You have heaped up treasure* [for the day of judgment]." Like Jesus, James also said earthly wealth is destroyed by moth and rust. In contrast, we can have "a good foundation for the time to come" (Timothy 6:19) if we lay up treasure for ourselves in heaven, because that's the only place it can't be destroyed.

Keeping in mind that everything we possess breaks down, rusts, decays, and can be stolen makes generosity easier. As we remember these things, earthly wealth loses value in our eyes and becomes easier to part with. Let me provide three other encouragements that also make generosity easier.

Give Generously Because You Can't Take It with You

I was not raised in a Christian home. I became a Christian in my early twenties, shared the gospel with my parents, prayed for their salvation for a few years, and—by God's grace—they became believers. I was able to baptize them. They moved to be with us in Washington, living only two houses down from us. Dad served as a deacon in the church I pastor.

A recent Sunday night, my mom called me terrified, begging me to rush to their house. My dad had Alzheimer's, so I thought he was angry or had wandered off, but the situation was much worse. He was unconscious on the floor, and he was not breathing. My good friend and associate pastor, Nathan, followed me to my parents' house and we both took turns administering CPR. The paramedics arrived and worked on my dad for more than an hour, but they were unable to revive him.

I don't know at what point my father passed away. The paramedics might say it was when he stopped breathing, his heart stopped beating, or his brain stopped functioning. But the Bible tells us it occurred when his spirit left his body:

- "The body *without the spirit* is dead" (James 2:26).

- "They stoned Stephen as he was calling on God and saying, 'Lord Jesus, *receive my spirit*'" (Acts 7:59).

- "Jesus cried out again with a loud voice, and *yielded up His spirit*" (Matthew 27:50).

The spirit is immaterial (nonphysical), and the body is material (physical). When the spirit leaves the body, it takes nothing material (physical) with it. We come into the world with nothing and leave the same way. I was thinking about this when the paramedics took my father's body away because they handed me his possessions, including his watch and hearing aids. He didn't need them any longer, and wouldn't be taking them with him to heaven:

- Job said, "Naked I came from my mother's womb, and naked shall I return" (Job 1:21).

- Korah said, "Wise men die; likewise the fool and the senseless person perish, and leave their wealth to others…When he dies he shall carry nothing away; his glory shall not descend after him" (Psalm 49:10, 17).

- Solomon said, "As he came from his mother's womb, naked shall he return, to go as he came; and he shall take nothing from his labor which he may carry away in his hand" (Ecclesiastes 5:15).

- Paul said, "We brought nothing into this world, and it is certain we can carry nothing out" (1 Timothy 6:7).

God asked the rich fool, "The things you have prepared, whose will they be?" (Luke 12:20 ESV). The answer? Not his! Whatever we accumulated during our life is left to others: friends, family, neighbors, the church, or the government. We don't know exactly where our wealth will go; we just know it won't go with us. This is the greedy person's worst nightmare: "I hated all my labor in which I had toiled under the sun, because *I must leave it to the man who will come after me*" (Ecclesiastes 2:18).

Proverbs 23:5 says, "Will you set your eyes on that which is not? For riches certainly make themselves wings; they fly away like an eagle toward heaven." Riches tend to fly away when we least expect it, and if there's one time they really fly away, it's when we die. John Piper said,

> At the greatest crisis of your life [when you die], when you need contentment, and hope, and security more than any other time, your money and all your possessions take wings and fly away. They let you down. They are fair-weather friends at best. And you enter eternity with nothing but the measure of contentment that you had in God.[1]

God repeatedly reminds us that we take nothing with us—not because He wants to discourage us, but because He wants to encourage us to live in light of this reality. Randy Alcorn said,

> When Jesus warns us not to store up treasures on earth, it is not just because wealth might be lost; it is because wealth will always be lost. We leave it when we die. Realizing its value is temporary should radically affect our investment strategy.[2]

When a rich man dies, people ask, "How much did he leave behind?" The answer is "All of it!" You never see U-Hauls behind hearses because we aren't taking anything with us. Keeping this in mind makes giving generously much easier.

Jim Elliot was a Christian missionary killed along with four other men while attempting to evangelize the Huaorani people of Ecuador. He famously said, "He is no fool who gives what he cannot keep to gain what he cannot lose." This quote applies perfectly to earthly wealth: We should be generous with money in this life because we can't take it with us when we enter the next life. But when we give money away in this life, we lay up treasures in heaven.

Give Generously to Send Wealth Ahead

We have two choices about what to do with our money. The first choice is to keep it for ourselves. This leaves us like the rich fool, who was prepared for this life but unprepared for the next. When we chose to enjoy our wealth now, we don't get to enjoy it in heaven, which leaves us eternally destitute:

> A rich man died and went to heaven. Abraham greeted him and said, "Welcome to heaven. Let me show you where you'll be staying."
>
> As they walked, the rich man saw beautiful mansions stretching out in every direction. They were constructed of gold and silver and precious gems. As they passed one mansion, the rich man said, "Who gets to stay here?"
>
> Abraham replied, "That's for your groundskeeper. He was a godly man who loved Jesus and served Him all his life. This is his reward."
>
> They continued past other mansions, until they reached an extremely large one. The rich man asked Abraham, "Is this one mine?"
>
> Abraham said, "No, this one belongs to your maid. On the little bit of money you paid her, she raised six children and gave to her church."
>
> They continued to walk until they came to a different section of homes that weren't as nice. As they walked up a small hill, they stopped in front of a shack made of tar paper and used sheet metal. The front door was cut out of an old refrigerator box. It was held together with bailing wire, twine, and duct tape. After pausing for a moment, the rich man asked, "Who lives here?"
>
> Abraham responded, "Why, this is yours!"
>
> The rich man couldn't believe it. He said, "There must be some mistake!"
>
> Abraham said, "No, there's been no mistake. We did the best we could with what you gave us!"[3]

How tragic that some people work so hard to prepare for the final years of this life but neglect the eternity that follows!

The second choice for how we handle our wealth is to send it ahead! What we give away on this side of heaven is kept for eternity. The best stewards in this life have much waiting for them in the next.

Give Generously Because You Enjoy Riches for Only a Short Time

Imagine there's a house you've wanted for as long as you can remember. One day the owner of the house hands you the keys and says, "You can have it!" You're excited, but then he adds, "The only catch is it's going to burn down in a short period of time." How excited are you now?

But this is also the case with everything the world offers, including our money. Think back to Jesus's and James's words about earthly treasures being destroyed by moth, rust, and rot. When viewed in light of eternity, everything we have will be burned down in a short period of time.

The Christian life must be lived by keeping the shortness of it in view. When Jonathan Edwards was only 19, he wrote 70 resolutions that he committed to practicing for God's glory. Number nine was, "To think much, on all occasions, of my dying." This might sound a little morbid, but he wanted to always remember how temporary this life is.

Jonathan Edwards isn't the only one who thinks we should focus on the shortness of this life. God wants us to do the same. We know that because He repeats this point throughout Scripture:

- "What is your life? It is even a vapor that appears for a little time and then vanishes away" (James 4:14).

- "My life is a breath!" (Job 7:7).

- "My days are consumed like smoke" (Psalm 102:3).

- "Man is like a breath; his days are like a passing shadow" (Psalm 144:4).

Generosity is also made easier when we focus on the temporary nature of this life because we recognize our wealth is enjoyed for only a short period of time. Adam Clarke said, "It requires but little of this world's goods to satisfy a man who feels himself to be a citizen of another country, and knows that this is not his [home]."[4]

The short enjoyment of riches is illustrated well in Daniel's life. Here's the background: Belshazzar was the king of Babylon, which was the superpower of the day. He threw a party, invited 1,000 lords, and drank from the vessels the Babylonians took from the temple when they conquered the Jews (Daniel 5:1-3). While they drank and praised their false gods, a hand appeared and wrote on the wall of the palace, terrifying Belshazzar (Daniel 5:5-6). Wanting to know what the writing meant, he said to Daniel:

> "If you can read the writing and make known to me its interpretation, you shall be clothed with purple and have a chain of gold around your neck and shall be the third ruler in the kingdom."

> Then Daniel answered, and said before the king, "Let your gifts be for yourself, and give your rewards to another; yet I will read the writing to the king, and make known to him the interpretation… And this is the inscription that was written: Mene, Mene, Tekel, Upharsin. This is the interpretation of each word: Mene: God has numbered your kingdom, and finished it; Tekel: You have been weighed in the balances, and found wanting; Peres: Your kingdom has been divided, and given to the Medes and Persians." Then Belshazzar gave the command, and they clothed Daniel with purple and put a chain of gold around his neck, and made a proclamation concerning him that he should be the third ruler in the kingdom.

> That very night Belshazzar, king of the Chaldeans, was slain. And Darius the Mede received the kingdom, being about sixty-two years old (Daniel 5:16-17, 25-31).

Daniel was offered the most common worldly desires: riches, fame, and position. He declined because he knew it was all temporary—Babylon would be conquered that night. Belshazzar gave Daniel the rewards anyway, but he possessed them for only a few hours.

It's tempting to say, "Sure it was easy for Daniel to decline Belshazzar's offer because he would enjoy everything for only a little while. What about the things I can possess for years or decades?" In light of eternity, whether it's a few hours, years, decades—or even if we could enjoy earthly possessions for centuries or millenniums—it is still only a short period of time. Wisdom dictates we should give generously to store up in heaven what we can enjoy for eternity.

A BETTER APPROACH TO GIVING

The rich should "be generous and ready to share" (1 Timothy 6:18 ESV), but are they the only ones expected to give? No. Everyone is expected to give. Poor people can be as guilty of stinginess, bad stewardship, and financial foolishness as the rich fool.

The obvious question, then—for the rich and poor alike—is, "How *much* should we give?" We'll answer this question in the following chapters. But first, let me provide some encouragement for what is to come. I know giving can be challenging, and in the Christian life we are frequently tempted to think the answer is simply trying harder. If we roll up our sleeves and give it our best shot, surely we'll become generous people, right? Wrong. Giving is a heart attitude (more about this in chapter 7!). Many people have experienced ongoing frustration when trying to be better at giving but finding little change—it is still difficult for them!

A better approach is to remember that if we are Christians, the power of the gospel is at work in our lives. While you read, keep in mind that it's not about you white-knuckling it. Instead, God's grace empowers you to obey: "It is God who works in you both to will and to do for His good pleasure" (Philippians 2:13). With God's help—with the Spirit's enablement—we can manage our finances well, and even enjoy giving!

CHAPTER 7

Give Willingly

———————

Giving, and the amount Christians should give, is a controversial topic. If you've been in the church for long, you've probably heard different opinions. And you may have your own thoughts based on your experiences up to this point. May I ask you a couple of questions?

First, have you been told that you should tithe?[1] If so, take a moment to consider whether New Testament verses cause you to think this way. I believe it's clear that Christians are commanded to give, but they're not commanded to give a tithe, which brings me to my second question.

Second, if you've believed that you must give a tithe, will you consider a different view if it is supported by Scripture? The obvious question you might ask is, "If we aren't commanded to give a tithe, then how much do we give?" That's the topic of the next chapter. In this chapter, I want to show that God calls us to give willingly.

Having asked those questions, here's a principle I'd like to ask you to begin applying in your heart: God wants us to give out of thankfulness rather than out of obligation. Keep in mind how much God has done for you so you're moved to give out of a heart of worship versus out of duty.

Please don't assume any of this is merely my opinion. I believe it is vital for us to be convinced by God's Word alone, and on this topic, understanding what Scripture teaches requires some technical information. Bear with me as we get this foundation in place!

THE NEW TESTAMENT DOESN'T COMMAND GIVING A TITHE

Not long after becoming a Christian, I heard that I should tithe. As my familiarity with the New Testament grew, my confidence in this claim waned because I couldn't find any supporting verses. Giving a tithe is clearly commanded under the Old Covenant, which is associated with the Mosaic law. But Christians today are under the New Covenant, which is associated with the law of Christ. Paul notes this distinction in the New Testament:

> To the Jews I became as a Jew, that I might win Jews. To those who are under the law, as under the law, that I might win those under the law; to those who are without the law, as without law (not being without law toward God, but *under law toward Christ*), that I might win those who are without the law (1 Corinthians 9:20-21).

Paul said to win Jews to Christ, he would put himself back "under the [Mosaic] law," which means he hadn't been adhering to the requirements of that law since coming to Christ. When he tried to win Gentiles ("those who are without [the Mosaic] law"), he ensured he wasn't under the Mosaic law. But to prevent readers from thinking he was without any law, he said he remained "under law toward Christ." The point is that there's a clear distinction between two different laws and how they relate to our giving:

- the Mosaic law, which is associated with the Old Covenant (which we are not part of), and its mediator, Moses, commands giving a tithe

- the law of Christ, which is associated with the New Covenant (which we are part of), and its mediator, Jesus, doesn't command giving a tithe [2]

The tithe was God's way of paying the priests who served God's people all through the Old Testament era up through the time of Jesus's earthly life. After Christ's death, burial, and resurrection, He became our great high priest (Hebrews 4:14). This produced a change, because "when there is a change in the priesthood, there is necessarily a change in the law as well" (Hebrews 7:12 ESV).

Two Categories of Commands

The Mosaic law was divided into two categories. First are the moral commands, or what we think of as the commonsense commands, such as, "You shall not murder…commit adultery…steal…bear false witness." These commands are based on God's nature, which defines morality for us. Because God's nature doesn't change, morality doesn't change, and because morality doesn't change, the moral commands don't change. Because the moral commands don't change, they are brought forward from the Old Covenant into the New Covenant. They're part of the law of Christ and are still binding for us today.

The second category is the ceremonial commands, which are amoral (not moral or immoral). These commands are not common sense in that we wouldn't intuitively come up with them. Think of the commands related to sacrifices and offerings, feasts and festivals, abstaining from certain foods (such as pork and rabbit), farming certain ways, and avoiding mixing certain fabrics. The command to give a tithe was also ceremonial, and thus it was not carried forward into the New Covenant and is not part of the law of Christ.

One fact that might surprise many people is God didn't even command giving a tithe in the Mosaic law. He commanded giving *multiple* tithes: one for the Levites, one for the use of the temple and the feasts, and one for the poor of the land (Leviticus 27:30-32; Numbers 18:21-32; Deuteronomy 14:22, 28-29; 26:12). All these tithes pushed the total closer to 25 percent. If people want to put themselves "under the law," as Paul said in 1 Corinthians 9:20, they should give closer to one-fourth of their earnings rather than one-tenth, for one-fourth is what the Old Testament Jews were commanded to give.[3]

Further complicating the situation for people who feel bound to give a tithe is the fact the Mosaic law commanded giving a tithe on grain, wine, oil, and animals. How would this apply today? I suppose the best we could do is give away one-tenth of our food, clothing, and possessions. Instead, God has a better (but tougher) way for us to give today.

A Higher Standard for Giving

Like many people, when I began reading the Bible, I started "in the beginning" with Genesis, which I loved. Exodus was also enjoyable, but then I reached Leviticus. Maybe some new believers have liked reading the 613 commands in that book for the first time, but I admit that I didn't. I moved to the New Testament and started reading through Matthew. I reached the Sermon on the Mount, and it changed my life.

At that time, I didn't know Jesus was contrasting the Mosaic law and the law of Christ, but I could tell He was raising the bar. Six times He quoted the Mosaic law, "You have heard that it was said…," followed by, "But I say to you…," revealing the higher standard the law of Christ set regarding murder, adultery, divorce, swearing, revenge, and love (Matthew 5:21-22, 27-28, 31-34, 38-39, 43-44).[4]

Because the law of Christ raised the bar in these areas, we can conclude that it raised the bar for giving too. As Christ's followers, ten percent shouldn't be seen as the end of Christian giving. It should be seen as the beginning!

No Mention of Tithing in the New Testament

The final reason we know we're not commanded to give a tithe (or any percent, for that matter) is that it's not commanded, or even recommended, in the New Testament. The word *tithe* appears only four times (Matthew 23:23; Luke 11:42; 18:12; Hebrews 7:5-9), and none of these passages are instructions for church-age Christians to give a tithe.[5]

The epistles are the instruction letters for New Covenant believers (those under the law of Christ), but there's no mention of giving a tithe. Considering there's extensive teaching on prayer, love, forgiveness, serving, and many other topics in the epistles, this silence is inconceivable if God expected us to give a tithe.

THE NEW TESTAMENT EXPECTS GIVING WILLINGLY

Why doesn't God command us to give a certain percent? Because He wants us to give willingly out of thankfulness, versus giving out of obligation to a command. Second Corinthians 8 and 9 provide the richest, most detailed teaching on giving in the New Testament. Keep these chapters in mind because we'll repeatedly draw from them to understand Christian giving.

Paul told the Corinthians, "See that you *excel in everything* [and that would include giving]. I say this *not as a command*" (2 Corinthians 8:7-8 ESV). This is interesting! Paul was an apostle, which means he had the authority to command his readers to give. We know he wanted them to give because that was the point of this portion of his letter, but right when it sounded like he was about to command them to give, he clarified that he was *not* doing that. Why? He wanted them to give willingly!

In the next chapter, Paul said,

> I thought it necessary to exhort the brethren to go to you ahead
> of time, and prepare your generous gift beforehand, which you

had previously promised, that it may be *ready as a matter of generosity and not as a grudging obligation*...let each one *give as he purposes in his heart*, not grudgingly or *of necessity*, for God loves a cheerful giver" (2 Corinthians 9:5, 7).

The Corinthian believers promised they would give, but they hadn't yet because it's much easier to talk about giving than to actually give. Paul reminded them of their promise by sending Christians ahead to get the gift, but he still wanted it to be a willing gift and not done under obligation. He didn't want to force the gift out of them. The words "grudging obligation" refer to the conditions when giving. We're not supposed to give because of external pressure, such as the demands of others. When giving is done this way, it resembles taxation more than worship.

Paul's words are clear, which is why it's disappointing when Christian leaders disobey them. We can't help but think of televangelists and pastors saying almost anything to get people to give. They will guilt, shame, lie, and make ridiculous promises if it helps them obtain one more dollar. They aren't trying to help people grow in their relationships with the Lord. Instead, they're motivated by greed and covetousness. Bible teacher Warren Wiersbe said,

> During my years of ministry I have endured many offering appeals. I have listened to pathetic tales about unbelievable needs. I have forced myself to laugh at old jokes that were supposed to make it easier for me to part with my money. I have been scolded, shamed, and almost threatened, and I must confess that none of these approaches has ever stirred me to give more than I planned to give. In fact, more than once I gave less because I was so disgusted with the worldly approach.[6]

Writer Mark Twain once quipped, "I was so sickened by the long appeal that I took a bill out of the plate."[7] We don't pass the plate at Woodland Christian Church because the Bible says people aren't supposed to give "of necessity." Instead, we offer different ways for people to give when and how they want. To give praise to God, I'll share that He has always taken good care of us. I can't think of one leadership meeting that has ever involved concern over our finances. You might think that's rare, but as elders, we keep coming back to how it's our position to trust God to provide, but it's not our position to tell the congregation how much to give. Instead, we encourage the congregation to pursue God in this area and seek His guidance on how much He would have them give.

WE MUST DECIDE HOW MUCH TO GIVE

Paul said, "Let each one give *as he purposes in his heart*" (2 Corinthians 9:7). Can I be honest with you? I don't like these words! I prefer black-and-white instructions. I have joked with my wife that I was born under the wrong covenant, and that I need the precision of the Mosaic law. I don't want to have to decide how much to give. I want God to tell me.

You can't miss the point, though: If we were commanded to give a tithe, Paul would have said, "Let each one give *a tithe*." But he didn't. This means no one can tell you how much to give, and that includes your pastor. You're welcome to email me when you finish this book. I love to hear from my readers! But if you say, "I read your whole book and I still don't know how much to give," I'll reply that you are correct because you must decide the amount on your own. The New Testament doesn't tell us how much to give, but it *does* give us principles to help us determine the amount, and we'll look at those in the next chapter.

For now, I can tell you we shouldn't decide casually or flippantly. I'm not saying we need to agonize over how much, or fast and pray for extended periods of time, but the decision shouldn't be taken lightly. In the Amplified Bible, 2 Corinthians 9:7 reads, "Let each one give [*thoughtfully and with purpose*] just as he has decided in his heart." We must put some effort into deciding the amount because God is looking at what's in our hearts versus our hands.

GOD SEES THE "HEART GIFT" VERSUS THE "HAND GIFT"

Imagine a man has a wallet divided into two sections. In one section he puts the money for the offering. In the other section he puts the rest of his cash, which is a considerably larger amount.

When the offering is taken, he accidentally reaches into the wrong part of his wallet, takes out the large amount of cash, and puts that in the plate. After the service he realizes what happened, tells the pastor, and comforts himself by saying, "It doesn't really matter, though, because I gave it to the Lord, and He recognized the amount I gave."

The pastor asked, "How much did you intend to give?"

The man answered, "I intended to give the smaller amount, but I accidentally gave the larger."

The pastor replied, "Then that's what God recognized because that's what you decided to give in your heart."

Wow, that's telling, isn't it? Think of it like this: If we want to give more but can't, God recognizes that, because He sees what's in our hearts. If the hand gives more than the heart wanted to give, God recognizes that, too, because He sees what's in the heart versus in the hand.

GIVING WILLINGLY IN THE OLD TESTAMENT

You might ask, "If God wanted His people to give willingly under the New Covenant, why did He command them to give a tithe under the Old Covenant?"

First, the tithe served a similar purpose as the taxes we pay today.[8] In the same way that our taxes support the government and its services, the Old Testament tithe supported the Jewish nation's priesthood and their services.

Second, even though God commanded specific tithes from the Israelites, He still wanted His people to give willingly even under the Old Covenant. Consider these examples.

In Exodus 25, God wanted Israel to build the tabernacle. Because it's the Old Testament, we might expect Him to say, "Every man must give a tithe so the tabernacle can be built." Instead, He said, "From every man *whose heart moves him* you shall receive the contribution for me" (Exodus 25:2 ESV). There's no mention of giving a tithe even though the Mosaic law had just been instituted in the previous chapter.

Later, Moses said, *"This is the thing which the* LORD *commanded,* saying: 'Take from among you an offering to the LORD. *Whoever is of a willing heart,* let him bring it as an offering to the LORD'" (Exodus 35:4-5). We might expect Moses to say, "The thing that the Lord has commanded is a tithe," but he appealed to the people's generosity because he wanted them to give willingly. A few verses later, parts of Exodus 35:21-29 record this:

> Everyone came *whose heart was stirred,* and everyone *whose spirit was willing,* and they brought the LORD's offering...They came...
> as many had *a willing heart* ...All the women whose *hearts stirred...*
> The children of Israel...whose *hearts were willing* to bring material

for all kinds of work which the LORD, by the hand of Moses, had commanded to be done.

The words "heart was stirred…spirit was willing…willing heart…hearts were willing" describe the willing giving God wanted even under the Mosaic law. There's a strong emphasis on the people themselves (their hearts and spirits) versus an external source, such as the priests or law. This prevented them from giving "of necessity" (2 Corinthians 9:7).

Regarding giving to the poor, Deuteronomy 15:10 says, "You shall *give to him freely*, and your *heart shall not be grudging* when you give to him" (ESV). This language is similar to 2 Corinthians 9:7: give freely and "not grudgingly." Again, Deuteronomy 16:10 says, "Keep the Feast of Weeks to the LORD your God with the tribute of *a freewill offering* from your hand."

Solomon described the giving that results in blessing: "One *gives freely*, yet grows all the richer; another *withholds* what he should give, and only suffers want" (Proverbs 11:24 ESV). Giving willingly is elevated, while giving reluctantly causes suffering.

Which one—a willing giver or a reluctant giver—better describes you? Often the best way to learn who we are and who we need to be is by example. Let's consider two Old Testament givers.

Jacob Demonstrates Giving Unwillingly

In the Old Testament, Jacob tricked his brother, Esau, out of his birthright. Jacob's mother, Rebekah, told him to flee because Esau wanted to murder him for his deception. Jacob had to leave his family behind, not knowing when or if he would see them again. At this low point in Jacob's life, God spoke to him in a dream and made him many wonderful promises. When Jacob woke, Genesis 28:20-22 tells us what happened:

> Jacob made a vow, saying, "If God will be with me, and keep me in this way that I am going, and give me bread to eat and clothing to put on, so that I come back to my father's house in peace, then the LORD shall be my God. And this stone which I have set as a pillar shall be God's house, and of all that You give me *I will surely give a tenth to You.*"

I read this and picture God sarcastically saying, "Wow, I can't believe it. Jacob, you'll give Me a full tithe!" Jacob hasn't been given the name *Israel* yet, which means he's still "heel grabber" versus "God prevails." He tried to manipulate everyone in his life, including God. The bargain he wanted to strike was that if God would do these things for him, then God would be his God and he would give Him a tithe. Jacob's loyalty and giving was conditional. He implied that if God didn't do these things for him, then God wouldn't be his God and he wouldn't give Him a tithe. But we don't make God our God and give because of what He will do for us. We make God our God and give because He *is* God and because of what He has *already* given us.

At times, we can be tempted to give unwillingly like Jacob. We might pray something like, "God, if You'll do this for me, then I'll do this for You. If You'll give me this raise…bonus…car…house…, then I'll give You this in return."

If we give unwillingly, consider what God can and can't bless. He can bless the gift, which is to say He can still use the money for His purposes. He doesn't look at the gift and say, "This was given unwillingly so I can't do anything with it." But can God bless us? It's hard to imagine any spiritual benefit for the giver when the giving is done reluctantly versus willingly. Let's consider Abraham's example to see what it looks like to give willingly.

Abraham Demonstrates Giving Willingly

When Abraham rescued his nephew, Lot, by defeating four kings, he came to possess considerable wealth. After returning from the battle, he met Melchizedek, and Genesis 14:18-20 records the encounter:

> Melchizedek king of Salem brought out bread and wine; he was the priest of God Most High. And [Melchizedek] blessed [Abraham] and said: "Blessed be Abram of God Most High, possessor of heaven and earth; and blessed be God Most High, who has delivered your enemies into your hand." And he *gave him a tithe of all.*

The "principle of first mention" states that God reveals the truest meaning of words the first time they're used in the Bible.[9] When the word *tithe* appears in Leviticus, it's part of the Mosaic law, which is to say it's commanded. But when the word *tithe* occurs for the first time in the above verses, this is 500 years before the law was given. This is the truest tithing because it demonstrates giving willingly apart from the law. Abraham gave "as he purposes in his heart, not grudgingly or of necessity" (2 Corinthians 9:7). He gave like a New Covenant believer under the Old Covenant!

Melchizedek was a king and priest who blessed Abraham. Abraham responded by giving willingly to him. Jesus is also a king and priest: He's the King of kings (Revelation 19:16) and great High Priest (Hebrews 4:14). Considering how much more Jesus has blessed us than Melchizedek blessed Abraham, how much more willingly should we give to Jesus than Abraham gave to Melchizedek?

THANKFULNESS PRODUCES BETTER GIVING THAN LAW

Because there was no law commanding Abraham to give to Melchizedek, his giving was motivated by thankfulness. Giving out of thankfulness is superior to giving out of obligation, as evidenced by these two Old Testament accounts.

We'll always be motivated to give more when we give out of thankfulness.

First, the people of Israel gave for the construction of the tabernacle. Exodus 36:3-6 records:

> [The builders of the temple] received from Moses all the contribution that the people...brought for doing the work on the sanctuary. [The people] still *kept bringing him freewill offerings* every morning. [The builders] said to Moses, "The people bring *much more than enough for doing the work that the* LORD *has commanded us to do.*" So Moses *gave command,* "Let no man or woman do anything more for the contribution for the sanctuary." So the people were restrained from bringing (ESV).

The people gave so willingly Moses had to tell them to stop! Here we see a command connected to giving, but it was a command to stop. This is what hearts of worship produce. While I doubt we'll ever be told to stop giving, I can say that we'll always be motivated to give more when we give out of thankfulness.

The second example might involve the greatest amount of wealth ever accumulated in the Old Testament. David wanted to build the temple, but God told him he couldn't because he had "shed much blood (1 Chronicles 22:8). Because David was eager to make the temple a success, he did everything he could to help, stopping short of doing the actual building. He collected all the materials, stating that it included "one hundred thousand talents of gold [7,500,000 pounds] and one million talents of silver [75,000,000 pounds], and bronze and iron beyond measure, for it is so abundant" (1 Chronicles 22:14). How was so much wealth accumulated? The people gave willingly and joyfully:

> [David asked], "Who then is *willing* to consecrate himself this day to the LORD?" Then the [people]...offered *willingly*...[They] *rejoiced*, for they had offered *willingly*, because with a loyal heart they had offered *willingly* to the LORD; and King David also *rejoiced* greatly. Therefore David blessed the LORD..."But who am I, and who are my people, that we should be able to offer so *willingly* as this?...As for me, in the uprightness of my heart I have *willingly* offered all these things; and now with *joy* I have seen Your people, who are present here to offer *willingly* to You" (1 Chronicles 29:5-17).

Again, this echoes the language of 2 Corinthians 9:7. The people gave willingly and joyfully (variations of each word used ten times), not reluctantly or under compulsion, and this prefigures the way God wants His people to give under the New Covenant.

It's important to observe that the Mosaic law wouldn't have produced this much generosity—the people would have stopped giving well earlier. Only thankful hearts can give this much because they've been moved to do so as an act of joyful worship.

This is another reason it's so sad when televangelists or church leaders try to get people to give out of obligation. What they should do is preach Christ and build people's love and thankfulness for Him. Then people will give willingly because of what He has done for them.

JESUS WILLINGLY GAVE MORE THAN A TITHE

Jesus gave Himself completely for us. This is illustrated no better than by the burnt offering, which is a wonderful picture of Christ.[10] The key verse is Leviticus 1:4: "[The priest] shall lay his hand on the head of the burnt offering, and it shall be accepted for him to make atonement for him." Let's consider how each part looks to Christ's sacrifice:

- "[The priest] shall lay his hand on the head of the burnt offering"—This communicated the transmission of sin to the animal, like our sins were transmitted to Jesus on the cross: "The LORD has laid on [Jesus] the iniquity of us all" (Isaiah 53:6).

- "...and it shall be accepted for him"—"Him" is the sinner, so this is substitutionary atonement. The animal died in the sinner's place, like Jesus died in our place.

- "...to make atonement for him"—The burnt offering made atonement for the sinner, just like Jesus "is the propitiation for our sins" (1 John 2:2).

Three verses—Leviticus 1:9, 13, and 17—record that "the priest shall burn *all of it* on the altar, as a burnt offering...with a pleasing aroma to the LORD." Paul applied this imagery to Jesus: "Christ also has loved us and given Himself for us, an offering and a sacrifice to God" (Ephesians 5:2). Burnt offerings were completely consumed, and Jesus is the true and greater burnt offering completely consumed for our sins. Instead of giving us 10 or 25 percent, Jesus gave us 100 percent. How could this truth not motivate us to give much better than any command?

SO WHY GIVE WILLINGLY?

We give because we're thankful. What an incredible gift God has given us in being able to worship Him this way! When we give willingly and not of necessity, we can be encouraged that we're giving the way God desires, "for God loves a cheerful giver" (2 Corinthians 9:7).

Because we're not commanded to give a tithe, in the next chapter we'll discuss the principles that help us decide on an amount. As you continue reading, keep Jesus in mind because only His radical act of self-giving can consistently move us to give as God desires—willingly out of thankful hearts of worship. Are you ready to jump in with me?

CHAPTER 8

Give Sacrificially

Early in our marriage, Katie and I were part of a home fellowship. A couple joined the group soon after being released from prison. Even though they hadn't been Christians for long, their affection for the Lord was evident. They were thankful that He had forgiven them, that He would want a relationship with them after the things they had done, and that He would allow them to begin new lives in Christ. Because of their decisions that led to their incarcerations, and the burned bridges with most—if not all—family members and friends, it wouldn't be too much to say that our home fellowship was just about all they had.

They were part of our group when Katie was pregnant with our first child, Rhea. Everyone was excited for us, but perhaps because this couple had no children or grandchildren, they seemed more excited than anyone else. They desperately wanted to give Rhea a gift when she was born, but as you can guess, they didn't have much.

They settled on a dirty, smelly blanket, which they put in a torn plastic bag. They were smokers, so we had to put the blanket on the sanitary cycle on our washer quite a few times, but we still couldn't get rid of the smell. While the blanket didn't cost much and was never useful to us, the gift was very meaningful. Why? Because they had so little, we knew the sacrifice they had made.

Giving is much bigger than the gift. If I can use two analogies, the gift is an iceberg above the water, and below the surface is what went into the gift. The gift is a tree, and the roots in the ground are what went into the gift. Please keep these illustrations in mind because I will refer to them throughout the chapter. Everything behind the giving is more important than the gift itself.

In Scripture, a great example of this is the believers in Macedonia. They gave a gift to the believers in Jerusalem, and so sacrificial was their giving that Paul used their example to challenge the Christians in Corinth. Please keep this in mind: The epistles weren't written only for the benefit of the church they were addressed to. The book of Romans wasn't just for the Romans; Ephesians wasn't just for the Ephesians; Corinthians wasn't just for the Corinthians. They were written to benefit all believers.

So, just as the believers in Macedonia challenged those in Corinth, they should also challenge us. When we examine all that went into the Macedonians' giving, we learn lessons to apply to our own giving.

THE MACEDONIANS—A GREAT EXAMPLE FOR THE CORINTHIANS AND US

Because the New Testament doesn't command giving a tithe (as we discussed in the previous chapter), how do we know how much to give? Although the New Testament doesn't tell us how much, it does give us principles to determine the amount. Most of these principles are found in two chapters: 2 Corinthians 8 and 9. If you want to read about Christian giving, go to these chapters. They provide the richest, most detailed teaching on giving in the New Testament, and we are going to dig into them in this chapter and the next.

The context for 2 Corinthians 8 and 9 is important. One of the major goals of Paul's third missionary journey was to gather a special offering for the poor Christians in Jerusalem. He wrote to the Corinthians to get them to give to the cause by telling them about the Macedonians. Just as Job is synonymous with suffering and Solomon is synonymous with wisdom, the Macedonians should be synonymous with giving. Paul wrote:

> We want you to know, brothers, about the grace of God that has been given among the churches of Macedonia, for in a severe test of affliction, their abundance of joy and their extreme poverty have overflowed in a wealth of generosity on their part. For they gave according to their means, as I can testify, and beyond their means, of their own accord (2 Corinthians 8:1-3 ESV).

The Macedonians gave "in a severe test of affliction." Macedonia was the northern region of Greece, where the churches of Philippi, Thessalonica, and Berea were located. This area had been ravaged by many wars, and even at the time of Paul's writing was still being plundered by Rome. This is a glimpse of the iceberg below the surface or the roots in the ground.

During trials, who do we tend to think about? Ourselves. Who do we tend not to think about? Others. But not the Macedonians! Even during their suffering, they still thought about, and gave considerably, to others.

Because the Macedonians gave so much, we would expect them to have been given so much (we would expect them to be rich), but it's the opposite! They gave while experiencing "extreme poverty." The Greek word translated "poverty" refers to a beggar with nothing and no hope of getting anything. And the believers in Macedonia weren't just in poverty, but "extreme poverty." When I think of first-century Christians, I think of people who were already deprived. For the Macedonians to be this poor means—financially speaking—they were the lowest of the low. But they still found a way to produce "a wealth of generosity." In chapter 6, we discussed the rich being commanded to give generously, but the Macedonians are a good example of the poor and afflicted giving generously too.

Paul said they gave "beyond their means." They gave more than they could afford. They didn't have the money, but they gave anyway. Considerable sacrifice went into their giving.

A Poor Widow's Giving

If the Macedonians are the best example in Scripture of corporately giving sacrificially, there's a familiar account that serves as the premier example of individually giving sacrificially:

> Jesus sat opposite the treasury and saw how the people put money into the treasury. And many who were rich put in much. Then one poor widow came and threw in two mites, which make a quadrans. So He called His disciples to Himself and said to them, "Assuredly, I say to you that this poor widow has put in more than all those who have given to the treasury; for they all put in out of their abundance, but *she out of her poverty* put in all that she had, her whole livelihood" (Mark 12:41-44).

I could bore you with a discussion of the different coins of the day and how much exactly this widow gave, but I don't think that's necessary. You can't miss that she gave a tiny amount.

Jesus called over His disciples to talk to them about what He had observed.

He wasn't impressed with the much that the rich put in. Instead, He drew their attention to the amount the widow gave. He watched "*how* the people put [in] money." The Greek word translated "how" is *pos* and means "in what way." Jesus wasn't just watching what people gave; He was watching *how*, or *in what way*, they gave. He looked beyond the gift to the giving.

First Samuel 16:7 says, "The LORD does not see as man sees; for man looks at the outward appearance, but the LORD looks at the heart." The widow is a good example because Jesus saw something that not even the disciples saw— she gave more than everyone else.

If rich people put in large sums and she put in a tiny amount, how could Jesus say she put in more than all of them? Clearly, He wasn't talking about the amount of money. He was talking about the *amount of sacrifice*. God sees our proportion versus our portion. The rich gave large sums, but they also retained large fortunes, which means they sacrificed little. The widow "put in all that she had, her whole livelihood," so she sacrificed much.

A few dollars given by some can be much more than hundreds or thousands given by others. Conversely, hundreds or thousands given by some can be much smaller than a few dollars given by others. George Muller said, "God judges what we give by what we keep."[1]

An Example of Eternal Rewards

If we get an elevated view of this account, it can serve as a window into the way the heavenly reward system works. The widow had no idea Jesus was watching her, just as we easily forget that the Lord is watching us. There's no indication the widow heard what Jesus said to the disciples, just as we don't know what the Lord thinks of our giving. When the widow put the coins into the treasury it's as though they were deposited into her heavenly account as well, just as we can lay up treasure for ourselves in heaven.

Considering Jesus said she put in more than everyone else, the amount she had deposited in eternity was greater than the amount she had deposited in the box. She put in two mites on earth, but "[laid] up for [herself much more] in heaven, where neither moth nor rust destroys and where thieves do not break in and steal" (Matthew 6:19-20). On the other hand, the "rich put in much" on earth, but little (maybe only two mites) in heaven.

Why God Cares About the Sacrifice Versus the Amount

The amount we give isn't of greatest importance to God because He doesn't need our money. He can accomplish His goals with or without our help. If we give a little but God needs a lot, He has no problem obtaining what He needs because "the highest heavens belong to the LORD your God, also the earth with all that is in it" (Deuteronomy 10:14; see also Psalms 50:10-11; 89:11; Haggai 2:8). God owns everything, so He doesn't ever think, *I sure hope so-and-so will give enough or I'm going to be in trouble.*

But this brings up a question: If God doesn't need our money, why does He want us to give at all? The answer is twofold. First, it is one of His ways of giving to us. He is graciously providing us the opportunity to participate in the work He's doing. Second, He is allowing us to worship Him. Because giving is an act of worship, and because God doesn't need the money, our worship isn't defined by the amount we give. Instead, our worship is defined by the amount we sacrifice.

Our Sacrifice Is Worship

Unfortunately, when we hear the word *worship*, we typically picture singing in church, but we should think of worship in terms of sacrifice. Under the New Covenant, we might believe there's no priesthood, high priest, temple, or sacrifices, but there's still a

- priesthood: "You [are]…a *holy priesthood*" (1 Peter 2:5).
- high priest: "We have a *great High Priest* who has passed through the heavens, Jesus, the Son of God (Hebrews 4:14).
- temple: "Do you not know that you are *the temple of God?*" (1 Corinthians 3:16; see also 6:19).

And there are still sacrifices! Just like New Covenant believers are priests and the temple, we're also expected to be sacrifices: "I appeal to you therefore, brothers, by the mercies of God, to present your bodies as a *living sacrifice*, holy and acceptable to God, which is your *spiritual worship*" (Romans 12:1 ESV). Did you catch the relationship between worship and sacrifice?

Under the Old Covenant, God accepted the sacrifices of dead animals as worship, but with Christ's sacrifice, dead animals are no longer acceptable. Instead, we worship by offering ourselves as living sacrifices, which means our very lives are to be lifted up in worship.

What does this have to do with giving? Giving can be worship, but it must involve sacrifice. Consider these three examples.

Sacrificial Worship with Abraham and Isaac

In the previous chapter, I explained the "principle of first mention." The first instance of the word "worship" occurred when Abraham was going to sacrifice Isaac: "Abraham said to [the two men who accompanied them], 'Stay here with the donkey; the lad and I will go yonder and *worship*, and we will come back to you'" (Genesis 22:5). It's hard to imagine that Abraham thought of sacrificing Isaac as worship. But because the greater the sacrifice, the greater the worship, this might be the greatest act of worship in the Old Testament.

Interestingly, who else did Abraham say would worship? Isaac! He said, "The lad and I will go...worship." How was Isaac worshipping? He was willing to be sacrificed! Because Romans 12:1 commands us to "present our bodies as a *living sacrifice*," aside from Jesus Christ Himself, there might be no better example of doing this than Isaac.

Sacrificial Worship with Animals

When people sin, there must be an accompanying death: "The wages of sin is death" (Romans 6:23). In the Old Testament, animals supplied the death in the sinner's place. These sacrifices were a temporary covering for sins that looked forward to Christ's substitutionary atonement: "[The sinner] shall offer the [animal] as a burnt offering...the priest shall make atonement on his behalf for the sin which he has committed, and it shall be forgiven him" (Leviticus 5:10).

If the animal's death was all that was needed to make atonement for the sin, why does Leviticus command 24 times that the sacrifices be "without blemish"? Animals that are old, sick, dying, and full of blemishes aren't good sacrifices because offering them doesn't involve much sacrifice.

Sacrificial Worship with David

David, who was a man after God's own heart, understood worship must involve sacrifice. God told him to build Him an altar on the threshing floor of Araunah the Jebusite. Araunah was a generous man who thought highly of David, so when David asked to buy Araunah's threshing floor, Araunah replied,

> Let my lord the king take and offer up whatever seems good to him. Look, here are the oxen for burnt sacrifice, and threshing implements and the yokes of the oxen for the wood. All these, O

king, Araunah has given to the king. May the LORD your God accept you (2 Samuel 24:22-23).

Araunah offered David everything needed for the sacrifice, including the threshing floor, animals, and the wood. But if David accepted all this, it wouldn't be David's sacrifice, it would be Araunah's; therefore, David replied:

> "No, but I will surely buy it from you for a price; *nor will I offer burnt offerings to the LORD my God with that which costs me nothing*." So David bought the threshing floor and the oxen for fifty shekels of silver (2 Samuel 24:24).

David wouldn't offer anything to the Lord that cost him nothing. He knew that a sacrifice that doesn't involve any sacrifice isn't a sacrifice.

Giving Without Sacrifice

The sacrifice behind the sacrifice (or the roots or iceberg below the surface) is what makes a sacrifice worshipful. Let's tie this back to giving. We want our giving to be worshipful, but if our giving doesn't involve any sacrifice, it isn't not worshipful. Giving without sacrifice is like offering animals that are full of blemishes, or offering a sacrifice paid for by someone else.

Erwin Lutzer said, "Those who give much without sacrifice are reckoned as having given little."[2] While I can't say how much we should give, I can say this: it must involve sacrifice. We should feel it. If we can't, we probably aren't giving enough.

Give According to Your Income

Giving is proportionate. God doesn't set a fixed percentage, but He does expect the amount to be relative to our income. The Macedonians "gave according to their means" (2 Corinthians 8:3 ESV). A few verses later Paul wrote, "For if the readiness is there, it is acceptable *according to what a person has, not according to what he does not have*" (verse 12 ESV). Both verses communicate giving is based on income. In Luke 12:48, Jesus said, "Everyone to whom much is given, from him much will be required." Although this is not directly about finances, it still communicates that if we're given more, we're expected to give more.

In Paul's previous letter, he said, "On the first day of the week let each of you lay something aside, storing it up *as he may prosper*, that there be no collections when I come" (1 Corinthians 16:2). They were to give according to the amount they prospered, which is to say according to their income. Donald Whitney said,

> The more you prosper, the higher should be the proportion of your giving. There is no percentage goal in giving. Giving ten percent of your gross income does not necessarily mean you have fulfilled the will of God. That's not a ceiling of giving to stop at, but a floor to move from.[3]

This principle reveals another problem with giving a tithe. Some people have prospered more than others, and therefore should give more. Others haven't prospered as much, and they can give less.

Giving in America

When you read, "Others who haven't prospered as much," you may have breathed a sigh of relief because you think that describes you. Maybe it does, but if you live in the United States, it's unlikely. As we've already noted, people in the US are typically the people who have prospered more than others. It's hard to imagine many Americans falling into the category of giving less because we make less. Most people in the rest of the world would love to prosper "as little as we do."

Although sadly, consider these statistics for American Christians:[4]

- Only five percent give ten percent of their income

- Eighty percent give only two percent of their income

- Thirty-seven percent of regular church attendees and evengelicals don't give money to the church

On average, American Christians give two-and-a-half percent of their income. To give that some perspective, during the Great Depression, it was almost three-and-a-half percent. On average, American Christians gave more during the Great Depression than we give now. Gene Getz said, "Statistics reveal that most Christians in America do not include God in their budgets. Sadly, God often gets what is leftover, if anything."[5]

The statistics are sad not because it means churches aren't getting enough money, although I'm sure that's the case in many congregations. It's sad because of what it reveals about the condition of American Christianity. Jesus said, "Where your treasure is, there your heart will be also" (Matthew 6:21). If we aren't giving much, what does that say about our hearts?

Prefigured in the Old Testament

The Old Testament foreshadows the New Testament, and this is true about giving according to our income:

> Then you shall keep the Feast of Weeks to the LORD your God with the tribute of a freewill offering from your hand, which you shall give *as the LORD your God blesses you*...Every man shall give as he is able, *according to the blessing of the LORD your God* which He has given you (Deuteronomy 16:10, 17).

Considering these words appear in the Old Testament, we might expect the verses to say, "Every man shall give a tithe," but they say to give "as the LORD your God blesses you," which means giving according to their income.

God blesses us financially so we can use that blessing to serve Him and others.

The above verses are from Deuteronomy, which means "second law." The book records Moses delivering the law to the new generation of people who would enter the Promised Land because the old generation had died during the 40 years of wandering in the wilderness. So giving according to income wasn't just foreshadowed in the Old Testament, it was foreshadowed in the law that commanded giving a tithe!

Again, I can't tell you how much to give, but I can say it should be according to your income. If you make more, God expects you to give more. God blesses us financially so we can use that blessing to serve Him and others.

The "Gift" of Giving

If people have the gift of teaching but they don't have the gift of mercy, can they say, "I'll teach, but I won't be merciful"? Or if they have the gift of leadership but they don't have the gift of service, can they say, "I'll be in charge, but don't expect me to serve"? Or, "I have the gift of ministry, but I don't have the gift of encouragement, so I'll minister, but I won't encourage"? Of course not.

While people with the gifts of mercy, service, and encouragement will find it easier to be merciful, serve, and encourage, other passages in Scripture command all believers to be merciful, serve, and encourage. In the Sermon on the Mount, in Luke 6:36, Jesus told His disciples to "*be merciful*, just as your Father also is merciful." Paul said, "You were called to freedom, brothers. Only do not use your freedom as an opportunity for the flesh, but through *love serve one another*" (Galatians 5:13 ESV), and "Encourage *one another and build one another up*, just as you are doing" (1 Thessalonians 5:11 ESV). Ephesians 4:11-12 says evangelists, pastors, and teachers—who we typically think are the ones gifted for ministry—are to be "equipping the saints *for the work of ministry*." All saints should see themselves in ministry. Those we most commonly think of as being in ministry are tasked with preparing others for ministry. Imagine someone saying, "I'm not an evangelist, so I don't share the gospel with others." We would think that's absurd, because while some are evangelists, all believers should be evangelistic.

Giving is also one of the gifts: "We have different gifts, according to the grace given to each of us. If your gift is…*giving, then give generously*" (Romans 12:6, 8 NIV). But giving is also commanded: "Each one *must give*" (2 Corinthians 9:7 ESV). So, is giving a gift or command? Both! Just as the person with the gift of service will find serving easier, those with the gift of giving will find giving easier. Giving isn't only something Christians *do*, it's something we are: *givers*.

What if we have a hard time being a giver? Let me give you two encouragements.

First, I once read about a stingy man who said, "The preacher told us to give until it hurts so I don't give at all, because just the thought of giving hurts." If we're like this man (which all of us are, to some extent), remember what we covered in this chapter: Worship is sacrifice, and the greater the sacrifice, the greater the worship. Those who find giving painful have the greatest potential to be worshipful in their giving.

Second, in the next chapter, we will consider God's generosity. As we think about all that God has given us, how can that not motivate us to be givers as well?

CHAPTER 9

God's Generosity Encourages Giving Cheerfully

Our God is a giver. He "gives to all life, breath, and all things" (Acts 17:25). He gives us abundant life: "I have come that they may have life, and that they may have it more abundantly" (John 10:10). He gives us wisdom: "If any of you lacks wisdom, let him ask of God, who gives to all liberally and without reproach, and it will be given to him" (James 1:5). He gives us gifts: "Every good gift and every perfect gift is from above, and comes down from the Father of lights" (James 1:17). The greatest gift God gave us is His Son: "God so loved the world that He gave His only begotten Son, that whoever believes in Him should not perish but have everlasting life" (John 3:16). Romans 8:32 says, "He who did not spare His own Son, but delivered Him up for us all, how shall He not with him freely give us all things?"

Ephesians 5:1 commands us to "be imitators of God," which means we should give too. Proverbs 21:26 says, "*The righteous gives* and does not spare." Why is giving righteous? God's actions define righteousness. Because God gives, giving is righteous and makes us imitators of Him.

GOD GIVES TO US SO WE CAN GIVE TO OTHERS

In the parable of the unforgiving servant, the master rebuked the man: "You wicked servant! I forgave you all that debt because you begged me. Should you not also have had compassion on your fellow servant, just as I had pity on you?" (Matthew 18:32-33). The wicked servant was condemned because he wouldn't forgive as God had forgiven him. This reveals an important principle in Scripture: We should do for others what God has done for us. For

example, we should love others because God loved us: "As I have loved you…
you also love one another" (John 13:34). We should forgive others because
God forgave us: "Forgive one another, even as God in Christ forgave you"
(Ephesians 4:32). Regarding giving, because God is a giver who has given so
much to us, we should give to others.

Some spiritual gifts, such as teaching and leadership, *seem like gifts* because
there's a benefit to the person receiving the gift. But other gifts, such as mercy
and serving, *don't seem like gifts* because they seem to benefit others more than
they benefit the people who received the gifts. This gives us insight into why
God gives us gifts, which we must consider because God's reason for giving
gifts can be different than our reason.

We typically give gifts to bless the recipient, but God gives gifts to bless
the recipient *and* so the recipient can bless others: "As each has received a
gift, *use it to serve one another*, as good stewards of God's varied grace" (1 Peter
4:10 ESV). We can enjoy the gifts God has given us—for example, God has
given me the gift of teaching, which I enjoy—but being good stewards of
our gifts means using them for others' benefit. This applies to all God has
given us, including our wealth.

Let's return to two of the parables we looked at earlier. First, in the parable of the talents, the third servant buried his talent (gift) in the ground and
was severely punished in response (Matthew 25:18, 30). The financial application is that when we keep our wealth to ourselves, we're acting like the
third servant—we're taking what God has given us and, in a sense, burying
it in the ground. Second, the parable of the rich fool reveals we aren't given
wealth to keep it for our ourselves. When we hoard our wealth, we're acting like the rich fool.

In both parables, the men failed to use God's generosity the way it is
intended: for others. God is generous with us so we can be generous with others.

REAPING AND SOWING

Many people, even those who have never opened the Bible, are familiar
with the phrase "You reap what you sow." These words are taken from two
passages in the New Testament. The first, and most well-known, is Galatians 6:7: "Do not be deceived, God is not mocked; for *whatever a man sows,
that he will also reap*." The second is in Paul's words about the Macedonian
believers' sacrificial giving, which served as an example to the Corinthians
(and to us): "The point is this: *whoever sows sparingly will also reap sparingly,*

and whoever sows bountifully will also reap bountifully" (2 Corinthians 9:6). The amount of the harvest is directly proportionate to the amount sown. The farmer who sows much seed will have a bigger harvest than the farmer who sows sparingly.

Paul leaned on this agricultural principle to encourage generosity. Although this can be applied to other areas of life—for example, we typically get out of relationships what we put into them—the context is giving. The blessing received for giving is directly proportionate to the amount given. The Christian who gives generously will have a bigger harvest than the Christian who gives sparingly.

When a farmer sows seed, he might feel like he's losing something as the seed he purchased falls from his hand to the ground. Similarly, we might feel like we're losing something when the money we earned leaves our hand and goes toward the offering. But just as the farmer gives in anticipation of receiving more in the future, we can give with the same expectation. On the other hand, if a farmer planted only a few seeds because he wanted to retain as much as possible, he would have more seed in his sacks, but at harvest time, he would have less grain in his barn.

We know this principle is important—it's one God doesn't want us to miss because it's repeated throughout Scripture:

- "You shall give to him freely, and your heart shall not be grudging when you give to him, because *for this the L*ORD *your God will bless you in all your work and in all that you undertake"* (Deuteronomy 15:10 ESV).

- "Honor the Lord with your wealth and with the firstfruits of all your produce; *then your barns will be filled with plenty, and your vats will be bursting with wine"* (Proverbs 3:9-10; see also Proverbs 19:17; 22:9; 28:27 ESV).

- "One *gives freely, yet grows all the richer;* another withholds what he should give, and only suffers want. *Whoever brings blessing will be enriched,* and one who waters will himself be watered. The people curse him who holds back grain, but a blessing is on the head of him who sells it" (Proverbs 11:24-26 ESV).

- "Bring the full tithe into the storehouse, that there may be food in my house. And thereby put me to the test, says the LORD of hosts, if I will not open the windows of heaven for you and pour down for you a blessing until there is no more need" (Malachi 3:10 ESV).

In King Hezekiah's day, the people gave generously to support the priests and Levites (2 Chronicles 31:5-7). When the chief priest described the situation, he said, "Since the people began to bring the offerings into the house of the LORD, we have had enough to eat and have plenty left, for *the LORD has blessed his people; and what is left is this great abundance*" (2 Chronicles 31:10). The people sowed generously, and God ensured they reaped bountifully.

Jesus loosely communicated the same principle: "*Give, and it will be given to you*; good measure, pressed down, shaken together, and running over will be put into your bosom. For *with the same measure that you use, it will be measured back to you*" (Luke 6:38). This imagery is uncommon to us, but it comes from the marketplace and would be familiar to Jesus's hearers. When people purchased grain in those days, it was given to them in a container. Consider these descriptive terms for a full picture of God's generosity:

- "good measure" means God gives generously versus meagerly
- "pressed down, shaken together" means God fills the empty spaces so the container holds as much as possible
- "running over" means God fills the container beyond its capacity

Although the imagery is from the marketplace, Jesus isn't giving us shopping advice. Instead, the word *parable* is related to our word *parallel* because parables put physical stories alongside spiritual truths. Luke 6:38 illustrates God's generosity to the generous, and God's repeated use of the words "you" and "your" make it personal. Jesus wants us thinking about this happening to us. John Bunyan wrote, "A man there was, though some did count him mad. The more he cast away the more he had."[1]

If We Give Enough Will God Make Us Rich?

God provides a return on the amount invested with Him: invest a little, receive a little; invest a lot, and receive a lot. Does this mean if we give a certain amount, God will give us more in return? For example, if we give the church $1,000 per month, will God then ensure our boss gives us a raise of $1,200 per month? That's not how it works.

Consider the situation with the Philippian believers, who resided in Macedonia and were among those who gave sacrificially to Paul. The apostle mentioned their generosity in Philippians 4:15-18, and then wrote in verse 19, "My God shall supply *all your need* according to His riches in glory by Christ Jesus." They were generous, and God would be generous to them. They would have every need met versus every want supplied. What are our needs? In 1 Timothy 6:8, Paul wrote, "If we have food and clothing, with these we will be content" (ESV). Our needs are food, clothing, and shelter. Fancy clothes, exotic food, and expensive mansions are wants. We don't give to receive, but God wants us to know that He doesn't ask that we give ourselves into poverty.

Do We Reap in This Life or the Next?

What do we reap from what we sow: is it physical, or spiritual, or both? Does the reaping occur in this life, the next, or both? John Calvin said we reap in this life and the next: "This harvest should be understood both in terms of the spiritual reward of eternal life and also referring to the earthly blessings with which God honors the [generous]. Not only in heaven does God reward the well-doing of the godly, but in this world as well."[2]

*We give now and experience God's blessings
in this life *and* we receive rewards in heaven
that we get to enjoy for eternity.*

Consider this interaction between Peter and Jesus. Peter knew he and the disciples had "sown much" to follow Jesus, so he wondered what he would "reap" in the future:

> Peter said, "See, we have left everything and followed you. What then will we have?"
>
> Jesus said to them, "Truly, I say to you, in the new world, when the Son of Man will sit on his glorious throne, you who have followed me will also sit on twelve thrones, judging the twelve tribes of Israel. And everyone who has left houses or brothers or sisters or father or mother or children or lands, for my name's

sake, will *receive a hundredfold and will inherit eternal life* (Matthew 19:27-29 ESV).

Receiving eternal life would be enough, but Jesus said we'll receive eternal life *and* "a hundredfold." I don't know exactly what this will look like, but I do know God is going to reward us with far more than what we have done for Him. He will ensure we don't outgive Him. With God, we will not be on the losing end. Because He tells us to avoid debt (Proverbs 22:7; Romans 13:8), we can be confident He won't be in debt to anyone.

There are short- and long-term benefits to giving. We give now and experience God's blessings in this life *and* we receive rewards in heaven that we get to enjoy for eternity.

GOD GIVES US GRACE SO WE CAN GIVE MORE

Paul said, "In a great trial of affliction, the [Macedonians'] abundance of their joy and their deep poverty abounded in the riches of their liberality" (2 Corinthians 8:2). For them, the formula was affliction and poverty equals joy and generosity—the opposite of what we would expect. It's reminiscent of the paradox two chapters earlier: "As sorrowful, yet always rejoicing; *as poor, yet making many rich*" (2 Corinthians 6:10). When we're sorrowful, we don't rejoice, and when we're poor, we don't make others rich. But this was the case for the Macedonians.

How could the Macedonians give so much when they were in extreme poverty? There's no natural answer, but the supernatural answer is in the previous verse: "We want you to know, brothers, *about the grace of God* that has been given among the churches of Macedonia" (2 Corinthians 8:1 ESV). In context, the word "grace" does not refer to spiritual graces, but to money and material needs. God supernaturally provided the Macedonians with what they needed. Their generosity is a good example, but God still receives the credit because His grace did it through them. Paul said something similar in the following chapter:

> Each one must give as he has decided in his heart, not reluctantly or under compulsion, for God loves a cheerful giver. And *God is able to make all grace abound to you*, so that having all sufficiency in all things at all times, you may abound in every good work (2 Corinthians 9:7-8 ESV).

The universals, or "alls," are truly staggering: "...*all* grace...*all* sufficiency in *all* things at *all* times...in *every* [or all] good work." Our resources are restricted. We have limited amounts of time, money, and energy, but God is unlimited. His infinite amount of grace allows Him to dispense it lavishly. He can "make all grace abound to [us], so that having all sufficiency [we] may abound in every good work."

The Greek word translated "sufficiency" means "a perfect condition of life in which no aid or support is needed." Because the context is giving, the idea is God supplies everything we need (no other support is needed) if we're generous. We can be confident that if we give, God gives us more so we can continue to give.

Think back to the principle of sowing and reaping. When it comes to sowing, we know it takes time to reap. We throw the seed into the ground and wait for it to grow. But Paul says that God replenishes while we give so we can give even more. We reap even while we're sowing. Farmers must wait for their harvests, but generous believers begin to reap immediately. One of the paradoxes of the Christian life is that we gain as we give. If we honor God with what He has given us, He will bless us with more so that we can give even more. We are blessed by God so we can be more of a blessing to others.

GIVE CHEERFULLY

I used to coach junior high wrestling. After one season, some of my wrestlers decided to buy me a gift. They pooled their money and purchased a nice plaque, which they planned to give me at the end-of-the-year banquet. While they were riding their bikes with the plaque, one of them accidentally dropped it in the road. They were so happy to give me the plaque that at first nobody told me why it was damaged. Finally, someone apologized and explained what had happened. But there was no need for apologies because I was blessed by how cheerfully they had given it to me. A gift, regardless of what it is, means so much more when given cheerfully.

I know what you're thinking: *Scott, in the last chapter, you said to give sacrificially, and now you're saying to give cheerfully. These don't go together! I can give sacrificially, or I can give cheerfully, but I can't do both! The more sacrifice that's involved, the less cheerful I am. The less sacrifice involved, the more cheerful I am.* But we can give sacrificially and cheerfully, and hopefully the Macedonians' example is evidence that we can do so!

The Macedonians gave sacrificially, and they gave with an "abundance of joy." Despite their difficult circumstances, they didn't merely have some joy when giving. They had an abundance of it! It's like they had so much joy they gave and had some joy left over!

How cheerfully did they give? They were "*begging us earnestly for the favor of taking part in the relief of the saints*—and this, not as we expected, but they gave themselves first to the Lord and then by the will of God to us" (2 Corinthians 8:4-5 ESV). That's cheerful giving! How many times have you heard of Christians begging to be able to give? The words "not as we expected" mean the Macedonians gave even more than Paul and his companions anticipated!

They called being able to give a "favor." The Greek word translated "favor" is *charis*, which is related to our English word *charity*. The same word is translated "grace" elsewhere in Scripture. It was "the grace of God" that allowed them to give. For the Macedonians, giving was such a joy that it's as though they asked for more grace to be able to give more.

The Greek word translated "taking part" is *koinonia*, which is often translated as "fellowship." The word means "strong association, community, or participation." The Macedonians wanted such strong fellowship with the Jerusalem believers they "[took] part in [their] relief," and associated with them in their suffering through their giving. When we give, we also associate with those who are suffering, and "bear one another's burdens" (Galatians 6:2).

Putting God First

Paul said the Macedonians "*gave themselves first to the Lord* and then by the will of God to us" (2 Corinthians 8:4-5 ESV). The word "first" isn't referring to time or chronology, but priority. They gave themselves *first* to the Lord, and that led to their generosity. As we discussed earlier, the way we handle our finances is an outpouring of our relationships with the Lord. The Macedonians demonstrate that if we put God first, not only will we give the amount He wants, we will give *the way* He wants—cheerfully.

Think about the Sermon on the Mount to understand how putting God first allows us to give cheerfully. Jesus preached on laying up treasures in heaven in Matthew 6:19-24. Immediately after that, in verses 25-34, He preached on not being anxious (or, in the NKJV, NIV, and NASB, not worrying) about our food, drink, bodies, clothing, or even the length of our lives. The word "anxious" (or "worry") occurs six times in ten verses.

Why would Jesus preach about not worrying immediately after preaching about laying up treasures in heaven? When we lay up treasures in heaven, which is to say when we give as God desires, it is tempting to wonder if we will have enough to eat, drink, clothe ourselves, and even keep ourselves alive. Jesus concluded by saying, "Seek first the kingdom of God and His righteousness, and all these things shall be added to you" (Matthew 6:33). If we put God first (as the Macedonians did), then we can give cheerfully because we trust Him to give us what we need.

A Wonderful Reason to Give Cheerfully

As Christians we should be familiar with what God loves, and there are quite a few examples in Scripture:

1. God loves those who keep His commandments (Deuteronomy 7:9).

2. God loves righteous deeds (Psalm 11:7).

3. God loves those who seek refuge from their adversaries at [His] right hand (Psalm 17:7).

4. God loves righteousness and justice (Psalm 33:5).

5. God loves those who love Him (Proverbs 8:17).

6. God loves those who pursue righteousness (Proverbs 15:9).

7. God loves the world (John 3:16).

8. God the Father loves those who love His Son (John 16:27).

9. God loves us while we are still sinners (Romans 5:8).

10. God loves those He disciplines (Hebrews 12:6; quoting Proverbs 3:12).

Second Corinthians 9:7 reveals one more thing God loves: "Each one gives as he purposes in his heart, not grudgingly or of necessity, for *God loves a cheerful giver.*" It doesn't just say God loves cheerful giving. Instead, it says He loves *people* who give cheerfully. The Amplified Bible says, "God loves a cheerful giver [and delights in the one whose heart is in his gift]." God loves everyone, but He has a special, unique love for cheerful givers. The Greek word translated "cheerful" is *hilaros*, which is related to our word, *hilarious*, and this is the only place it occurs in Scripture. The idea is God wants giving from hearts that find it enjoyable and entertaining.

How Do Parents Want Their Children to Give?

If you're a parent, think about your child giving you a gift. If we're honest, unless your child is very talented, the gift probably isn't something we would normally purchase if we saw it in a store. My point is the gift isn't valuable to us because of its quality. The gift is valuable because of the heart behind it—think again about the iceberg or roots below the surface. Our children want to bless us. We take pleasure in their gifts because they're signs of their love for us.

The Greek word translated "reluctantly" means "with grief, sorrow, or sadness." Picture people who give through clenched teeth with the gift (figuratively speaking) having to be pried from their hands. Imagine your child gives you a gift and says,

- "I hope this makes you happy, but I bet you would never give me something like this."

- "You better appreciate this because you wouldn't believe how difficult it was for me to get it."

- "I don't really want to give this to you, but I know it's your birthday, so I hope you enjoy it."

See the application? We wouldn't want our children giving us gifts with terrible attitudes, and our heavenly Father doesn't want His children giving Him gifts with terrible attitudes. God wants glad givers, not sad or mad givers. Robert Rodenmeyer said, "There are three kinds of giving: grudge giving, duty giving, and thanksgiving. Grudge giving says, 'I have to'; duty giving says, 'I ought to'; thanksgiving says, 'I want to.'"[3] God wants the third type of giving.

GIVE WITH THE RIGHT HEART

If we take our minds back to the principle of reaping and sowing, when a farmer sows seed, his heart doesn't matter. If he has good soil, sows good seed, and is the beneficiary of good weather, he can experience a good harvest regardless of his heart. The farmer in the parable of the rich fool is a perfect example. He was a selfish man who thought only about himself, yet he still experienced a great harvest. But this couldn't be further from the case for Christians because our motive for doing almost anything is vitally important.

Paul didn't just say we should give. He said we should give cheerfully (2 Corinthians 9:7). Giving is a heart issue, for "the Lord looks at the heart" (1 Samuel 16:7).

In the Sermon on the Mount, Jesus condemned things we would expect Him to, including murder, adultery, lying, and retaliation (Matthew 5:21-41). In the next chapter, He condemned things we would *not* expect Him to, such as praying, fasting, and giving. Why? When the right things are done with the wrong heart, they become the wrong things. Jesus said,

> Beware of practicing your righteousness before other people in order to be seen by them, for then you will have no reward from your Father who is in heaven. Thus, when you give to the needy, sound no trumpet before you, as the hypocrites do in the synagogues and in the streets, that they may be praised by others. Truly, I say to you, they have received their reward (Matthew 6:1-2 ESV).

Wanting to be seen by others reveals a heart that is giving wrongly. So serious is this offense that regardless of the amount given, it results in loss of reward. In case we missed this warning the first time Jesus said it, He repeated it a second time in the following verse. He really wanted to help us avoid losing our reward! He again gave instructions about giving with the right heart:

> When you give to the needy, do not let your left hand know what your right hand is doing, so that your giving may be in secret. And your Father who sees in secret will reward you (Matthew 6:3-4 ESV).

Of course, hands don't have minds of their own. We can't hide from one hand what the other hand is doing. The point is we should give in a way that nobody knows what we are doing except the Lord. Giving secretly is admirable because it's not being done to impress others. Instead, it's being done to please our heavenly Father. We are giving with the right heart when it's enough to know that He sees and will reward us.

THREE ENCOURAGEMENTS FOR GIVING

The Corinthians were rich compared to the Macedonians, so it seems strange that they needed to be encouraged to give when God had given them so much. But consider how strange it is that we need to be encouraged to give when God has given us even more.

Maybe you find it difficult (as I do) to give the way we should: willingly, sacrificially, cheerfully, generously, and with the right heart. If this is you (as it is me), let me give you three encouragements that I also give myself.

Encouragement One: Confession and Prayer

Confess your struggle with giving and pray that God helps you to grow. Ask Him to replace your unwillingness with willingness, your joylessness with joyfulness, your cheerlessness with cheerfulness, your stinginess with generosity, and your wrong heart with a right heart.

Encouragement Two: Scripture Memorization and Meditation

Go to Scripture to grow in the area of giving. Read the verses that apply, meditate on them, and memorize them. Write them on notecards and put them in places where you will see them regularly, such as on your refrigerator, mirror, or car dashboard. A great place to start is the verses we covered on the Macedonians, and in especially 2 Corinthians 9:6-8.

Encouragement Three: Reflection on God's Greatest Gift

We looked at many verses in 2 Corinthians 8 and 9 because they're the clearest chapters in the New Testament on giving. Second Corinthians 9:15, which is the last verse of the chapter, reads: "Thanks be to God for His indescribable gift!" Why did Paul conclude his teaching on giving with these words? He knew that encouraging us to reflect on God's greatest gift would motivate us to give. C.H. Spurgeon said,

> Christ is the ultimate example of giving. He is the great Giver. Because of Him we give freely and generously. Our Lord Jesus is ever giving, and does not for a solitary instant withdraw His hand... the rain of His grace is always dropping, the river of His bounty is ever-flowing, and the wellspring of His love is constantly overflowing. As the King can never die, so His grace can never fail.[4]

Giving is the appropriate response from people who realize how much they've been given. We should view giving as a privilege because of all that has been done for us. Consider this: Is there a higher, better reason we can have for giving? No.

I'm not going to tell you that God is going to suffer if you don't give, because He doesn't need our money. I'm also not going to tell you that giving earns (or improves) your salvation, because nothing can do that; we can't give to earn favor with God. Instead, we give *because of the favor that's been given to us* through Christ. The greatest reason to give is this: Giving is a way to worship the God who has given us so much, including His own Son.

CHAPTER 10

Good Stewardship
Toward the Poor

W hen I was growing up, I became friends with a boy my age who lived in a trailer park. As we got to know each other, I noticed his parents were always home. I thought dads woke up and, on most days, went to work. Then they came home in the evening. That's what my dad did, as well as the other dads I knew. I projected that expectation on my friend's father and was surprised when this wasn't the case.

One time he invited me into his parents' little trailer, and they were playing Nintendo. When we left, he told me, "That's what my parents do." Along with eating and sleeping, that seemed to be about all they did. I never even saw them go outside. Because this was before I knew what welfare was, I wondered how they had money for living expenses.

There has been much debate about our responsibility to the unemployed, uninsured, and uneducated in our society. Many of the people affected by economic downturns or other unfortunate circumstances desire to work but can't find employment. On the other side of the spectrum are those who have become generational welfare recipients, preferring to remain on the government dole. How should we as Christians respond to these scenarios?

A BETTER APPROACH TO CHARITY

Under the Mosaic law, the welfare system in Israel instructed farmers, "When you reap the harvest of your land, you shall not wholly reap the corners of your field when you reap, nor shall you gather any gleaning from your harvest. You shall leave them for the poor and for the stranger: I am the LORD your God" (Leviticus 23:22).[1] Our government gives people handouts that require little more than standing in line or walking to a mailbox to collect a check. I believe God's approach was better for two reasons:

1. It provided for the poor by encouraging those who were capable of being productive to also be generous. This stands in contrast to the redistribution of wealth that our nation promotes by taking from those with more to give to those with less.

2. It required effort from the poor. God did not tell farmers to harvest everything and then give to the poor. Instead, He told farmers to leave enough for the poor to gather it themselves. Work gives people a sense of purpose, productivity, and dignity, which is why involving the needy in the process was to their benefit.

Ruth showed the beauty of this approach. She asked Naomi, whom she was caring for, "Please let me go to the field, and glean heads of grain after him in whose sight I may find favor" (Ruth 2:2). She could have said, "I'm with my mother-in-law, and we're both childless widows. We're weak and vulnerable, so everyone should give to us out of pity." Instead, she went to the field and gathered an ephah of barley, which is about 26 quarts (Ruth 2:17). Her example is a strong rebuke to those who could contribute to meeting their needs instead of expecting handouts.

Because we aren't in the Old Testament under God's welfare system, knowing who to give to requires balance and wisdom. As true as it is that giving is part of being a good steward, it is equally true that knowing when *not* to give is also part of being a good steward.

A COMMAND VERSUS SUGGESTION

Scripture provides us with guidelines on when to give and when not to give. The instruction we need is in 2 Thessalonians 3:6-15, so we will consider this passage carefully. In verse 6, Paul wrote, "We command you, brothers, in the name of our Lord Jesus Christ, that you keep away from any brother who is walking in idleness and not in accord with the tradition that you received from us" (ESV).

The strong language "we command" carried Paul's apostolic authority;

therefore, this is a binding order versus a suggestion or recommendation. The Greek word translated "command" is *paraggello*, which is a military term meaning "an order handed down from a superior officer." The same word is used four times in this passage, in verse 4, verse 6, and twice in verse 10 because the church is an army:

- Second Timothy 2:3-4 says a Christian "must endure hardship as a good soldier of Jesus Christ…that he may please him who enlisted him as a soldier."

- Philippians 2:25 and Philemon 1:2 call Epaphroditus and Archippus fellow soldiers.

- Ephesians 6:11-17 commands Christians to wear armor and carry a sword.

If soldiers do not obey orders, the result is disorder. Unfortunately, some of the Thessalonians were "idle" or in "idleness" (verses 7 and 11). The Greek word is *ataktos*, and it means "out of ranks, often so of soldiers." The same Greek word is in 1 Thessalonians 5:14 where it's translated as "insubordinate." We are commanded to keep away from these people, as well as those not following "the tradition," which refers to part of Paul's previous letter: "Aspire to lead a quiet life, to mind your own business, and to work with your own hands, as we commanded you" (1 Thessalonians 4:11).[2]

Here's the point that we must consider: If we should keep away from people who call themselves Christians but are idle or lazy, it is hard to imagine that God would expect us to give them money.

A GOOD EXAMPLE TO FOLLOW

Paul modeled what he preached, so he frequently told believers to imitate him.[3] Although it seems odd to imitate anyone other than Christ, in 1 Corinthians 11:1, Paul said, "Imitate me, just as I also imitate Christ." Because Paul imitated Christ, by telling others to imitate him, he was indirectly telling people to imitate Christ. There's application for us in this passage because all Christians should see themselves as examples through whom others see Christ.

In the following verses, Paul urged people to follow his example—he himself was a hard worker and not idle:

You yourselves know how you ought to imitate us, because we were not idle when we were with you, nor did we eat anyone's bread without paying for it, but with toil and labor we worked night and day, that we might not be a burden to any of you. It was not because we do not have that right, but to give you in ourselves an example to imitate (2 Thessalonians 3:7-9 ESV).

Paul gave up his right to receive financial support, choosing instead to work to meet his needs and the needs of others. In his previous letter, he wrote, "You remember, brethren, our labor and toil; *for laboring night and day, that we might not be a burden to any of you*, we preached to you the gospel of God" (1 Thessalonians 2:9). This lightened the financial burden on the infant church and silenced accusers—nobody could say Paul was in the ministry for the money. In every city there were itinerant teachers trying to get as much money as possible from people, and Paul didn't want to be classified with them. As he wrote in 1 Corinthians 9:18, he wanted to "present the gospel of Christ free of charge," so money wouldn't be a hindrance.

But the fact Paul did not receive money brings up a good question that has financial implications for us: Should church leaders be paid?

GOOD STEWARDS SUPPORT THEIR CHURCH LEADERS

While church leaders have the right to set aside financial support like Paul did, his example is descriptive versus prescriptive. Other pastors don't need to do the same, and most couldn't even if they wanted to, especially those with a wife and children (which Paul did not have). Elsewhere, he wrote that church leaders have the right to receive support from their congregations:

- "Do you not know that those who are employed in the temple service get their food from the temple, and those who serve at the altar share in the sacrificial offerings? In the same way, the Lord commanded that those who proclaim the gospel should get their living by the gospel" (1 Corinthians 9:13-14 ESV).

- "Let him who is taught the word share in all good things with him who teaches" (Galatians 6:6).

- "Let the elders who rule well be counted worthy of double honor, especially those who labor in the word and doctrine. For the

Scripture says, 'You shall not muzzle an ox when it treads out the grain,' and, 'The laborer is worthy of his wages'" (1 Timothy 5:17-18).

Jesus taught the same principle:

- When He sent out the 12, He said, "Acquire no gold or silver or copper for your belts, no bag for your journey, or two tunics or sandals or a staff, for the laborer deserves his food" (Matthew 10:9-10).

- When He sent out the 70, He said, "Remain in the same house, eating and drinking such things as they give, for the laborer is worthy of his wages. Do not go from house to house" (Luke 10:7).

Even though Scripture is clear that church leaders should be compensated adequately for their labor, many of them are overworked and underpaid. Consider the following excerpts from articles on pastors' salaries:

> The National Association of Evangelicals did a 2015 study of more than 4,000 ministers nationwide and found that half make less than $50,000 per year. More than three in four knew someone who left ministry due to financial stress. I've talked to denominational leaders who found that many millennial pastors, a few years into ministry, had significant doubts about continuing due to inadequate pay.[4]

> Many pastors are under extreme stress because they do not have adequate income to meet their financial obligations. Like anyone else who is under heavy financial burdens, a pastor can find his thoughts consumed with worry. Because he is so distracted, he naturally is less effective in his ministry. Both he and his family feel the pressure.

> Some pastors leave their churches because of pay issues. You will not likely hear a pastor announce in his resignation that he is leaving because of financial pressures. The reality is that, for a number of pastors, the issue of compensation is a major push from one church to another, or from the church to a secular vocation. It's

not that the pastor is in his job for the money; it's that the com-
pensation for his vocation is insufficient to meet his family's needs.[5]

I serve as a regional facilitator over Washington and Oregon for Church
and Family Life. Many of the pastors I communicate with are forced to work
secular jobs too. They tell me how grueling it is to be bivocational. What
does this have to do with giving to the poor? Sadly, many pastors are poor!
Be a good steward by giving to your local church. Not only will you help
support your pastor, more importantly, you will please God.

One of the nice things about giving to your church is the elders or church
leadership can then determine the best uses of the money, such as paying the
pastor(s), supporting ministries and missionaries, and handling benevolence.
A few years ago, one of the women in the church I pastor said, "So-and-so
asked me for money. I told her to ask you, because I thought you would be
better able to determine whether to help." I agreed with her, because church
leaders typically are in a better position to investigate benevolence issues
and determine whether to give and, if so, and how much. Church leaders
can also offer other resources that are needed, such as counseling and books,
and figuring out ways to get needy people plugged into a church. If all we
do is help people financially but don't help them spiritually, then we have
hardly helped them. We haven't provided lasting solutions that enable them
to become self-sufficient. Most importantly, we want to give people the gospel to help them eternally.

DISTINGUISHING BETWEEN TWO GROUPS

What about when we face situations that can't be given over to elders or
church leaders? For example, while driving, we see someone standing on the
street corner asking for money. We can't roll down the window and say, "Go
ask my pastor." How do we know whether to give or not give?

The early church faced a situation that helps us determine what to do. Acts
2:45 says they "sold their possessions and goods, and divided them among
all, as anyone had need." The new believers were happy to care for those
who couldn't care for themselves, but some took advantage of the generosity,
became freeloaders, and lived off others' sacrifices. Paul attempted to combat
this: "Even when we were with you, we commanded you this: If anyone will
not work, neither shall he eat" (2 Thessalonians 3:10). This command was
so important he also communicated it in person ("when we were with you").

The words "will not work" allow us to distinguish between two completely different groups: those unable to work and those unwilling to work. Let's examine how we should respond to both groups so we can be good stewards.

Good Stewards Give to Those Unable to Work

Some people experience physical handicaps or family responsibilities that prevent them from working. Others need financial help because of unfortunate circumstances: "The fallow ground of the poor would yield much food, but it is swept away through injustice" (Proverbs 13:23 esv). They worked hard enough that their fields would produce abundant food, but they lost it because of conditions outside of their control.

God's Word gives us insight into His heart for the less fortunate and expectation that we will help them. In the New Testament we see these passages:

- Jesus said, "He who has two tunics, let him give to him who has none; and he who has food, let him do likewise" (Luke 3:11).

- "If a brother or sister is naked and destitute of daily food, and one of you says to them, 'Depart in peace, be warmed and filled,' but you do not give them the things which are needed for the body, what does it profit?" (James 2:15-16).

- "Whoever has this world's goods, and sees his brother in need, and shuts up his heart from him, how does the love of God abide in him?" (1 John 3:17).

The Old Testament contains similar instruction:

- "If among you, one of your brothers should become poor, in any of your towns within your land that the Lord your God is giving you, you shall not harden your heart or shut your hand against your poor brother" (Deuteronomy 15:7; see also 24:12 and Proverbs 31:9).

- "He who despises his neighbor sins; but he who has mercy on the poor, happy is he" (Proverbs 14:21).

- "The righteous considers the cause of the poor, but the wicked does not understand such knowledge" (Proverbs 29:7).

So important was it to care for those in need that God said He would bless those who did so:

- "You shall surely give to [the poor] freely, and your heart should not be grieved when you give to him, because *for this the LORD your God will bless you in all your works and in all to which you put your hand*" (Deuteronomy 15:10).

- "He who has a generous eye *will be blessed*, for he gives of his bread to the poor" (Proverbs 22:9).

- "He who gives to the poor *will not lack*, but he who hides his eyes will have many curses" (Proverbs 28:27).

Josiah was arguably the greatest king of the southern kingdom of Judah. God attributed the nation's prosperity to his care for the poor: "[Josiah] judged the cause of the poor and needy; *then it was well*" (Jeremiah 22:16).

We talked about the principle of sowing and reaping, and it is in effect when we give to the poor: "He who has pity on the poor lends to the LORD, and *he will pay back what he has given*" (Proverbs 19:17; see also Proverbs 11:24). We give to serve God, versus giving to receive, but at the same time, God says He will provide a return on our investment.

When helping the less fortunate, if you have children, you can come together as a family and say, "These people are struggling, and we are privileged to be able to help them. God has blessed us, and we get to bless them. Let's pray for them and give thanks for this wonderful opportunity, because, as the Lord said in Acts 20:35, 'It is more blessed to give than to receive.'"

What about neglecting those in need? God says they

- insult Him: "Whoever oppresses a poor man *insults his Maker*, but he who is generous to the needy honors him" (Proverbs 14:31 ESV; see also 17:5).

- will be ignored by Him: "Whoever shuts his ear to the cry of the poor will also cry himself *and not be heard*" (Proverbs 21:13).

- will become poor themselves: "He who oppresses the poor to increase his riches, and he who gives to the rich, *will surely come to poverty*" (Proverbs 22:16).

- will lose their lives: "Do not rob the poor…for the LORD will plead their cause, and *plunder the soul of those who plunder them*" (Proverbs 22:22-23).

- will be punished: "*I will not turn away its punishment,* because [the Israelites] sell the righteous for silver, and the poor for a pair of sandals. They pant after the dust of the earth which is on the head of the poor, and pervert the way of the humble" (Amos 2:6-7; see also 4:1; 5:11-12; 8:4-10; Isaiah 3:13-15; 10:1-4).

Although homosexuality is the sin most associated with Sodom, the city was also condemned for ignoring the less fortunate: "Behold, this was the guilt of your sister Sodom: she and her daughters had pride, excess of food, and prosperous ease, but *did not aid the poor and needy*" (Ezekiel 16:49 ESV).

These passages reveal just how important it is to care for those in need. God offers blessings to those who do so and discipline to those who don't. But what about people who are poor not because of unfortunate circumstances, but because of their own choices? Scripture helps us understand how to respond to them as well.

Poor Stewards Give to Those Unwilling to Work

Proverbs 21:25 says the lazy man's "hands *refuse to labor.*" This is the person in 2 Thessalonians 3:10, who "is not willing to work" and therefore should "not eat" (ESV). As important as it is to give to those who through no fault of their own find themselves struggling financially, it is equally important to avoid giving to those who *through fault of their own* find themselves struggling financially. The Bible discusses a few causes of poverty, and laziness is one of the most common: "*Lazy hands make for poverty,* but diligent hands bring wealth" (Proverbs 10:4 NIV; see also Proverbs 13:4; 20:4, 13; 24:34).

As important as it is to give to those who through no fault of their own find themselves struggling financially, it is equally important to avoid giving to those who through fault of their own find themselves struggling financially.

When well-meaning people disobey the command *not* to give to those unwilling to work (yes, Paul said "we commanded you" in 2 Thessalonians 3:10, so it is a command), they often defend their actions by saying something like, "Well, if they're not going to use the money wisely, then that's on them. I'll just let God sort it out." No. It's on us because we're disobeying a command. He wants us to sort it out.

Common sense tells us we can't give to every need. Even the wealthiest philanthropists must decide what to do and not do with their money. Saying yes to something means saying no to something else in most areas of life, but it is especially true when our resources are limited, such as time and money. Hypothetically, even if we had the money to give at every opportunity, doing so would make us poor stewards because there are times when giving does more harm than good. Enabling is not loving. As is the case with all disobedience, there are negative consequences. Let's consider the four reasons it is detrimental to give to those unwilling to work.

Detriment One: Wastes Money

As a pastor, I've had weeks that I have had more people ask for money than for prayer. There are some differences in the requests: sometimes it's a phone call, while other times it's a person coming to the church. But one thing variable that is almost always the same is there's a story that describes the most unfortunate circumstances imaginable; Job looks blessed compared to many of these people. Dealing with them is one of the most unenjoyable parts of my job not because I don't want to help, but because as soon as they can tell that I will not give them money, they want nothing else to do with me.

In my years pastoring, I can think of only one person we helped financially who later communicated his appreciation. I can't think of anyone we helped financially who was helped spiritually. In other words, the money we gave didn't lead to salvation, sanctification, or regular church attendance. Maybe God did do something through our gift, but if He did, it was unknown to me.

Granted, whenever we help, no strings should be attached. We are not looking for a pat on the back or any sort of repayment. But because I have seen so little fruit from giving money to people who have asked, I'm left wondering how much better of a steward I might have been if I had given that same money to one of our missionaries or to someone with a proven need instead.

Detriment Two: Hinders Repentance

Those who are not willing to work should not be given anything because that can shortchange the work God wants to do in their lives—they're prevented from experiencing the consequences of their actions. It is in their best interest to reach the low point that can lead to repentance. That is what happened with the prodigal son in Luke 15:16-18:

> He was longing to be fed with the pods that the pigs ate, and *no one gave him anything*. But when he came to himself, he said, "How many of my father's hired servants have more than enough bread, but I perish here with hunger! I will arise and go to my father, and I will say to him, 'Father, *I have sinned against heaven and before you*'" (ESV).

How much damage would've been done if well-meaning people "helped" the prodigal son? He reached the point of repentance because nobody gave him anything. Everything that works against repentance is detrimental, even if it looks loving, as charity does.

Those who are "not willing to work" should "not eat" because hunger can motivate them to find employment. But if they're given charity, then hunger is prevented from being the strong incentive God desires that can lead to repentance.

Detriment Three: Enables Further Sin

When we give to people who are unwilling to work, we may very well be indirectly encouraging them to engage in other sins. When people aren't spending their time and energy profitably, they often find unprofitable ways to spend them. Paul described this in the next verse of the passage we've been unpacking: "We hear that some among you walk in idleness, not busy at work, but busybodies" (2 Thessalonians 3:11 ESV).

When people aren't busy working, they become "busybodies." Idleness breeds compromise and is a foundation for other sins. Apparently the Thessalonians hadn't learned, because Paul wrote in his first letter: "Aspire to lead a quiet life, to *mind your own business*, and to work with your own hands" (1 Thessalonians 4:11). If they were busy with work, they wouldn't have the time or energy to worry about others. First Timothy 5:13 says something similar: "They learn to *be idle*, wandering from house to house, and *not only idle but also gossips and busybodies,* saying things which they ought not." They weren't busy working, so they became busy gossiping.

When I was an elementary schoolteacher, I knew that keeping students busy is the best way to manage their behavior. When students are working, they don't have the time to get into trouble. The same is often true with adults. As a pastor, I have found that it is often people with too much time on their hands that are overly concerned with others. People who are busy serving don't have the time to worry about others. If David had been with his men in battle, he would have been too busy to see Bathsheba. C.H. Spurgeon said, "A man who wastes his time in sloth offers himself to be a target for the devil, who is an awfully good rifleman. In other words, idle men tempt the devil to tempt them."[6]

Knowing this, Paul continued, "Such persons we command and encourage in the Lord Jesus Christ to do their work quietly and to earn their own living (2 Thessalonians 3:12 ESV). This is the fourth command (previously in verses 4, 6, and 10), and he added an exhortation with two parts: First, "work quietly" instead of causing division and disruptions. Second, "earn [a] living" versus receiving charity.

What does this have to do with giving? When we give to those who are unwilling to work, not only are we enabling them to continue in their sin, but we are also allowing them to engage in further sin through their idleness. The best gift to give lazy people is not food or money, but a job.

Detriment Four: Prevents Shame

Let me explain what shame is, biblically speaking, so we can understand why it's important for those who are unwilling to work to experience it. Genesis 2:25 says Adam and Eve "were both naked...and were not ashamed." This is the opposite of the way they should have felt because many verses associate nakedness with shame.[7] Some of the verses are about pagans who aren't prone to experiencing shame, yet even they felt shame when naked; therefore, why didn't Adam and Even experience any?

Shame can only be produced by the knowledge that you have done something wrong. For example, imagine you enter the home of people who always take their shoes off, but you don't know that's their practice. You walk around feeling fine until the owner says, "We always take our shoes off." Then you feel ashamed. Or, have you ever started eating only for someone to say, "Why don't we say grace and thank God for the food?" Now you're ashamed.

Because Adam and Eve hadn't yet eaten of the tree of the knowledge of good and evil, they didn't know there was anything wrong with what they were doing; therefore, they felt no shame. In Genesis 3:5, Satan said, "God knows that in the day you eat of [the tree] your eyes will be opened, and you will be like God, *knowing good and evil.*" This was true! Satan mixes truth with lies because then the lies sound more convincing. They ate, and "at that moment their eyes were opened, and they suddenly *felt shame at their nakedness.* So they sewed fig leaves together to cover themselves" (Genesis 3:7 NLT). The tree of the knowledge of good and evil gave them the knowledge it was wrong for them to be naked, and they were ashamed. So they tried to clothe themselves.

What does this have to do with giving? When people are not willing to work but we give them money, we are showing them our support. This prevents them from developing the knowledge that their unwillingness to work is wrong. Hence Paul's continued instructions: "As for you, brothers, do not grow weary in doing good. If anyone does not obey what we say in this letter, take note of that person, and have nothing to do with him, *that he may be ashamed*" (2 Thessalonians 3:13-14). It is detrimental to give to those not willing to work because it prevents them from experiencing shame that can lead to their repentance.

KEEP DOING GOOD

Let me draw your attention to Paul's encouragement to "not grow weary in doing good." We should read these words as though God is saying them to us because He is! The Thessalonians needed this encouragement, and we do too. It is easy to become cynical, stop giving, and neglect the genuinely needy just because some people are not willing to work.

We have all needed people's help at times in our lives, and there are times God wants us to help others in need. There are people who, through no fault of their own, are struggling financially. They shouldn't suffer further just because there are others who happen to take advantage of our giving. We want these less fortunate people to see Christ through our charity.

Let me leave you with this one great encouragement: When we help the genuinely needy, it as though we are helping Christ, who said, "Truly, I say to you, as you did it to one of the least of these my brothers, you did it to me" (Matthew 25:40 ESV).

CHAPTER 11

Spending Problems
Versus an Income Problem

Most people throughout history have wanted necessities, but the more common problem today is having too much stuff. In the past, people wanted food and clothing, but we have too many clothes and we eat too much food. Mark Twain once defined civilization as "a limitless multiplication of unnecessary necessities."[1] We spend too much money and accumulate too much stuff. It's no surprise that storage-space facilities are one of the fastest-growing industries. An article titled "Self-storage: How Warehouses for Personal Junk Became a $38 Billion Industry" reads:

> Despite recessions and demographic shifts, few building types have boomed like self-storage lockers. The self-storage industry made $32.7 billion in 2016, nearly three times Hollywood's box office gross. Self-storage has seen 7.7 percent annual growth since 2012, and now employs 144,000 nationwide. One in eleven Americans pays an average of $91.14 per month to use self-storage. The United States has more than fifty thousand facilities and roughly 2.31 billion square feet of rentable space. To give that perspective, the volume of self-storage units in the country could "fill the Hoover Dam twenty-six times with old clothing, skis, and keepsakes.[2]

When I drive down the road and pass storage units, I wonder what's in them that people don't need and can't get to easily, but still feel the need to keep. How many owners are still paying off the credit cards (see next chapter!) they used to buy that stuff in the first place?

Typically when we have too much stuff, we should recognize two things: First, we are spending too much money. And second, we don't have an income problem; we have a spending problem.

If we have spending problems but blame our income, this creates another problem. We don't make appropriate changes because we put the blame in the wrong place: We blame our income when we should blame ourselves. We complain about our paycheck when we should handle our finances differently.

Even people with low incomes are still able to enjoy commodities that years ago would've been considered luxuries—cell phones, cars, computers, televisions. Most of us can comfortably live off much less if we avoid the spending problems that plague us. I use the word *most* because some people genuinely work hard, and are truly financially wise, yet still struggle to make ends meet. For the rest of us, let's figure out how to make our money go further by examining the most common spending problems.

SPENDING PROBLEMS OFTEN RESULT FROM SMALL PURCHASES THAT ADD UP

Sometimes we struggle financially because of large purchases costing thousands of dollars. More often, though, we struggle because of many small purchases made over several years. These frequent expenditures take place without a second thought for three reasons:

- Small purchases are easier to justify—we can tell ourselves, "It is only five dollars...or ten dollars...or twenty dollars" without considering that, over time, this adds up to thousands of dollars.

- Small purchases don't seem detrimental—we recognize how tragic it is to waste thousands of dollars, but it's much tougher to recognize the damage caused by wasting a few dollars. We would probably be surprised to learn how much we have spent on small purchases we thought had little effect on our finances.

- Small purchases don't look wrong—we don't think eating out, going to the movies, or swinging by the coffee shop is all that bad, so it's easy to end up spending a lot through many small expenditures.

It's surprising how easily people who are struggling financially will justify their small expenditures. Scripture does not condemn these purchases, but it does condemn purchases we can't afford. We have the liberty to spend our money the ways I've listed above, but not if we don't have the money.

AMC Entertainment is America's most popular movie theater chain.[3] Using their prices, the average movie costs $26 per person (ticket $11, soda $6, and popcorn $9).[4] This is over $50 for a couple, and as kids are added, the price quickly reaches $100. How can this be justified when a movie rental or subscription service is a fraction of the price?

Then there are the high-end coffee outlets. Imagine a man we will call Joe. On Joe's way to work each morning he spends five dollars on coffee. If he does this for five years, it will cost him almost $7,000 dollars. Then imagine Joe starts to struggle financially. A caring friend tries to talk to Joe about his casual spending. Sadly, Joe responds that he has an income problem: "If only I made more money; then I wouldn't be in this predicament. The problem is my boss doesn't pay me enough."

Joe's friend tries to press in a little more and draw his attention to his daily coffee purchases, but Joe responds, "It is only five bucks. There's no way these purchases could be the problem. Quit judging me. You can't tell me that I can't buy coffee! Where does Scripture forbid that?"

These examples may seem harmless because they involve movies and coffee. But the point is that many small purchases add up. Imagine what happens when you add up all the other small purchases, such as eating out or grabbing that extra item at the store that you don't really need.

SPENDING PROBLEMS OFTEN RESULT FROM WORTHLESS PURCHASES

By "worthless" I don't mean the item has no value. If that were the case, hopefully we wouldn't have made the purchase in the first place. I'm referring to the item's value to us years, months, weeks, or sometimes even days ahead. If the item is valuable at the moment but it has no value to us in the future, it has been a worthless purchase.

Let me illustrate this by sharing something I used to witness when I was a schoolteacher. Because I was a Christian, I used to be concerned with my students' academics *and character*. I taught math, reading, and writing, but I also tried to spend time teaching about forgiveness, honesty, hard work, and generosity.

There were a few times each year I would have the opportunity to discuss finances with my students. One regular opportunity occurred prior to field trips. When kids are at a museum, aquarium, or tourist attraction, they are tempted to throw away their money on souvenirs. I would tell my students:

> Do not waste your money on any of the items you see in the shops. If you do, let me tell you exactly what will happen. You are going to buy something, be excited about it for a short period of time—probably only a few hours, but maybe only a few minutes—and then lose interest. Each year at the end of field trips, after the students exit the bus when we get back to the school, I walk down the aisle and see these souvenirs left in their seats. They had already gotten bored of their purchases. I don't want you to make the same mistake.

These were worthless purchases. It is easy to listen to this story and pass judgment on students, but how often do we do the same thing as adults? How many times have we bought something and forgotten about it a week or two later? How much stuff do we have in our homes that isn't being used for any profitable reason in our lives? If we're honest, most of us would be surprised—and probably embarrassed—by the number of purchases we've made that provide no lasting benefit. And these worthless purchases add up.

SPENDING PROBLEMS OFTEN RESULT FROM SELF-ENTITLEMENT

Before we jump into this next warning, let me remind you that one of the purposes of the Old Testament is to provide examples for us to learn from. Romans 15:4 says, "Whatever things were written before [referring to the Old Testament] *were written for our learning*." First Corinthians 10:6 and 11 say, "These things [in the Old Testament] *became our examples*…these things [in the Old Testament] happened to them *as examples*, and they were *written for our admonition*."

The Old Testament provides a backdrop for New Testament instruction. Some individuals serve as positive examples through their obedience, while others serve as negative examples through their disobedience. Let's consider three people who serve as examples of the danger of self-entitlement.

Eve's Entitlement

Satan has many names in Scripture: prince of darkness, prince of the power of the air, prince of this world, and another fitting title would be "prince of entitlement." When he tempted Eve, he said, "God knows that in the day you eat of it your eyes will be opened, and you will be like God, knowing good and evil" (Genesis 3:5).

In essence, Satan said, "God does not want you to be like Him or know as much as Him. He's always telling you what not to do. You deserve to be happy. Do what you want!" The devil tried to make Eve feel entitled, and it worked.

Amnon's Entitlement

David had a son, Amnon, who desired his half sister, Tamar. Amnon knew it was wrong to pursue her, but he did not control his mind and take his thoughts captive. He lusted after her until he made himself sick, even to the point of losing weight. An evil man, Jonadab, helped Amnon come up with a plan to have his way with Tamar. He began by saying, "Why are you, *the king's son*, becoming thinner day after day? Will you not tell me?" (2 Samuel 13:4).

Essentially, Jonadab said, "You are the king's son. You should have what you want. You should not have to go without. If you want her, you should take her." Jonadab made Amnon feel so entitled that he raped Tamar.

King Ahab's Entitlement

King Ahab wanted a vineyard that belonged to Naboth, a godly man. Naboth would not give Ahab the vineyard, so Ahab pouted. First Kings 21:4 says he "went into his house sullen and displeased because of the word Naboth the Jezreelite had spoken to him...And he lay down on his bed, and turned away his face, and would eat no food."

Ahab's wife, Jezebel, came to him and said, "*You now exercise authority over Israel!* Arise, eat food, and let your heart be cheerful; I will give you the vineyard of Naboth the Jezreelite" (verse 7). Jezebel basically said, "You are the king of Israel. If you want this vineyard, you should have it!" Jezebel made Ahab feel so entitled that he murdered Naboth and took his vineyard.

Beware of Self-Entitlement from Any Source

All three individuals—Eve, Amnon, and Ahab—gave in to temptation because they felt entitled. This serves as a warning to us for those times when we feel entitled. Often this temptation comes from our flesh telling us, "You shouldn't have to go without. Other people have this, and you should too. Reward yourself. You've earned it!" Often, all we've really earned is a worse financial situation.

Many people are in debt, with little savings, simply because of these three little words: "I deserve this."

Other times, temptation comes from a friend, like Jonadab with Amnon, or a family member, like Jezebel with Ahab. Those closest to us might mean well, but they hurt us when they say things like, "Everyone wants you to have this, and you should have it too. You owe it to yourself to be happy."

Regardless of the source of the temptation, we need to be on guard against statements that make us feel entitled. Many people are in debt, with little savings, simply because of these three little words: "I deserve this."

SPENDING PROBLEMS OFTEN RESULT FROM IMPATIENCE

We don't like to wait. When we want something, we want it now. In contrast, Scripture calls us to be patient and informs us of patience's several benefits. Here are a few examples:

- Patience allows our prayers to be answered: "I *waited patiently for the* Lord; and He inclined to me, and heard my cry" (Psalm 40:1).

- Patience is a source of strength: "Those who *wait on the* Lord *shall renew their strength*; they shall mount up with wings like eagles, they shall run and not be weary, they shall walk and not faint" (Isaiah 40:31).

- Patience permits fruit to be produced in our lives: "[The seed] that fell on the good ground are those who, having heard the word with a noble and good heart, keep it and *bear fruit with patience*" (Luke 8:15).

- Patience provides spiritual maturity: "My brethren, count it all joy when you fall into various trials, knowing that the testing of your faith *produces patience*. But *let patience have its perfect work, that you may be perfect and complete, lacking nothing*" (James 1:2-4).

- Patience helps us learn and prevents us from saying things we shouldn't: "Let every man be swift to hear, *slow [or patient] to speak*" (James 1:19).

Finances is one area in which patience can be beneficial. Proverbs 21:5 says, "The plans of the diligent lead surely to plenty, but those of *everyone who is hasty, surely to poverty*." The hardworking have an abundance, but the impatient end up poor. Many people admit having given in to four words that have led to bad financial decisions: "I want it now!" The issue is instant gratification. Rushing into a purchase often leads to regret later. Let's consider another example from the Old Testament.

Don't Be an Esau!

Let's turn to a familiar account about Jacob and Esau. Esau came back from the field tired and hungry. He wanted some of his brother's stew. Jacob said, "I'll give you some if you'll give me your birthright." It is hard to believe Jacob asked something so outrageous, but his name means "deceiver" or "heel catcher," so it was fitting of him to do this.

The only thing more outrageous than Jacob's request was Esau's response. In Genesis 25:32, he said, "I am about to die; so what is this birthright to me?" However, Esau wasn't in danger of starving. He was being dramatic to justify his behavior, just like we are sometimes dramatic to justify our behavior: "I need this...I have to have this...If I don't get this..."

Esau didn't care what the stew cost him. He wanted the stew, and he wanted it now. His impatience is shown in two ways. First, and most obviously, he wouldn't wait for food. Second, he wouldn't wait to enjoy his birthright, which would have been a big blessing to him later. But because it didn't benefit him at the moment, he did not want it.

Did Esau go on to regret his impatience? Absolutely! When he realized he had given up his birthright and would receive no blessing from his father, "he cried with an exceedingly great and bitter cry...For you know that afterward, when he wanted to inherit the blessing, he was rejected…though he sought it diligently with tears" (Genesis 27:34 and Hebrews 12:16-17). It's sad picturing a grown man sobbing and begging his father to give him something. He was impatient and it caused him regret, and we, too, can be impatient in ways that lead us to regret.

Philippians 3:19 describes people "whose god is their belly." They are controlled by "their appetites," or whatever they want at the moment. This describes Esau, but it can describe us too. We should ask ourselves: "Am I like Esau? Is my god my belly? Are my purchases controlled by my appetites and whatever I want at the moment? Am I an impatient type of person who ends up with regret?"

The Stanford marshmallow experiment was a series of studies conducted on children. They were given one marshmallow and told they could eat the marshmallow immediately, but if they waited until the person conducting the experiment returned 15 minutes later, they would receive a second marshmallow. The children fell into two categories—those who ate immediately and those who waited and received a second marshmallow.

In follow-up studies on the children when they were older, the researchers found the children who waited tended to have "better life outcomes as measured by SAT scores, educational attainment, body mass index, and other life measures."[5] Their patience—or impatience—dramatically affected their behaviors later in life, including their financial decisions.

Wait Two (or More) Weeks

In our home we found a simple, practical way to avoid making purchases we will regret. We wait a few weeks before buying. Wait two weeks (or four weeks if you really want to be sure) and see if you still want to make the purchase. Obviously, we don't have to follow this principle for everything we buy, but the lower the price that you are willing to apply this principle, the better the chances that you'll save money and avoid remorse.

If you wait a few weeks and you still want to make the purchase, there's a better chance you won't regret it. Often when people experience regret, it occurs within a few days. Waiting can help you avoid this. You'll find yourself sitting back and saying, "I sure am glad I didn't make that purchase," versus "I can't believe I bought this." While I've heard many people share their regret associated with impulsive purchases, I've never heard anyone say, "I regret the time I spent waiting to buy this."

SPENDING PROBLEMS OFTEN RESULT FROM MISUNDERSTANDING "GOOD DEALS"

Have you ever noticed that whenever you want to buy something, regardless of the season of the year or your geographic location, you are able to find a "good deal"? It is not a coincidence! I was a business major in college. I took marketing and learned that successful salespeople make customers think they're getting a good deal when they are not. If sellers were giving buyers that good of a deal, they wouldn't stay in business.

Proverbs 20:14 says, "'It is good for nothing,' cries the buyer, but when he has gone his way, then he boasts." We try to spend less money by complaining to the seller that the item is not worth the price, but after buying it, we brag that it was a good deal. Think of the times you have heard people discuss their purchases. How often have they said, "What was I thinking? I paid way too much and got ripped off!" Instead, you hear, "This was a once-in-a-lifetime opportunity. You would not believe the deal I got!" Listening to the way many people talk about spending money, you would wonder how any retailer can stay in business. You would think every salesperson should be fired because they're practically giving everything away to the great bargain hunters.

HOW DO WE KNOW WHEN TO SPEND MONEY?

Because we know we must spend money, and because there *are* times when you really will find a good deal—many people have saved hundreds or thousands of dollars finding the right purchase at the right time—how do we know when to buy something?

Let me first suggest this: Regardless of how attractive it looks, if you must take on debt (more about debt next chapter), don't make the purchase. Without the money, it is not a good deal *for you*. You might be tempted to say, "If I don't get this now, I'll never find this good of a deal again." That's probably not the case. With patience, you'll probably find another good deal in the future when you have the money to make the purchase.

But assuming you have the money, let me give you two principles to help you determine when to make a purchase.

First, Do Your Research

Doing your research is the only way to know for certain you are getting a good deal. If you're unfamiliar with the average prices of the item you're considering buying, then how will you know whether you should make the purchase or keep looking?

Earlier, I suggested you wait some time before buying. This will give you the time you need to do your research. Talk to people who can give you input: "Where there is no counsel, the people fall; but *in the multitude of counselors there is safety*" (Proverbs 11:14; see also Proverbs 15:22; 24:6). Apply this to your finances. If you're considering buying a vehicle, who do you know who knows vehicles? If you're considering a new sink, lighting system, or patio, what recommendations can you receive from friends who are plumbers, electricians, or woodworkers?

Also, be sure to include your husband or wife as you do your research. Your spouse might not be an expert on the product, but this is the person you should trust God to help you more than anyone else in your life. He or she might say, "I don't think we should do this now," or "I think we should buy this instead." Katie and I talk about most purchases ahead of time, and there have been plenty of times one of us, fortunately, put on the brakes. If you're a child, ask your parents for their advice.

A few years ago, we needed to purchase a vehicle because our growing family could no longer fit in our seven-passenger minivan. We decided to take the plunge and purchase a fifteen-passenger van. I started my research by creating a spreadsheet with columns that included price, year, mileage, and average review from the Internet. I developed a simple formula that allowed me to assign each van a rating based on the data I accumulated. Soon I had a spreadsheet full of information, and I added to it each day when more vans were put on the market.

One day a van showed up and the rating was much higher than any previously. My research indicated this van was an incredible deal. It turned out a restaurant owner had purchased the vehicle and thought he would use it for the business, but drove it only a few times. He told a friend he just wanted him to get rid of it for him. When I arrived to buy the van, the friend said, "You must be getting a great deal, because I've already had fifty other offers since you first called."

Second, Let God's Commands Serve as Fleeces

This principle can help not just with purchases, but with figuring out God's will in general. We've been given commands in Scripture that can serve as fleeces, or litmus tests, to direct us. Obeying them enables us to determine what to do.

Let's consider something specific, such as buying a house. Many people would say that God's Word doesn't tell us what house to buy, but I would disagree. No, we are not told directly, but indirectly the commands in Scripture can help us make the right decision. For example:

- We are commanded to be involved in a local church: "Not forsaking the assembling of ourselves together, as is the manner of some, but exhorting one another, and so much more as you see the Day approaching" (Hebrews 10:25).

- We are commanded to care for our family members: "If anyone does not provide for his own, and especially for those of his household, he has denied the faith and is worse than an unbeliever" (1 Timothy 5:8).

- Parents are commanded to spend time with and raise their children: "You shall teach [God's words] diligently *to your children*... older women [should]...admonish the young women to...*love their children*...Fathers [should]...*bring [up their children]* in the training and admonishment of the Lord" (Deuteronomy 6:7; Titus 2:3-4; Ephesians 6:4).

If we keep these commands in mind while looking at a house, we can ask ourselves these questions:

- Is this home close enough to a local church that we will be able to get involved in?

- Am I going to be able to take better care of my family with this home?

- Will this home decrease my time on the road to and from work, thereby giving me more time with my children?

Just as these questions help us determine whether our reasons for buying a specific house are godly, we should also consider whether our motivations are ungodly. For example, could we be motivated by...

- pride—we want a new house that makes us feel better about ourselves and improves our self-image and reputation. Instead of having our identity in Christ, our identity is in this purchase: "All that is in the world—the lust of the flesh, the lust of the eyes, and the pride of life—is not of the Father but is of the world" (1 John 2:16).

- covetousness—we have a home that meets our needs and has served us well for years, but our best friend moved into a new place and invited us over to see it. Suddenly, our house doesn't look so good anymore. Now we want a new house that rivals our friend's: "[Jesus] said to them, 'Take heed and beware of covetousness, for one's life does not consist in the abundance of the things he possesses'" (Luke 12:15).

- entitlement—we have worked hard for years and made many sacrifices. Our faithfulness in the workplace and our diligence with our finances have left us in a good position. We begin to tell ourselves, "I deserve it. I owe it to myself." But Jesus said, "If anyone desires to come after Me, let him deny himself, and take up his cross, and follow Me" (Matthew 16:24).

Although young people might not be looking for a home, if you're a young person reading this and you're still under your parents' authority, how do your parents feel about whatever you are considering buying? Do you have their blessing? Ephesians 6:1-3 says, "Children, obey your parents in the Lord, for this is right. 'Honor your father and mother,' which is the first commandment with promise: 'that it may be well with you and that you may live long on the earth.'" Considering these verses, if parents don't want their children buying something, it is possible that God would not want the children to buy it and is conveying that through the parents.

There is one more fleece that we will consider at length in the following chapter, and that is debt. Because the Bible speaks so strongly about debt (as we will see), if we are thinking about buying something but we are not taking debt into consideration, we are disregarding one of the clearest ways God can direct us.

When we look at what God's Word says about debt, family, marriage, children, pride, covetousness, entitlement, selfishness, materialism—and the list could go on—we have enough information to make the right decisions with purchases (and most other areas of life). The issue isn't usually a lack of knowledge. Instead, the issue is twofold: First, are we willing to take the time to study Scripture to learn what God wants? Second, after we learn what God wants, are we willing to obey?

An Example from Our Lives

When we moved to Washington in 2010 to pastor Woodland Christian Church, we lived in the parsonage. A few months later my parents moved to be near us, and they settled on a home that was only a few hundred feet away. In 2019, the church hired an associate pastor who wanted to live in the parsonage. My dad had Alzheimer's, and we knew he would need greater care in the future than my mom could provide, so we looked at purchasing a home together.

In making this decision, we had two convictions that served as fleeces to direct us. First, we knew we wanted to remain debt-free (Proverbs 22:7; Romans 13:8). Second, we knew we needed to honor my parents (Exodus 20:12; Ephesians 6:2-3).

We thought the first command would be easy to obey because after putting our money together, we knew how much we could spend. But we quickly found that our obedience to even this command was tested. We fell in love with one house that was $25,000 more than our budget would allow. If the house had been $250,000 more than we could afford, then we could have more easily said no. But because the amount of new debt seemed so small, we were tempted to say, "It's only $25,000. We could quickly pay this off." By God's grace, we stuck to our conviction and passed on this house.

The second command was also difficult to obey. We looked at many houses that Mom, Katie, and the kids liked, but Dad disliked. He always had an odd, and at times even unreasonable, issue. We were tempted to say, "He has Alzheimer's and isn't thinking correctly, so we don't need to listen to him." Instead, we said, "If God wants us to buy a house, He can give Dad peace about it."

As the house hunting stretched on, the temptation to compromise on our fleeces only increased. Finally, a house right next to my parents became available, and it was priced at barely under the amount of money that we had available. Everyone liked it, but we knew the real test was with Dad. Mom talked to him about the house, and she told us he liked it. Just to be sure, I talked to Dad about it too, and he also assured me that he liked it.

Katie, the kids, and I moved into my parents' house, and my parents moved into a new and smaller house next door. We were able to live near each other and near the church. We were all happy with the houses, the arrangement, and the peace that came from knowing we had obeyed God. We felt thankful that we didn't compromise on one of the fleeces and possibly miss out on God's best.

JESUS'S EXAMPLE

To increase our motivation to obey the teaching in this chapter, we need look no further than our Savior. Consider the following from when He was tempted:

> When the tempter came to Him, he said, "If You are the Son of God, command that these stones become bread…If You are the Son of God, throw Yourself down. For it is written: 'He shall give His angels charge over you,' and 'In their hands they shall bear you up, lest you dash your foot against a stone'" (Matthew 4:3, 6).

The devil was not doubting whether Jesus is the Son of God. Instead, he was trying to make Jesus feel entitled. Often when the Bible uses the word *if* it means "since" or "because," so it is as though the devil said, "*Because* You are the Son of God, You should not have to be hungry. You should not have to go through this. Throw Yourself down so the angels can catch You, and all this will be over."

The devil sounded like Jonadab. Jonadab said, "Why are you, the king's son, becoming thinner day after day? You should have what you want!" Satan said, "Why are You, the Son of God, becoming thinner day after day out here in the wilderness? Turn these stones into bread so You have something to eat!"

Jesus's Self-Denial

Just as Jonadab wanted to make Amnon feel entitled, the devil wanted to make Jesus feel entitled. If anyone could ever be entitled, it was Jesus! As the Son of God, He should have what He wants when He wants it; He should not have to go without. He could have said no to any discomfort, but "He humbled Himself and became obedient to the point of death, even the death of the cross" (Philippians 2:8). He denied Himself for us.

Contrast what the devil said to Jesus and what Jonadab said to Amnon with what Jesus says to us: "If anyone desires to come after Me, let him deny himself, and take up his cross daily, and follow Me" (Luke 9:23). While these words do not directly apply to finances, they have plenty of indirect application. We will have victory over self-entitlement when we obey Jesus's words.

Jesus's Patience

As we consider the devil's temptation of Jesus, we're reminded of Esau. Matthew 4:2 says Jesus "fasted forty days and forty nights, afterward He was hungry." Jesus was much hungrier than Esau. Like Esau, Jesus was also going to eat again. The Father's plan for the Son was that He die on a cross, not starve to death in the wilderness. The devil's real temptation was, "You do not have to be patient. Eat now. Don't wait!"

The difference between Jesus and Amnon is Jesus resisted the temptation to be entitled. He denied Himself. The difference between Jesus and Esau is Jesus resisted the temptation to be impulsive. He was patient. As Amnon and Esau show us what not to do, Jesus shows us what to do.

When you need the encouragement to be disciplined with your finances, put off spending problems, and avoid purchases that displease God, focus on Jesus. Meditate on His self-denial and patience. He was the model for us in His earthly life, "leaving us an example, that you should follow in His steps" (1 Peter 2:21).

CHAPTER 12

God's View of Debt

A man came home with a fancy new car. His wife asked, "Why did you buy that? We can't afford a new car, and there was nothing wrong with our old car."

The man answered, "Our old car needed a new battery."

His wife replied, "Then why didn't you just buy a new battery?"

The man said, "Well, I was faced with a choice. A new battery cost $100 and a new car cost $25,000, and they wanted me to buy the battery with cash."

Many people can relate to this man. We think debt is a blessing because it allows us to buy things with money we don't have.

Just to let you know ahead of time, you might have more trouble with this chapter than any other in this book. Is it because avoiding debt is more difficult than obeying the other teachings in the book? No, not at all. In fact, giving is probably more difficult for many people than avoiding debt.

You might have more trouble with this chapter because the principles in it are so contrary to the world's approach to money. For example, if I tell you it is important to give, save, and plan for retirement, you can find plenty of non-Christians who agree. But if I tell you to avoid debt, you can find plenty of financial advisors who will disagree and tell you that not only is debt acceptable, it is necessary and beneficial.

I will be the first to say that we should consider the counsel of financial advisors. When I do counseling, I have recommended people visit them. But let me ask you this before we go any further: Whose counsel should we value *the most*? Whose instruction should trump all others? God's!

The question is not "What makes the most sense financially?" or "What do financial advisors recommend?" The question is, "What does God want?"

Your Finances God's Way received its title because it is about managing finances the way God wants, and the Bible tells us how to do things God's way. Walking by faith means obeying God when it doesn't appear to make sense or goes against the counsel of others. As Peter said, "We ought to obey God rather than men" (Acts 5:29). So what does God say about debt?

GOD'S VIEW OF DEBT

To learn the Bible's teaching on debt, we must understand the difference between law and wisdom literature. The law (think Leviticus) contains commands forbidding sin, while wisdom (think Proverbs) contains principles that help us navigate through life. Let's consider what the law and then wisdom literature have to say about debt.

The Law and Debt

The law does not condemn lending and borrowing. Instead, it condemns usury (exorbitant interest) and promotes generosity:

- "If you lend money to any of my people with you who is poor, you shall not be like a moneylender to him, and *you shall not exact interest from him*" (Exodus 22:25 ESV).

- "If one of your brethren becomes poor, and falls into poverty among you, then you shall help him, like a stranger or a sojourner, that he may live with you. *Take no usury or interest from him;* but fear your God, that your brother may live with you (Leviticus 25:35-36).

- "At the end of every seven years you shall grant a release...every creditor shall *release what he has lent to his neighbor*" (Deuteronomy 15:1-2 ESV).

The point to notice is debt is not a sin because the law does not forbid it.

Wisdom and Debt

Wisdom literature also discusses lending and borrowing: "O LORD, who shall sojourn in your tent? Who shall dwell on your holy hill? He who... *does not put out his money at interest...* The wicked *borrows but does not pay back,* but the righteous...is *ever lending generously*" (Psalm 15:1-2, 5; 37:21,

26 esv). Jesus is "the wisdom of God" (1 Corinthians 1:24, see also verse 30 and Colossians 2:3), so His words also tell us what wisdom says about debt: "Give to him who asks you, and *from him who wants to borrow from you do not turn away*" (Matthew 5:42). We see (1) lending and borrowing aren't discouraged, (2) usury and failing to pay what's owed are condemned, and (3) generosity is praised.

Up to this point, debt hasn't sounded bad. But now we must consider one of the most well-known financial verses in the Bible: "The rich rules over the poor, and the borrower is the slave of the lender" (Proverbs 22:7 esv). How do we understand debt sounding acceptable elsewhere, but unacceptable now? Combining the teaching on debt from the law and wisdom literature, we find the biblical balance is this: Because debt is not forbidden in the law it is not necessarily sinful, but because wisdom warns against it, we are wise to try to avoid it. The danger is debt makes us slaves to the one we owe money to. If we're going to be slaves of anything, we should be "*slaves of righteousness*...so now present your members as *slaves to righteousness* [and]... *slaves of God*" (Romans 6:18, 19, 22).

Proverbs 22:7 is a cautionary alert to, as much as possible, not make someone else our master. Some people in debt feel enslaved to creditors. They dread going to the mailbox because they're afraid of receiving another bill they can't afford—they don't know how they're going to pay their master. Rod Rogers said,

> What does God have to say about the impact of debt on His people? In the Old Testament world if you couldn't pay your debt on time you became the slave of the lender until you worked off your debt. In our day, if you borrow money you become the lender's slave by giving much or most of your income back to the lender.[1]

EVEN CHURCHES CAN BE WRONG

The biggest threat to viewing debt biblically might not be the world or financial advisors. Sadly, it might be churches! We shouldn't be surprised when the world acts like debt is a blessing, but we should be surprised when churches do. I don't like to criticize churches, but I feel obligated to do so because I fear you could read this chapter and think, *We shouldn't worry about debt, because I remember when that church went into debt.* Churches aren't the standard. They don't always do what's right.

It is sad when churches go into debt to supposedly accomplish the Lord's work, when the same Lord they're claiming to serve might condemn the debt they're embracing. This often happens when churches get huge loans for buildings, which is an ironic situation. They want a building to worship the Lord in, but that same Lord warns against the debt they embraced to purchase the building. As Jesus said, "God is Spirit, and those who worship Him *must worship in spirit and truth.*" We must worship God according to the truth, which means worshipping Him according to the truth in His Word.

The situation is made worse when churches justify their actions by saying, "The Lord led us to do this." As soon as people attach God to something, nobody can disagree because then it would be disagreeing with God. But if God did not lead the church leaders to go into debt, then how bad is it to claim He did?

If a church goes into debt but struggles financially, the leadership often turns to the congregation and pleads (or guilts) the people into giving more money for the cause God supposedly wanted. Perhaps the pastor will even rebuke the people for not giving more. But what if it was the church leadership's fault for acting outside God's will in taking on the debt?

When the leadership says, "The Lord led us to do this" but they don't have the money to continue the work they claim God wanted, God looks bad—He called His people to do something, but then didn't give them what they needed to do it. He led His people to step out in faith but didn't honor their faith.

Hudson Taylor was a missionary and the founder of the China Inland Mission. He said, "God's work done in God's way *will never lack God's supply.*"[2] This is true, but when church leadership say it was God's will to get a building loan and then can't afford the payments, they make God's work appear to *lack God's supply.* God looks unfaithful and unable to be trusted.

Christians must keep in mind that churches are led by fallible men who do not always make the best decisions. While I would like to be able to encourage you to look at what churches do and follow the examples of pastors and elders, the standard is not what men do. The standard is the Bible.

DEBT IS YOUR ENEMY VERSUS YOUR FRIEND

Let me first say that people aren't always in debt for bad reasons. Some situations put people in debt against their wishes. There could be health issues that cause bills to pile up, a job loss and accompanying inability to pay expenses, or an unforeseen accident that drains emergency funds. People experiencing such circumstances should not feel condemned by this chapter.

What's important to note here is that the above examples are all situations outside of people's control. They didn't invite the debt into their lives. Sadly, when most people are in debt, it was completely within their control—it was their choice. They put themselves in debt when they gave in to sins such as covetousness, discontentment, materialism, or self-entitlement.

You might read this chapter and think I'm being judgmental or harsh, especially if you have been taught that debt is a blessing. The truth is that I'm trying to help you! As a pastor, I have watched debt cause enough problems that it would be unloving of me not to warn you. Please hear me clearly: Debt is not your friend!

Think about this logically: If God warns us about something in His Word, how often could it be His will to act against that warning? Not often! If Scripture cautions us about something, how cautious must we be about allowing it into our lives? If we answer these questions honestly, we must approach embracing debt with great apprehension.

Let's get an elevated view of debt by considering the situation in our country. Then we can zoom in and look at the situation in households.

OUR NATION'S DEBT

Michael Farris is a lawyer and the founder of the Home School Legal Defense Association (HSLDA) and Patrick Henry College. In 2001 he wrote,

> We should demand that our government respect the economic freedom of our children and grandchildren by eliminating the national debt. In the fall of 1992, the national debt was $4 trillion. That is $16,000 for every man, woman, and child in America. A $4 trillion stack of $1000 bills would be 245 miles high.[3]

The national debt was $4 trillion in 1992, $6 trillion in 2001, $15 trillion in 2011, and it is expected to reach $30 trillion in 2021.[4] Why do we have a debt ceiling if we keep raising it? If the purpose is to prevent debt from exceeding a certain level but we raise the ceiling when it's reached, haven't we defeated the purpose? We should get rid of the pretenses that have no real significance and be honest about our actions: We take on debt recklessly.

Biting the Bullet

The way our nation is accruing debt is unsustainable, and ultimately, there are only three possible ways to change the course we're on. The first possibility is to raise taxes. The second possibility is to spend less. But most economists believe either strategy compromises the economy.[5] Lowering taxes stimulates growth and spending, but also increases the debt. As the government spends money or engages in "quantitative easing," also known as stimulus spending (injecting large amounts of money into the economy), the economy grows, but so does the debt. It should also be noted that some economists believe when the government stops stimulus spending, the economy returns to where it would have been without it, but with one exception: an increased national debt.[6]

The third solution is, to put it bluntly, bite the bullet. Suffer through difficult years, including economic slowdowns, and lower the quality of living until the debt is in check. But could a political candidate win if he talked about making these kinds of sacrifices? I doubt it. People want a candidate who promises prosperity versus poverty. Also, as the percentage of our nation receiving entitlements grows, so too will the number of voters who want candidates promising more rather than less spending. Sadly, I hope this famous quote doesn't define our nation:

> A democracy cannot exist as a permanent form of government. It can only exist until the voters discover that they can vote themselves largesse from the public treasury. From that moment on, the majority always votes for the candidates promising the most benefits from the public treasury with the result that a democracy always collapses over loose fiscal policy, always followed by a dictatorship. The average age of the world's greatest civilizations has been 200 years.[7]

If I can paraphrase: A democracy only lasts until the people learn they can vote themselves the greatest amount of immediate prosperity. At that point, the nation will be crushed under the weight of the people's selfishness.

Sacrificing Our Children's Future for Our Present

We have an amazing capacity to sacrifice the future for the present, but what's surprising is we will even sacrifice our children's future for the present.

The preamble to the US Constitution states the purpose of it is to secure the blessings of liberty to us and to our posterity (children), something we are not doing. One of our founding fathers, Thomas Jefferson, said,

> The question whether one generation has the right to bind another by the deficit it imposes is a question of such consequence as to place it among the fundamental principles of government. We should consider ourselves unauthorized to saddle posterity with our debts, and morally bound to pay them ourselves.[8]

Again, if I can paraphrase: Our generation should not be able to hurt the next generation by "kicking the can down the road" and giving them the consequences of our actions. Although the debt negatively affects us, our children will suffer the most.

The Bible's Condemnation

Proverbs 13:22 says, "A good man leaves an inheritance to his children's children." I don't know if there's a better verse describing *the opposite* of what our nation is doing. It would be one thing if we were only failing to leave our children an inheritance, but our sin goes beyond that because we're robbing them of their futures. They will be burdened with the problems that are being created today.

Psalm 37:21 says, "The wicked borrows but does not pay back" (ESV). We currently borrow 40 cents of every dollar. You could argue that our nation has never defaulted on its debt, but we were within days of doing so in 2011.[9] We lost our triple-A bond rating with Standard & Poor's and received a negative outlook for the future, indicating risk of a further downgrade if the government's fiscal discipline weakened or the economy deteriorated further.[10] China's official Xinhua news agency said, "The U.S. government has to come to terms with the painful fact that the good old days when it could just borrow its way out of messes of its own making are finally gone."[11]

You might be saying, "I'm not in government. I didn't make these decisions. What do our nation's debt and spending problems have to do with me?" The answer is our nation is people: you and me. We are part of the problem. Most Americans don't spend or view debt any differently than the government.

INDIVIDUAL DEBT

Let me share some numbers with you. Using multiple sources, as of 2020, on average, people have the following debts:

- Credit card debt is $6,500
- Automobile debt is $18,500
- Student loan debt is $39,000
- Household debt is $145,000
- Mortgage debt is $210,000[12]

Let's look at a few of these categories of debt so we can manage our finances God's way.

Credit Card Debt

A Bankrate survey found 30 percent of Americans have more credit card debt than they have saved up for emergencies.[13] If people have $6,500 in credit card debt, are charged the average APR of 19 percent,[14] and pay the minimum each month (3 percent, which is roughly $190), they would stay in debt for more than 17 years, put more than $5,800 toward interest, and pay back more than $12,300. Pay back $12,300 to borrow $6,500? Why would we think this is anything other than foolish?

Embracing credit card debt is one of the worst financial mistakes we make. Ted Rossman, industry analyst at CreditCards.com, explains how detrimental it can be:

> Credit card rates are at record highs 17.73 percent, and that's for people with good credit. Many people with lesser credit are paying 20 to 25 percent on their cards. Paying these kinds of rates for any length of time is really going to hold you back financially. Credit card rates are three to five times what we typically see on mortgages, auto loans, and student loans.[15]

The problem with credit cards is they seem like free money—you can buy something today and pay for it later. Because the bill doesn't arrive for weeks, you feel as though you didn't spend a cent. Even when the bills arrive, the purchase still doesn't seem painful because the payments are only smaller installments of the entire cost.

We must keep in mind that, in the end, we pay back more than twice the initial purchase. For example, a $10,000 purchase at 20 percent interest, paid off over 8 years, requires monthly payments of only $210, but the total paid back is $20,115. That means $10,115 in interest! Would you still make that $10,000 purchase if it were $20,000 instead? Hopefully not.

While I would highly discourage credit cards, if you are going to use them, be sure to pay off the balance each month. Wise people never pay the exorbitant interest tacked on to their credit card purchases. They pay off the balance each month, thereby using the card without it using them.

Automobile Debt

A close second behind the damage of credit card debt is automobile debt. You have probably heard that new vehicles are terrible purchases because they lose value when driven off the lot. Let me reinforce that point by giving you some numbers. Fifteen percent is the average value lost, which means if you purchase a vehicle for $30,000, you lose $4,500 within minutes. Let that sink in. A casino is probably the only other place you can lose that much money that quickly. Sixty percent of the value of a vehicle is lost within the first five years.[16] New vehicles are one of the worst investments people make, yet plenty of people still purchase them.

The average car payment is $545 per month. This doesn't include the extra money for auto insurance, which is more expensive on a new car. The average new car loan is 68 months, which means the average car costs more than $37,000 when paid off completely. If you invested the same amount of money with a 12 percent rate of return, you would earn more than

- $125,000 in 10 years
- $500,000 In 20 years
- $5.4 million in 40 years[17]

Even if we use a smaller car payment of $415 per month and a more conservative interest rate, we are still out the following amounts:

- $390,000 in 30 years with a 6 percent APR
- $570,000 in 30 years with an 8 percent APR
- $820,000 in 30 years with a 10 percent APR[18]

Wouldn't you want to avoid throwing away this much money by purchasing your vehicles with cash? By doing that, you can wisely use the extra money in other ways, such as paying off your mortgage. Let's take a look at why that is a good idea.

Student Loan Debt

The student loan debt in the United States is now more than $1.57 trillion, which exceeds credit card debt by more than $780 billion.[19] Student loan debt has increased almost 160 percent since 2007, also making it the fastest-growing type of debt.[20] Sixty-two percent of students graduate with student loan debt,[21] the average monthly payment is $393,[22] and the average repayment period is 21.1 years.[23] Instead of making these payments, if 21-year-olds invested $393 every month with a 10 percent return, they would have 4.5 million dollars when they reach 67 years of age.[24] How many graduates can say the money they made from their degrees exceeded the money they could've made if that same amount were invested?

Three misconceptions have contributed to the problem. Let's look at each of them.

Misconception One: A Degree Always Improves Your Life

While some graduates found degrees improved their lives, others experienced the opposite. Fifty-three percent who took out student loans say they regret doing so, and 43 percent say they regret going to college altogether.[25]

Student loans can become a gateway to greater debt. When people have tens of thousands of dollars of college debt, a few thousand more seems insignificant. Student loans can create bad financial habits that graduates take with them throughout life.

Misconception Two: You Need a Degree to Succeed

Many high-end professionals will tell you they wouldn't be where they are without their degree, while others would tell you they have never used their degree (think of the discussion about "worthless purchases" in the previous chapter). How do you know if you need a degree? The answer is contained in one word in that question: *need*. Those who work in some professions, such as medicine, law, and education, *need* degrees. Those who work in other professions, such as firefighters, insurance agents, cooks, plumbers, exterminators, medical assistants, landscapers, construction workers, and phlebotomists, don't need degrees, and some of these jobs pay as much or more than those requiring degrees.[26]

A gentleman who has been doing some remodeling on our house lamented the money he spent on a degree he isn't using. Many people (myself included) have college degrees that have gone unused. I have a bachelor's in business and two masters (education and biblical studies), and I rarely use the information I learned in those programs. My biblical studies degree has helped me as a pastor, but if I used all that time spent writing papers and taking tests, I believe I could have learned as much or even more on my own.

Misconception Three: You Must Go into Debt to Get a Degree

A woman in my church wasn't sure whether she should go to college. She wanted to get married, have children, and be a stay-at-home mom, but she knew that might not happen for years. She decided to go to college, but she didn't want to go into debt, so she prayed that God would give her the money she needed to go to school for as long as God wanted. She attended for a few years, the money ran out, she stopped going, and soon afterward, she got married.

There are two things I like about her approach. First, she chose to remain debt-free. Perhaps you work while going to college and pay for classes as you make the money for them. Your four-year degree takes eight years, but you graduate with no student loans. Instead of living on campus, perhaps you live with your parents to save money.

Second, she put the matter in God's hands. I do not bring this up to discourage anyone from attending college, but the decision should be a matter of careful research and prayer. Do your homework (no pun intended!) and bring the matter before the Lord to determine whether college is the best course for you.

Mortgage Debt

For simplicity's sake let's divide our expenses into two categories: nonessential (such as vacations, eating out, entertainment) and essential (food, clothing, and housing). Debt should be avoided for nonessential expenses (such as vacations and flat screen televisions) and it can be avoided for most essential expenses. The one exception is housing because many people don't have the money to buy a home with cash. If you're wondering how much to spend on housing, the general rule is 30 percent of your income, whether it's rent or a mortgage payment.[27]

Some people consider themselves to be debt-free when the only debt they have is a mortgage. This is an odd perspective because a mortgage alone could be larger than multiple other loans combined. When people have a mortgage, unless they are close to paying it off, they should not consider themselves close to being debt-free.

Our Story

When Katie and I first got married, we still owed $160,000 on our mortgage (originally $164,000). Katie also owed about $6,000 in school loans. We owned two vehicles that were paid off. We didn't (and still don't) own credit cards.

We considered not paying off our mortgage because of the tax deduction we could receive, but we were deterred for three reasons. First, we were given *The Total Money Makeover* by Dave Ramsey as a wedding gift and we read it on our honeymoon. Regarding the tax deductions from a mortgage, he wrote:

> If you have a home with a payment of around $900, and the interest portion is $830 per month, you have paid around $10,000 in interest that year, which creates a tax deduction. If, instead, you have a debt-free home, you would, in fact, lose the tax deduction, so the myth says to keep your home mortgaged because of tax advantages.
>
> If you do not have a $10,000 tax deduction and you are in a 30 percent bracket, you will have to pay $3,000 in taxes on that $10,000. According to the myth, we should send $10,000 in interest to the bank so we don't have to send $3,000 in taxes to the IRS. Personally, I think I will live debt-free and not make a $10,000 trade for $3,000.[28]

Second, we were sickened to think about the amount we would end up repaying the bank. Over the 30 years of the loan, the total would be $372,000, which would be more than twice the amount of the loan itself.

Third, and most importantly, as I said at the beginning of the chapter, we wanted to be guided by God's Word and not man's wisdom. Even if it seemed to make the most sense to keep our mortgage, we were convicted to pay it off because the Bible cautions against debt.

Being Upside Down

Some people think a mortgage is an acceptable form of debt because homes appreciate, making them investments. This contrasts with other assets—such as automobiles, boats, or electronics—that typically depreciate with time. The problem is many people have found themselves upside down in their mortgages (the value of the home is less than the loan amount). During the subprime mortgage crisis (2007 to 2010), also known as the Great Recession, 11 million Americans, or 23 percent, of the nation's homeowners were upside down.[29] Once the crisis was over, the number peaked at 31 percent in the third quarter of 2012.[30]

The situation improved, but *The New York Times* reported in January 2015 that "about 17% of all homeowners are still 'upside down' on their mortgages."[31] A 2013 article in *NPR* titled "You Be the Judge: Is the Housing Market Really Improving?" reads, "The number of 'underwater' homeowners may be down, but it's still extremely high, with an estimated one in five owing more than the home's worth."[32] A 2016 article titled "A Decade Out from the Mortgage Crisis, Former Homeowners Still Grasp for Stability" reads:

> Homeowners across the U.S. confronted the reality that their houses were worth a fraction of what they paid for them. Now, a decade later, even though the recession is over, more than six million homeowners are still upside down on their mortgages.[33]

We live in a fallen world. When one trial concludes, another begins. As I write this, in 2020, we are dealing with COVID-19. CBS News reports,

> 6.7 million households could be evicted in the coming months. That amounts to 19 million people potentially losing their homes, rivaling the dislocation that foreclosures caused after the subprime housing bust.[34]

The above statistics reveal there is simply no guarantee that a house will appreciate. Many people can attest to the financial problems they experienced when unforeseen circumstances, such as a recession, caused their home's value to plummet.

As James 4:14-15 says, "You do not know what will happen tomorrow. For what is your life? It is even a vapor that appears for a little time and then vanishes away. Instead, you ought to say, 'If the Lord wills, we shall live and do this or that.'" We don't know how the economy will fare, what trials we will face, what emergencies will occur, what expenses we will have to pay for, or even what our job or income will look like. Many people have thought they would make the same amount of money, or more, for the rest of their lives, only to find themselves laid off when their company experienced hard times and downsized. The list of situations that can lead to a home fore-closure is endless.

A mortgage is a major commitment to make when the future is unknown. We must exercise extreme caution (and prayer) before locking ourselves into decades of payments that are dependent on our financial situations remaining the same. People become indebted to the loan company for up to 30 years (sometimes more if they refinance or take out a second mortgage). Think (and pray) carefully before embracing a mortgage you might pay off for the rest of your life. Consider that even if you do pay off the mortgage accord-ing to the payment schedule, the result is that you've given the bank more than twice the amount of the loan itself. This alone is a great reason to strive to pay a mortgage off early. When viewed this way, we must examine every mortgage and consider whether it is a good use of God's money.

Don't delay getting out of debt. Dedicate yourself to making changes that will put you on the road to freedom from bondage.

TRUST GOD TO HELP YOU

Let me conclude with this: Don't delay getting out of debt. Dedicate yourself to making changes that will put you on the road to freedom from bondage. In the following chapter, we will discuss how we can eliminate debt given time, wisdom, and sacrifice. But for now, let me leave you with the following encouragement.

The battle to become debt-free is fought in the heart because this is where we're tempted to be selfish and covetous. The Lord can enable you to resist these temptations, giving you the needed selflessness and contentment. Believe He wants to help you: "Commit to the LORD whatever you do, and he will establish your plans" (Proverbs 16:3 NIV).

If you are a Christian, you are God's child, and just like earthly parents want to see their children manage their finances well, our heavenly Father wants to see us manage our finances well. Assuming God wants you to be debt-free, He will equip you to reach that wonderful goal.

CHAPTER 13

Avoiding and Eliminating Debt

When couples in the church I pastor give birth to a child, I try to bring them a meal, meet the baby, see if they need anything, and pray with them. When Robert and Katy Cunningham had their fifth son, I went to see not only them and their new baby, but also their new living situation. They (seven people, including five energetic young boys) had moved into a broken-down motorhome that was sitting on the property where Robert was building their house.

When I returned home, I told my wife two things. First, I shared how proud I was of Robert and Katy for their commitment to being debt-free and all the sacrifice that was involved in sticking with that conviction. Second, I said, "We don't have very much to complain about!"

Not long ago, Robert finished the construction. They were able to move out of the motorhome and into their new house debt-free.

Maybe you have said, "People can't buy a home with cash." I have heard this argument many times, and Robert and Katy's testimony (as well as many others) reveals it is not true. I have watched young and old people alike, inside and outside my church, purchase homes without mortgages. Here are three points of advice to help you do the same.

AVOIDING A MORTGAGE

First, Consider a Rental

Many people argue that it's better to buy a house because if you rent, you're throwing money away. The idea is the money would be better off put toward the cost of your house. This appears to be true until you consider how much of a mortgage payment goes toward the interest versus the principal. The money going toward the interest isn't going toward the price of the house any more than rent goes toward the price of the house. If you want your money to go toward the price of the house, save up the money and buy your house with cash.

Second, Live Modestly

We have friends who lived in a basement until they could buy their first home with cash. Some other friends lived in a two-bedroom rental with seven children. Did these situations involve sacrifice and living modestly? Definitely. But how good do you think these people feel now as they live in their homes with no debt?

Third, Purchase a Starter Home

When I talk about buying a home with cash, it might be more accurate to say *homes*. Who says you need to live in your dream home in your twenties or thirties? A better approach is to purchase a smaller starter home with cash and save up for your next home. Then sell your starter home, which is hopefully worth more than when you bought it, and use that money, along with the money you've saved up, to purchase your next home. As your family and income grow, so does your home.

If You Decide to Purchase a Mortgage

If, for whatever reason, you still decide to go ahead with a mortgage, let me offer you two points of advice.

Understand "Qualifying"

Real estate agents and loan officers want you to sign for the most amount of money. This has left people with much larger mortgages than they can afford simply because they were told they "qualified." They were locked into high payments that paralyzed them for decades, leaving them unable to save, be generous, or prepare for emergencies. A much wiser approach is a smaller mortgage that can be paid off faster and easier.

Choose a 15-Year Versus a 30-Year Mortgage

There are many benefits to a 15-year versus a 30-year mortgage:

- lower interest rates
- less interest over the life of the loan
- quicker equity built into the property
- less likelihood of being upside down if the housing market crashes

The only downside to a 15-year mortgage is larger monthly payments, but most people would be surprised to learn they're not *that much larger*. For example:

- The monthly payment on a 30-year, $300,000 mortgage with a 4 percent APR is $1,432, for a total repayment of $515,609 ($215,609 in interest).
- The monthly payment on a 15-year, $300,000 mortgage with a 4 percent APR is $2,219, for a total repayment of $399,431 (interest $99,431).

The difference is $787 per month, but the interest is more than cut in half: $99,431 versus $215,609, which saves you $116,178.

STRATEGIES TO ELIMINATE DEBT

What if you are already in debt, whether from a mortgage, credit cards, school loans, automobile loans, or all the above? You need strategies that help eliminate the debt you have.

Sacrifice

Remember, every cent counts. All the money we avoid spending puts us that much closer to being debt-free. This requires being frugal and intentional with purchases. We must often say no to things we want. The most popular and effective approaches to finances can't prevent us from having to go without certain enjoyments. While formulas and budgeting techniques can be helpful, there's no substitute for sacrifice.

Instead of being one strategy, think of this as the umbrella over all the strategies because each of them requires sacrifice. If we expect to eliminate debt, we must live in a way that others might consider extreme. Our society is so indulgent that if we live "normally," we will never be debt-free.

Live Below Your Income

The worst approach you can take with your money is spending it as though you make more than you do—living off $7,000 per month when you make $6,000. This will increase your debt month by month. The reasonable approach is spending at your income level—living off $6,000 when you make $6,000. But if you make $6,000 dollars per month, is the solution to live as though you make that amount? No. This will have you living paycheck to paycheck, spending all the money you make. You won't increase your debt, but you also won't eliminate any debt. The best approach is spending as though you make less than you do—living off $4,000 when you make $6,000. This will allow you to pay off almost $100,000 in four years (4 years x 12 months x $2,000 per month).

Eliminate Unnecessary Expenses

As you consider your expenses, try to eliminate whatever is unnecessary, such as going to the movies and eating out. Cancel subscriptions you don't need, such as cable television and extra phone lines. When you travel, bring food with you. Preparing meals at home saves money. While Katie and I were trying to get out of debt, if we ate out for a birthday or anniversary, we usually used a gift card. It may seem impossible to live without certain pleasures you've always enjoyed, but remember: The more expenses you eliminate, the faster you'll be out of debt.

Buy Used

As a ministry family, we've had lots of clothes and other items given to us. When all our bases weren't covered, we were able to find what we needed at yard sales and thrift and consignment stores. When you need "new" stuff, you can spend a fraction of the price buying used.

Stay Home

If you asked those who are closest to us, many people would say, "Scott and Katie never go anywhere!" Traveling is expensive. Eat, play, and laugh at home. You'll save on gas, lodging, and put less wear and tear on your vehicles. There are three keys to success with this strategy.

First, Build Relationships

When your children feel connected to you and each other, they will be more interested in staying at home because this is where they can be with those who are closest to them.

- Limit screen time: If "family time" involves a television or computer, kids are more likely to feel closer to the electronic device than their family members.

- Look for ways to connect: Can Friday evenings become "game night" or "make your own pizza night"? We purposefully end each day in the living room with everyone relaxing, visiting, and mellowing out before evening prayer and bedtime.

Second, Avoid Conflict

It is especially important for parents to have a healthy marriage because they set the example and tone in the home. The love and peace, or contention and strife, between husband and wife trickles down to the children. Children want to be in a home filled with harmony, but they will want to move away from one filled with quarreling.

Third, Invest in Your Home

Doesn't this conflict with our goal of saving money? Yes, but sometimes we need to spend money to save money. By staying home you'll save money, and you'll be more inclined to stay home if you have invested in it. Use some of the money you saved from not traveling and invest in your home to make it a place you and your family enjoy.

Avoid Lavishness

Even when you invest in your home (or making any purchases, for that matter), you should avoid extravagance. You can be nice, tidy, spacious, comfy, and modest. When eliminating debt, settle for simplicity. If you purchase new furniture, make sure it's because you need new furniture. Buying new furniture simply because you're bored with your current set is a waste of money and reveals a discontent heart. We still have much of the same furniture from when we got married.

Proverbs 13:7 says, "There is one who makes himself rich, yet has nothing; and one who makes himself poor, yet has great riches." Some people appear wealthy through their expensive homes, vehicles, and vacations, but if they're buried in debt, they "[make themselves] rich, yet have nothing." If their debt exceeds the value of their possessions, then they have less than nothing because they're in the negative. Others "[make themselves] poor" through their humble living, but they have "great riches" because they have money saved and no debt.

Avoid "Going Big"

Holidays, birthdays, and anniversaries can really add up. Our honeymoon was free because my parents let us use their timeshare in Palm Springs. How sad that many young couples limp out of the starting gate financially. They begin their marriage with thousands of dollars of debt, not from purchasing a home or car, but from their wedding and honeymoon. Save the "dream trip" for when your debt is paid off. Make it a reward.

For birthdays for each of our children, we buy one gift, and we ask the grandparents to buy only one gift. We also celebrate the child by having dinner and a cake that Katie prepares. For Christmas, our children buy their siblings small gifts. Katie and I have mutually agreed not to spend much on each other. We try to do most of our shopping after the holidays are over when things are discounted. For example, we have a tradition of buying all the discounted candy and eggs after Easter and having our own hunt then.

A minimalist approach not only keeps expenses and expectations low, it also minimizes stress and covetousness. For some people, the joy of special occasions is overshadowed by their financial anxiety.

Throughout the year we allow our kids to be bored instead of trying to entertain them. Not only does this save money, it causes them to find things to do. We encourage them to engage in activities that foster creativity, such as music, art, reading, writing, and building. We purchase books, musical instruments, and art supplies. Because we want our kids to play outside, we also invest in bikes, skates, scooters, jump ropes, and sidewalk chalk. We haven't introduced them to video games.

Most children have toys they don't play with. Figure out which toys your kids like and invest in those. For us, Legos, Duplos, and K'Nex have shown to be tried-and-true. We typically avoid toys that require batteries or electricity.

Avoid Expensive Hobbies

There's something wrong when people are thousands of dollars in debt yet they're spending thousands of dollars on activities, hobbies, and events that they really cannot afford. Until you are debt-free, you should try to avoid those activities that cost a lot of money.

Enjoy Cheap or Free

Have you been led to believe that you must spend money to enjoy yourself? There are many activities that are free or nearly free. Find something that you and your spouse and family love that doesn't cost much, or better yet, is free. Here are some examples:

- Visit a museum, aquarium, or zoo—Many of these offer free admission on certain days.

- Read—By yourself, with your spouse, or to your children. Combine this with another free activity, such as taking a trip to the library or bookstore. Many of these have children's play areas.

- Watch a movie—Didn't I discourage this in the last chapter? Yes, when frequenting a theatre, but not when watching something much cheaper or even free. While you're at the library getting your next book, you can also check out a DVD.

- Play games—A board game, puzzle, or deck of cards is a wonderful way to be together and pass the time.

- Attend church activities—Weekly Bible studies and home fellowships are free and have added spiritual benefits.

- Volunteer—Serve at your church, a soup kitchen, or pregnancy center. If you have children, they can be involved, which teaches them important lessons.

- Visit the farmers' market—Take in the sights, sounds, tastes, and smells while supporting your local community. Sometimes you can find fruits and vegetables in larger quantities and for cheaper prices than at the grocery store.

- Spend time outdoors—Take a walk, jog, garden, have a picnic, hike, or go on a bike ride. If you want to do something athletic you can play basketball or join a sports team in your community.

- Create—Cook a meal, make a photo album, draw, paint, or write.

- Develop a skill—There are free tutorials online to learn new skills, such as a foreign language, knitting, photography, or a musical instrument.

- Be hospitable—Invite friends or neighbors to your home. Make it a potluck to ease the labor and financial burden for everyone.

- Be productive—Clean the house, finish a project that's been nagging at you, plan a trip, polish your resume, or write a letter.

- Host a yard sale—Get rid of unwanted clothes, furniture, and other items while making money, decluttering, and blessing others.

Keep the End in Mind

Eliminating debt is difficult, and applying this strategy will help you apply the other strategies and give you the needed motivation to keep going. We paid off our mortgage after seven years by dreaming about what it would be like to be debt-free:

- Bills kept (primarily) limited to utilities

- Purchases made without having to worry if we had the money we needed

- More money put toward savings and giving

- No longer being slaves to a lender

We kept these blessings in mind while telling ourselves no purchase, trip, or luxury was worth trading for them. Keep reminding yourself of the joys you will experience when you are debt-free.

Continue Giving

I know this doesn't look like a strategy to becoming debt-free, but you will see why it is in a moment. For now, consider this illustration of the temptation you'll face. A man had two prize-winning calves that provided him with thousands of dollars. He told his wife, "Honey, this is wonderful. God has blessed us with these two calves, so I'm going to honor Him by giving Him one of them. One will belong to God, and one will belong to us. Whatever God's calf brings in financially, we are going to give to Him. Whatever our calf brings in financially, we are going to keep for ourselves."

The man came home one day looking sad and discouraged. His wife said, "Honey, what's wrong?"

The man said, "I can't believe it. God's calf died."

We want to let God's calf die versus our own. As you strive to pay off your debt, money will be tight and you'll be tempted to avoid giving to God. You must resist this temptation.

Giving and paying off debt seem mutually exclusive, as though doing one is choosing not to do the other. But they're compatible. If you want to honor God by paying off your debt, you must also want to honor Him by continuing to give. God says, "Those who honor Me I will honor, and those who despise Me shall be lightly esteemed" (1 Samuel 2:30). We shouldn't expect God to honor our desire to be debt-free if we stop honoring Him by no longer giving. God can help you pay off your debt better using less of your money than you can pay off your debt using all your money; therefore, continuing to give is a strategy.

Rod Rogers said, "If you want God's help to get out of debt, you must put God first in your giving. It flies in the face of conventional wisdom, but I have seen many families give their way out of debt."[1] I'm not promising everything is going to go perfectly if you give, but I can just about guarantee that things will go poorly if you do not give. Will God allow people to prosper financially if that is the very area in which they disobey Him? God loves us too much to let that happen. Do not expect to get ahead if you withhold what the Lord expects you to give. C.H. Spurgeon said, "Many are poor because they rob God."[2]

Katie and I had some friends who wanted to become debt-free, but at first, they approached it wrongly. They said, "We stopped giving. We were going to resume giving when we were out of debt, but we kept falling further behind. It wasn't until we gave again that we were able to pay off our debt."

PUT EXTRA MONEY TOWARD DEBT

As you apply the above strategies, you will be tempted to spend any extra money that comes your way. Decide right now that you'll put it toward repaying your debt. When you receive your tax return, Christmas or birthday cash, inheritance money, or income earned on the side, put it toward debt repayment.

When Katie and I were trying to eliminate debt, all our extra money went toward the mortgage. Some months it was a few hundred dollars, and other months it was a few thousand. When Katie inherited $10,000 dollars, we didn't think twice before putting it toward the mortgage. Every tax return went toward the mortgage. One year I worked part-time for a church while working full-time as an elementary schoolteacher. The entire pastor's salary, and much of the teaching salary, went toward the mortgage.

WHAT ABOUT WHEN YOU'RE OUT OF DEBT?

When we are out of debt, what are we going to do with the extra money we have available? First, hopefully we will increase our giving out of thankfulness to God for helping us to become debt-free. Second, we should increase our savings (more on this next chapter). Third, we can loosen up…a little.

Just because you are debt-free doesn't mean you should revert to the lifestyle that made you a slave in the first place. Continue applying the principles that helped you eliminate your debt so you can remain free.

When we were out of debt, we made some purchases we wouldn't have made while were still in debt, but our lifestyles didn't change that much. We still apply many of the same principles today, such as paying with cash, discussing purchases ahead of time, being patient, doing our research, buying used, and pursuing modesty. The goal should be to remain debt-free for life, not bounce in and out of debt. Just because you are debt-free doesn't mean you should revert to the lifestyle that made you a slave in the first place. Continue applying the principles that helped you eliminate your debt so you can remain free.

POSSIBLY MISSING OUT ON GOD'S BEST

Let me leave you with this final encouragement: If you don't have the money to make a purchase, the answer might be *not yet* instead of *no*. The door might be closed only until God enables you to come up with the money you need. He can do so by

- prompting you to improve on your ability to save
- convicting you about being more frugal
- showing you things you can sell
- helping you avoid costly expenses
- giving you greater wisdom for how to handle the money you have

But if you buy something when you don't have the money to do so, you might be missing these and other wonderful blessings God has in store for you. You don't want to have to wonder whether God would have helped you obtain the money you needed to avoid debt. Be patient and trust Him, so you don't end up settling for far less than His best.

Think about these two questions:

1. Is it God's will for you to own something?

2. Is it God's will for you to avoid debt?

If the answer to these two questions is *yes*, then God will enable you to buy with cash. And if it is God's will for you to buy with cash, you can be confident He will help you to reach that goal. He will "*equip you with everything good* that you *may do his will*, working in us that which is pleasing in his sight" (Hebrews 13:21 ESV).

Once your debt is paid off, you are ready to start saving. In the following chapter, we will talk about the right and wrong ways to do so.

CHAPTER 14

Saving the Right and Wrong Way

A fter health- and fitness-related New Year's resolutions, such as exercising more, going on a diet, and losing weight, the second-most-common resolutions are financial.[1] This would be good news, except that only 64 percent of New Year's resolutions last longer than the first month, and only 46 percent last longer than six months.[2] Changing is hard! As a pastor, I've heard many people say, "I'm going to stop this," or "I'm going to start that," but then nothing changes. We get into the habit of doing things one way and it's difficult to do things differently. This is why the Bible warns us about losing good habits and developing bad ones:

- "Do not be deceived: 'Evil company corrupts *good habits*'" (1 Corinthians 15:33).

- "They *get into the habit* of being idle and going about from house to house" (1 Timothy 5:13 NIV).

- "Not neglecting to meet together, as is *the habit of some*, but encouraging one another, and all the more as you see the Day drawing near" (Hebrews 10:25).

In chapters 11 and 13, we discussed avoiding going to the movies, eating out, or buying high-end coffee because all these purchases add up. The other risk is these activities become habit-forming.

WE DEVELOP THE HABIT OF SPENDING OR SAVING MONEY

Notice the word *or* in the subhead above. We can't develop the habit of spending *and* saving money. They are mutually exclusive. Think of a plane trying to fly in two different directions. I've spoken with people who habit-ually spend money and defend their actions by talking about how much they have saved. They still develop the habit of spending money, but they've found a way to justify it.

For some people, spending money moves from a habit to an addiction. Consider these testimonies from the *Los Angeles Times*.[3] Although women are in view, men can have similar problems:

> Michelle feared the day her husband might discover her secret stash of credit cards, her secret post office box or the other tricks she used to hide how much money she spent shopping for her-self. She said, "I make as much money as my husband and if I want a $500 suit from Ann Taylor, I deserve it and do not want to be hassled about it. So the easiest thing to do is lie." Last year, when her husband forced her to destroy one of her credit cards, she went out and got a new one without telling him. She also said, "I do live in fear. If he discovers this new Visa, he'll kill me.
>
> "Men just don't understand that shopping is our drug of choice," even while admitting that some months her entire salary goes to paying the minimum balance on her credit cards. She added, "Walking through the door of South Coast Plaza is like walking through the gates of heaven. God made car trunks for women to hide shopping bags in.
>
> "Shopping is my recreation. It is my way of pampering myself. When you walk into [a mall] and you see all the stores, it is like something takes over and you get caught up in it."

Three in five women admit to hiding purchases from their husband.[4] These women are slaves to spending money, and as I said a moment ago, men have this problem too.

The good news is all of us can change. Even if you're the biggest spender, you can develop the habit of saving money. The same fervor you had for spend-ing, can be turned into a fervor for saving. You can become as excited about maxing your retirement account as you used to be about buying things. You can reach the point that you view every purchase as money you are unable to save. To put it simply: As much as spending used to be your habit, sav-ing can become your habit.

THE BIBLE'S VIEW OF SAVING

As negatively as the Bible speaks of debt, it speaks equally positively of saving: "The wise store up choice food and olive oil, but fools gulp theirs down" (Proverbs 21:20 NIV). Foolish people spend (gulp down) what they have, but wise people save (store up). Earlier I mentioned Proverbs 13:22 to condemn government debt: "A good man leaves an inheritance to his children's children." But what would this verse look like when followed? You would have people who save so much it is passed down not just to their children, but to their children's children. In the New Testament, Paul affirmed, "Children are not obligated to save up for their parents, but parents for their children" (2 Corinthians 12:14).

Folly fritters away and is unprepared for the future, but wisdom conserves and makes provision, as the ant demonstrates:

- "[An ant stores] her supplies in summer, and gathers her food in the harvest" (Proverbs 6:8).

- "Four things…are little on the earth, but they are exceedingly wise; the ants are a people not strong, yet they provide their food in the summer" (Proverbs 30:24-25).

Ants are "exceedingly wise" because they know how to save. Recognizing a coming need and preparing today is wise. Doing so enables us to care for ourselves, family members, friends, and neighbors. A great example of this is when Joseph stored up for a coming famine:

> During the seven *plentiful years* the earth *produced abundantly*, and he *gathered up* all the food of these seven years, which occurred in the land of Egypt, and put the food in the cities. He put in every city the food from the fields around it. And Joseph *stored up* grain in great abundance, like the sand of the sea, until he ceased to measure it, for it could not be measured…The seven *years of plenty* that occurred in the land of Egypt came to an end, and the seven *years of famine* began to come, as Joseph had said. There was famine in all lands, but in all the land of Egypt there was bread (Genesis 41:47-49, 53-54 ESV).

What is saving if not gathering up or storing up during "plentiful years" that produce abundantly so we're prepared when lean "years of famine" come? Because of Joseph's efforts, "many people [were] kept alive" (Genesis 50:20).

AVOIDING FINANCIAL REGRETS

Sadly, despite the importance of saving, 69 percent of Americans have less than $1,000 in their savings accounts, and 34 percent have no savings at all.[5] More than 70 percent say they would be in a difficult situation if their paycheck was delayed even one week.[6]

I tell my congregation that one of the worst things to have to say is, "I wish I could go back and do things differently." How much better our lives would be if we never had to make this statement. On the other hand, one of the best things to be able to say is, "I'm so glad I made the decision I did." If you ask people what their biggest regret is, many will tell you about a financial decision they made that they have never been able to recover from. Statistically, more than three in four Americans have at least one financial regret.[7] The most common regrets are taking on too much debt and not saving early enough.[8] I want you to avoid being part of these statistics by saving the way the Bible prescribes.

ACCUMULATING MONEY THE RIGHT WAY

Proverbs 13:11 gives us insight into how to save correctly: "Wealth gained dishonestly will be diminished, but *he who gathers by labor will increase.*" This encourages consistent, steady saving week after week, month after month, and year after year.

Take your mind back to the parable of the talents:

> He who had received the five talents went *at once* and traded with them, and he made five talents more...But he who had received the one talent went and dug in the ground and hid his master's money. But his master [said to] him, "You wicked and slothful servant! You knew that I reap where I have not sown and gather where I scattered no seed? Then you ought to have invested my money with the bankers, and at my coming I should have received what was my own *with interest*" (Matthew 25:16, 18, 26-27).

By looking at what the first servant did right and the third servant did wrong, we see what we must take advantage of to save the right way. The key words are "at once" and "with interest."

Taking Advantage of Time and Interest

The first servant knew it was important to serve the master, so he got right to putting his talents to work. Unfortunately, the third servant did not follow the first servant's example—he buried his talent in the ground. This was a common practice in Jesus's day, akin in our day to putting money in drawers or mattresses (where it also gains no interest). God rebuked the third servant for failing to invest the money and gain interest.

Time, versus money itself, is the greatest tool
we have to increase the value of money.

We are being poor stewards when we waste money on trivial purchases, but we are also being poor stewards when we allow money to sit for years (or decades) without growing in value. When inflation is factored in, the money is losing value. The solution is to invest as early as possible.

Time, versus money itself, is the greatest tool we have to increase the value of money. The sooner we start, the greater our return. This also means that procrastinating (like the third servant) is one of the greatest threats to making money. The longer we put off investing, the more money we lose.

Contrast Peter and Paul

Consider these examples:

- Peter is 30 years old and he invests $200 per month at 7 percent interest. When he turns 60, he will have $244,000.

- Paul is 20 years old and he invests $200 per month at 7 percent interest. When he turns 60, he will have $525,000.

Starting 10 years earlier results in more than twice as much money—a difference of $281,000. Dave Ramsey said, "The current average annual return from 1926, the year of the S&P's inception, through 2011 is 11.69%."[9] Assuming the stock market continues the same pattern it has shown historically, consider these examples:

- Paul invests $2,000 per year starting at 19 years old. When he turns 26, he does not invest another penny, which means he

invested $16,000 over 7 years. When he turns 65, he will have
$2,288,996.

- Peter invests $2,000 per year starting at 27, the year after Paul
  stopped investing, and continues until he's 65, which means he
  invested $78,000 over 38 years. When he turns 65, he will have
  $1,532,166.

Although Peter invested almost five times as much as Paul over five times
longer than Paul, he has over 30 percent less money. The following chart
illustrates the reality:

	Paul		Peter	
Age	Invested	Total	Invested	Total
19	$2,000	$2,240	$0	
20	$2,000	$4,749	$0	
21	$2,000	$7,558	$0	
22	$2,000	$10,706	$0	
23	$2,000	$14,230	$0	
24	$2,000	$18,178	$0	
25	$2,000	$22,599	$0	
26	$2,000	$27,551	$0	
27	$0	$30,857	$2,000	$2,240
30	$0	$43,352	$2,000	$10,706
35	$0	$76,802	$2,000	$33,097
40	$0	$134,646	$2,000	$72,559
45	$0	$237,293	$2,000	$142,104
50	$0	$418,191	$2,000	$264,665
55	$0	$736,995	$2,000	$480,660
60	$0	$1,298,837	$2,000	$861,317
65	$0	$2,288,996	$2,000	$1,532,166
	Total Invested $16,000	Total Return $2,288,996	Total Invested $78,000	Total Return $1,532,166

This chart demonstrates the importance of investing as soon as possible. In our younger years, it's easy for us to assume we have plenty of time
to get started and thus we're not as careful or frugal with our money as we

should be. But when we put off investing, we lose the greatest tool we have for making money: time.

Do yourself a favor and start investing as soon as possible, regardless of your age. If you are young, keep these two truths in mind: First, the money you are saving now is money for your family in the future. And second, the money you are wasting now is money you are taking away from your family in the future.

ACCUMULATING MONEY WRONG WAYS

Before we jump into the specific ways we should avoid accumulating money, consider this Old Testament account that encourages us to trust God will provide for us when we obey Him. I hope this gives you the motivation to avoid accumulating money in any of the following wrong ways.

Amaziah was king of the southern kingdom of Judah and he hired 100,000 mercenaries for 100 talents (about 7,500 pounds) of silver from the apostate northern kingdom of Israel:

> A man of God came to [Amaziah], saying, "O king, do not let the army of Israel go with you, for the LORD is not with Israel"...
>
> Amaziah said to the man of God, "But what shall we do about the hundred talents that I have given to the troops of Israel?"
>
> And the man of God answered, "*The LORD is able to give you much more than this*" (2 Chronicles 25:7, 9).

Amaziah's immediate concern was the money he would lose. We might be quick to judge him, but I remember feeling this way after I became a Christian and had to throw away compromising possessions, such as movies, music, and clothing. Sadly, my concern was, "I paid so much for all this."

The prophet said God was able to give him "much more" than he would lose. God has no trouble providing for us when we obey Him with our finances. If you're ever tempted to compromise financially, go to this passage. I have used it in counseling to encourage people to do what's right with their money, even if that meant they would make less, or perhaps even lose money.

A friend of mine started DJing Christian events, but soon found himself taking increasingly worldly gigs (think foul music, drunkenness, immodest clothing, and sinful behavior) to make more money. One time he shared with me about an upcoming event, and I told him God wouldn't want him to do it. He agreed, but then said he would be out the $1,000 he was supposed to make. I replied that the Lord was able to give him so much more. Sadly, he wasn't willing to trust God's provision, so he took the gig.

As is the case with so many things in the Christian life, motive is crucial. Doing the right thing (saving) the wrong way makes it the wrong thing. Let's talk about a few of the wrong ways to save, or accumulate, money.

Avoid Gaining Money Corruptly

Proverbs 11:1 says, "*A false balance is an abomination to the* LORD, but a just weight is his delight" (ESV).[10] Notice that not only is it a sin to acquire money dishonestly, it is also an abomination. Although theft most commonly comes to mind, the Bible discusses other compromising ways of gaining money. Consider these present-day examples with the accompanying verses that condemn them:

- Earning money illegally—"*Treasures of wickedness* profit nothing, but righteousness delivers from death" (Proverbs 10:2).

- Lying on tax returns—"*Getting treasures by a lying tongue,* is the fleeting fantasy of those who seek death" (Proverbs 21:6).

- Overcharging—"One who *increases his possessions by usury and extortion* gathers it for him who will pity the poor" (Proverbs 28:8).

- Failing to pay workers what they are owed—"Indeed the wages of the laborers who mowed your fields, which you *kept back by fraud,* cry out; and the cries of the reapers have reached the ears of the Lord of [Hosts]" (James 5:4).

A bank officer approached a junior clerk and secretly asked, "If I gave you $50,000, would you help me alter the books?"

The clerk replied, "Yes, I would."

The officer asked, "Would you do it for $100?"

The clerk replied, "No way! What do you think I am, a common thief?"

The officer said, "We have already established that you are a thief. Now we must determine the price."[11]

Ungodly people can be bought. Balaam is one of the best examples in Scripture. He was willing to curse Israel for Balak, the king of Moab (Numbers 22).

Second Peter 2:15 says he "loved gain from wrongdoing" (esv). The Israel-ites executed him for his sin (Joshua 13:22), and the New Testament strongly condemns him (Jude 11; Revelation 2:14). He serves as a sober warning to anyone who makes money corruptly.

A friend's son wrecked the family vehicle. The father lied to the insurance company and said he was driving to save money. I thought, *You're that wor-ried about money, but now you think you're in a better place after lying? You're in a worse place financially because you've taken yourself outside God's will.*

Imagine you are tempted to deceive the insurance company, fudge on your tax returns, shortchange someone, or step on others to get ahead. It would be better to do what's right and experience loss: "When you do good and suffer for it you endure, this is a gracious thing in the sight of God... If you should suffer for righteousness' sake, you will be blessed...It is bet-ter to suffer for doing good, if that should be God's will, than for doing evil" (1 Peter 2:20; 3:14, 17). You might be tempted to say, "I've already invested so much...There have been all these expenses...If I don't do this..." Remind yourself of two truths: First, "the LORD is able to give you much more than this." Second, anything gained corruptly should be viewed as cursed instead of blessed. Only wealth earned with integrity has God's fingerprints on it. No amount of money is worth being able to peacefully lay your head down at night because you're right with the Lord.

Avoid Gaining Money Quickly

Just as Proverbs 13:11 tells us how to save correctly ("whoever gathers lit-tle by little will increase it"), we're also told how to save incorrectly: "Wealth *gained hastily* will dwindle" (esv). Similarly, "He who *hastens to be rich* will not go unpunished...A man with an evil eye *hastens after* riches, and does not consider that poverty will come upon him" (Proverbs 28:20, 22). To most people, few things are more attractive than obtaining money swiftly. There's a reason many advertisements use the phrase, "Get rich quick!"

The desire to obtain money quickly is fueled by impatience and often laziness. Proverbs 12:11 says, "Those who work their land will have abundant food, but those who chase fantasies have no sense" (niv). Get-rich-quick schemes fall into the category of fantasies, so when they present them-selves, they should be avoided. Beware of people who promise wealth with-out expecting work or risk on your part: More than a few trusting people have lost their savings in a "sure thing" that turned out to be a scam. The proper way to gain money is found in the words "work their land," or simply put, working hard.

What About Gambling?

One of the most obvious ways people try to get rich quickly is through gambling. Not only is this a terrible stewardship of God's money, there is also a strong potential for addiction. Casinos use many marketing tactics to entice people to risk as much money as possible. They also offer inexpensive or even free alcohol, which encourages drunkenness and decreases our decision-making ability. Everything in casinos is rigged to take money and give nothing in return, except fleeting pleasures and regret.

Lotteries, which are a form of gambling, are often participated in by people who can least afford to waste their money on them. Although the chances of winning are minuscule, the fantasy of being rich remains a great temptation for desperate people.

The proceeds from gambling or lotteries can be used in godly ways, but the ends don't justify the means. Just because money from stealing or selling drugs could be given to God doesn't mean we should steal or sell drugs. Similarly, just because money from gambling or lotteries can be given to God doesn't mean we should gamble or buy lottery tickets.

Is the Stock Market Gambling?

If we define gambling as risking money with the goal of making money, the stock market can be considered gambling because there is no guarantee the money will increase in value. A friend I respect equates the stock market with gambling, so he elected to purchase gold. Others might put their money in real estate. These approaches are acceptable, but they also carry the same danger as the stock market—losing value—which means they are also a gamble. You can put your money in a savings account with little potential loss of value, but there's also an interest rate that's so low there's little potential for reasonable returns.

Yet there are important differences to note between gambling at a casino and buying stocks. Foolish gamblers risk money to make it quickly, and they are not investing in any kind of equity with value. When investors buy stock, they obtain partial ownership of a company with the intent of making money over time as the company grows in value. The money is spent on something that possesses actual equity, even if there's a possibility that equity could decrease over time.

The difference comes down to intent. If you "play" the stock market to "get rich quickly" then, yes, that is gambling. If you invest in the stock market long-term, patiently waiting for your money to grow as the company in which you've invested grows, then you are taking a biblical approach. Anything that requires "luck" above wisdom and planning should be avoided.

With this said, if you still feel convicted about investing in the stock market, do not let me lead you to violate your conscience (1 Corinthians 8:12).

TEACH YOUR CHILDREN TO SAVE

Whether we as parents do this intentionally or not, we are training our children how to spend or save money, and we do this in two ways: First, we do this directly through our teaching; and second, we do this indirectly through our example.

We train our children through what we teach them about spending and saving. And if we aren't teaching them to save, then we are teaching them to spend because that is their default desire. Whether it's toys, trips, clothes— and the list goes on—kids grow up asking their parents to spend money. If we don't teach our children to save, our lack of instruction teaches them to follow their natural propensity to spend.

Second, we train our children through our example. They watch us and learn from us. If we habitually spend money, embrace debt, fail to give, and make other poor financial decisions, we are teaching our children to do the same. If we save money, avoid debt, give, and make wise financial decisions, we are teaching our children to do the same.

Once again, Proverbs 13:22 says, "A good man leaves an inheritance to his children's children." Parents obey this verse, not by giving their children enough money that some of it reaches the grandchildren, but by teaching their children to save. If they don't, then no matter how much the children receive, none of it will reach the grandchildren. Solomon, the richest man to ever live, lamented, "I must leave [my wealth] to the man who will come after me, and who knows whether he will be wise or a fool?" (Ecclesiastes 2:18-19). Parents can help their children to not be fools by instructing them.

Invite your kids on the adventure with you. Share the vision with them. Let them know your plans to save. Make it sound attractive. Ask them for ideas. Offer some sort of inexpensive reward or celebration for when you pay off the last dollar.

Have your children open savings accounts at an early age. When they receive money, whether from allowances or gifts, have them put the money in their accounts. Family members and friends give our children money to spend for birthdays and holidays. We tell them we will double the amount if they save it instead of spending it.

Recently, a man handed each of my children a dollar when we were in front of The Dollar Tree because he wanted them to be able to buy something. I could see their excitement. Here's how the conversation went:

> My children: "He gave us a dollar! He gave us a dollar!"
>
> Me: "This is exciting, isn't it?"
>
> My children: "Yes, it is!"
>
> Me: "We can put this money in your savings accounts."
>
> My children without the joy they had earlier: "Are you serious?"
>
> Me: "Yes. Do you want to spend that dollar on some worthless toy you are going to forget about by tomorrow, or do you want to put it in the bank?"
>
> What I wanted my children to say: "We want to put it in the bank!"
>
> What my children actually said: "We want to buy something!"
>
> Me: "I know you do, but this is why God gave you parents, so you would not waste money on cheap toys. Now let's go put that money in your savings accounts."
>
> What I wanted my children to say: "Thanks, Dad. You are so wise."
>
> What they actually said with disappointment: "Okay."

If your children are anything like mine, they probably aren't going to appreciate you making them save. That's okay. They will appreciate it later.

Maybe you are reading this thinking, *Wow, you are such a cheapskate! You wouldn't even let your kids spend a dollar at The Dollar Tree? It is just a dollar!* You're right that it's "just a dollar," but I wasn't concerned about the dollar. I was concerned with the habit that could develop. When children learn to waste a dollar when they are young, it becomes ten dollars, twenty dollars, or a hundred dollars when they are older.

You might handle the same situation differently than me. Perhaps you see this as an opportunity to teach your children to spend with discernment—to use their dollar toward something necessary (because Dollar Tree sells essentials) or something good (such as a greeting card to encourage someone) instead of on a worthless toy.

Whatever approach you take, train your children from a young age that every dollar counts. Compliment them when they make the choice to save versus spend. Show them their accounts are growing, which will get them excited. Each time we take our kids to the bank to deposit money, they love to get the receipt showing their new total. If they start saving when they are young, it can more easily become a habit when they're older.

HELPED BY GOD

Saving—like giving, eliminating debt, and most other principles in this book—takes time and sacrifice. Keep in mind that God is for you. He wants you to make the right decisions with the money He has entrusted to you. After all, not only has God given us commands for our good, He also helps us obey those commands.

As you strive to save, be encouraged that "[God's] divine power has given to us all things that pertain to life and godliness" (2 Peter 1:3). Because finances are such a big part of "life and godliness," we can be confident that God will empower us to be good stewards.

CHAPTER 15

Retiring Well

K atie and I were part of a wedding reception that took place on a golf course in a retirement community. We saw a room next to the restaurant filled with elderly people. They went there each morning to drink Bloody Marys for breakfast and then spend their day golfing and socializing.

While this might seem like a dream come true to many people, I suspect you recognize this is not the most honorable way to retire. While God doesn't prohibit retired people (or any people for that matter) from enjoying golf, social functions, or other pleasurable pursuits, these activities shouldn't be the focus of our lives. As 1 Corinthians 6:12 says, "All things are lawful for me, but all things are not helpful. All things are lawful for me, but I will not be brought under the power of any." Many hobbies are "lawful," but when are we being "brought under the power of [them]"? I can't answer this for you as it's an issue of discernment, but I can say the Holy Spirit will be faithful to convict you when you're spending too much time in unprofitable ways.

The Bible never talks about people reaching a point when they can stop working and start living selfishly. It's tragic when older people who have run most of the race and now have more freedom than ever to serve the Lord simply squander the time they have left on meaningless activities with no eternal value.

Take your mind back to the parable of the rich fool. Luke 12:19 says, "I will say to my soul, 'Soul, you have many goods laid up for many years; take your ease; *eat, drink, and be merry.*'" Sadly, this captures what comes to mind for some people when they think of retirement, but this shouldn't be the desire for Christians. If our view resembles that of someone Jesus calls a fool, then we should repent and change our thinking.

There is nothing wrong with retiring from a secular profession, but there are right and wrong ways to retire. We should view retirement similarly to the way we view money: it is amoral but just as people can use money morally and immorally, people can use retirement morally and immorally. Before we go any further, let's understand how the world's idea of retirement developed so we can avoid this approach.

A HISTORY LESSON

Retirement began as an inappropriate response to social issues. Before the Industrial Revolution, people's jobs could change more easily as they got older. For example, an aging farmer could let his sons do the harvesting while he performed fewer and less-intensive chores, and a businessman could hire out the more difficult work and act as a mentor to those under him.

When the Industrial Revolution took place, an obsession with productivity and economic growth arose. There were machine-based jobs that could do the work of multiple people at a faster pace and a cheaper price. This was the one moment in history to pinpoint when elderly employees became viewed as liabilities. They couldn't work as quickly as younger people, and they were prone to more mistakes. This slowed production, increased expenses, and made younger employees more attractive. In response, corporations pushed the government to enforce retirement to remove an aging workforce in favor of a younger one.

Because the elderly were viewed as being useless, when they retired, they did nothing. They had been told they had little to contribute and it was best if they simply got out of the way, so they spent their remaining years in unproductive ways.

A prominent man in all of this was Dr. William Osler. He was an expert in the field of gerontology (the scientific study of aging). On February 22, 1905, he delivered a speech titled "The Fixed Period." He said,

> The effective, moving, vitalizing work of the world is done between the ages of twenty-five and forty, when [people] are energetic and creative. Workers from age forty to sixty are tolerable. Workers over age sixty are useless.

Dr. Osler said people should be forced to retire. They should have one year to settle their affairs, and then be "peacefully extinguished by chloroform."

Osler's speech made headlines, with reports claiming, "Dr. Osler recommends chloroform at sixty."[1] The concept of mandatory euthanasia for humans after a certain age, often 60, became a recurring theme in twentieth-century literature. For example, Isaac Asimov's 1950 novel, *Pebble in the Sky*, called pneumonia "the old man's friend" because it allowed elderly people a quick and painless death.[2] The important point to notice is the concept of retirement came from a worldly, and even somewhat morbid, view of elderly people.

The Great Depression worsened the situation. Younger men needed jobs to support their families, so eventually President Franklin Roosevelt developed Social Security. Workers could pay into a fund that they could draw on once they turned 60, encouraging them to retire and leave employment for the younger generation. To convince older people that retirement benefitted them as well as the nation, the government joined with labor interest groups to sell the idea that work was for the young, and the old "deserved" to relax. Retirement became an expectation—something people felt, and still feel, entitled to have.

Considering the origin of the concept of retirement should discourage us from seeing it as an acceptable Christian pursuit, at least the way it's engaged in by unbelievers. Looking at what the world does often gives us a good idea of what *not* to do.

So how should Christians retire? The Bible doesn't mention 401(k) plans or IRAs, but there are principles that direct us.

RETIRE INTO CHRISTIAN SERVICE

One reason it is so important to retire well is Luke 12:48 says, "To whom much is given, from him much is required." If we have been able to retire, then God has blessed us, and we must be good stewards of that blessing. We can do so by keeping this truth in mind: We retire from secular professions and retire into Christian service. God has simply given us more time to serve Him! We might retire from an earthly job, but we never retire from serving Christ. God changes the address of our workplace, and He changes our role, but He doesn't change our need to be faithful servants. John Piper said,

> Finishing life to the glory of Christ means resolutely resisting the typical American dream of retirement. It means being so satisfied with all that God promises to be for us in Christ that we are set free from the cravings that create so much emptiness and

uselessness in retirement. Instead, knowing that we have an infinitely satisfying and everlasting inheritance in God just over the horizon of life makes us zealous in our few remaining years here to spend ourselves in the sacrifices of love, not the accumulation of comforts.[3]

What does Christian service look like during retirement? Scripture provides three recommendations that are found in 1 Timothy 5 and supported elsewhere in the Bible.

Retired People Can Mentor

Retired people can serve well by mentoring others, in particular, the younger generation. Titus 2:3-5 says, "Older women…are to *teach what is good, and so train the young women* to love their husbands and children, to be self-controlled, pure, working at home, kind, and submissive to their own husbands" (ESV). Older women are told to teach young women, and they're told what kinds of guidance they should pass along.

First Timothy 5:1-2 says, "Do not rebuke an older man but *encourage him as you would a father,* younger men as brothers, *older women as mothers,* younger women as sisters, in all purity" (ESV). Young men should look up to older men the way they look up to their father, which implies older men should see themselves as fathers to young men. Young ladies should look up to older women the way they look up to their mothers, which implies what Titus 2 instructs: Older women should see themselves as mothers to young ladies. And what do fathers and mothers do? They teach, train, disciple, and mentor.

We've all heard, "You should respect your elders," and according to Scripture, that's true! If any older people are reading this, I can imagine them saying, "Amen! Preach it! These younger people should look up to us!" Yes, they should, but the older people should also take on mentoring roles.

Psalm 71:18 makes this clear: "Even to old age and gray hairs, O God, do not forsake me, until *I proclaim your might to another generation, your power to all those to come*" (ESV). This reveals the desire godly, elderly people should have: telling the younger generation about the Lord. Mentoring and instructing younger people is one of the primary ministries God has given to older people. Often it is older, retired saints who, after a lifetime of walking with God, can convey the truths of God's Word by relating to younger people how God has worked in their lives.

Second Corinthians 12:14 states, "Children ought not to lay up for the parents, but the parents for the children." This is speaking financially, but if adults should pass along earthly riches, how much more should they pass along the "riches of the glory of…Christ" (Colossians 1:27). By far, the greatest riches are found in a spiritual heritage: "the riches of the glory of [Christ's] inheritance in the saints" (Ephesians 1:18). This heritage should be passed down from the older generation to the younger one.

When Katie was a young mother, she benefited greatly from the investment of older, godly women. They had gone before her and could share their wisdom and experience with her.

When I became a father, I was blessed by older men who had raised godly children and have helped me in my journey. As a father of nine, I have had many questions about parenting. I am thankful for each man who has taken the time to tell me what they did with their children.

I could provide many examples, but I will keep it to one that stands out. I was friends with a young man who impressed me, and he attributed his godly character to his father. Although I didn't know his father, I contacted him and asked if we could speak so I could learn from him. On a long drive, he talked to me for more than three hours about the things he did with his three sons. I still remember and apply some of the teaching he shared with me.

Retired People Can Pray

Generations of people have been impacted by the faithful prayers of elderly people. Prayer is perhaps the most fruitful ministry outlet for those who have retired:

> Honor widows who are really widows. But if any widow has children or grandchildren, let them first learn to show piety at home and to repay their parents, for this is good and acceptable before God. Now she who is really a widow, and left alone, trusts in God and *continues in supplications and prayers night and day* (1 Timothy 5:3-5).

Paul says widows who have outlived their husbands can commit themselves to prayer. Anna the prophetess is a good example. These verses about her make it sound like she lived at the temple fasting and praying:

> [Anna] was advanced in years, having lived with her husband…
> and then as a widow until she was eighty-four. She did not depart
> from the temple, *worshiping with fasting and prayer night and day*
> (Luke 2:36-37 ESV).

The alternative to serving the Lord is serving self. If a widow chooses this, God says, "She who lives in pleasure is dead while she lives" (1 Timothy 5:6). There are two possible reasons for this language. First, it is as though she's already dead because she's not doing anything productive for the kingdom of God—as though God says, "Because she isn't serving Me, she might as well be dead." The other possibility is she is dead, not physically, but spiritually. She lives such a selfish lifestyle it's evidence she's unsaved.

Although this is about widows, it's no stretch to say if this is how God views them for living for pleasure, this is how He views anyone who lives for pleasure. There is no reason to think widows would be held to a higher standard than anyone else.

Retired People Can Assist

Paul continues in 1 Timothy 5:9-10:

> Let a widow be [supported by the church] if she is not less than
> sixty years of age, having been the wife of one husband, and hav-
> ing a reputation for good works: if she has brought up children,
> has shown hospitality, has washed the feet of the saints, has cared
> for the afflicted, and has devoted herself to every good work (ESV).

God doesn't prohibit Christians from living off pensions, or even living off support from the church, but they must meet three requirements: First, they have no family to support them, which is the point of verses 4 and 5. Second, they must be at least 60. Third, they must minister to the Lord and other believers. This reveals not just the possibility but the expectation that older people do not retire from Christian service.

Are older people expected to serve with the same vigor and energy they exhibited when they were younger? No. Let's consider two examples from Scripture that are instructive because they show us the right and wrong ways to handle slowing down.

Slowing Down the Wrong Way

David's terrible sins of adultery and murder took place when he failed to go to battle with his men. He learned his lesson, but later, he swung the pendulum the other way. He didn't retire from fighting and went out to battle when he should have remained behind:

> When the Philistines were at war again with Israel, David and his servants with him went down and fought against the Philistines; and *David grew faint.* Then Ishbi-Benob, who was one of the sons of the giant, the weight of whose bronze spear was three hundred shekels, who was bearing a new sword, thought he could kill David. But Abishai the son of Zeruiah came to his aid, and struck the Philistine and killed him. Then the men of David swore to him, saying, "*You shall go out no more with us to battle,* lest you quench the lamp of Israel" (2 Samuel 21:15-17).

David "grew faint" and one of Goliath's sons almost killed him. Just as David should've retired from fighting, we should retire from certain things when we get older. Otherwise, we can end up hurting ourselves or someone else.

As we age, we can't do everything we used to do when we were younger, but we can still find reasonable ways to serve God. We may lack the energy we had earlier in life, but we should still be as committed to using the energy we still have for God's glory.

Slowing Down the Right Way

The Bible always does things better than the world. We find a great example of retiring well in the Mosaic law:

> The LORD said to Moses, "This applies to the Levites: Men twenty-five years old or more shall come to take part in the work at the tent of meeting, but at the age of fifty, *they must retire from their regular service and work no longer. They may assist their brothers in performing their duties* at the tent of meeting, but they themselves must not do the work. This, then, is how you are to assign the responsibilities of the Levites" (Numbers 8:23-26 NIV).

Levites started working in the tabernacle and later the temple when they were 25. At the age of 50, they retired from regular service because of the physical demands. Then the strenuous work could be given to younger men. When the older Levites retired, they would "assist" the younger Levites, but they never stopped working completely, nor did they live only for themselves. They continued serving, but in a way that was appropriate for their age.

Whatever ability God has given you, more than likely there is a way to use it in your later years.

If retired people in our day want to help, they should have no trouble finding ways. They can take meals, send cards, volunteer to lead ministries, visit the sick, and provide counseling. Older women can help younger women with their children. My mom takes one of our kids during the week for reading. Older men can find younger men to help with trades and skills.

In December 2019, two church members were murdered at a church in Texas before Jack Wilson, a 71-year-old man, prevented anyone else's death by shooting the gunman. Mr. Wilson was a former reserve deputy sheriff who chose to spend his retirement providing security for his church. Whatever ability God has given you, more than likely there is a way to use it in your later years.

COMBINE FAITH AND WISDOM WHEN PLANNING FOR RETIREMENT

What about the financial side of retirement? Should we have faith that God will provide for us, or should we do some planning ourselves? Yes!

Let me explain by asking you to imagine parents who say, "We let our children play in the road because we have faith God will protect them," or people who say, "I don't lock my doors at night because I have faith God will keep us safe." We wouldn't say these people have faith. We would say they're being foolish. Imagine people who say, "I need a job, but I just sit at home because I have faith God will provide one." We wouldn't say these people have faith. We would say they're being foolish. And lazy.

Faith and wisdom are not mutually exclusive. Walking by faith doesn't have to involve neglecting wisdom. Being wise doesn't mean we are not trusting God. As Christians, we should always choose the path of faith *and* wisdom. Wisdom dictates we don't let our children play in the road, we lock our doors at night, and if we don't have a job, our full-time job is looking for a job. As a pastor, of course I love people coming to church on Sundays. But during the winter months, when the roads are icy, some people stay home and watch our service online. I don't condemn them by saying, "They're fearful, lacking faith, and disobeying God." As much as I desire to have them with us in person, I recognize this is the path of faith and wisdom for them.

When it comes to retirement, we must also combine faith and wisdom. Imagine someone saying, "I trust God will provide for me, so I don't plan for retirement." This person might have faith, but he lacks wisdom. Imagine someone else saying, "I have taken matters into my own hands and am planning everything for my own retirement." This person might have wisdom, but he lacks faith.

The balance is we should plan for retirement (wisdom) while trusting God (faith). Look at your bank accounts, examine your current spending patterns, and estimate your future financial needs. At the same time, pray for God to give you wisdom and direct your efforts.

Recognize that the goal of retirement is not pleasure and a lavish lifestyle. Work to have enough money saved to care for yourself and be generous toward others. Strive to keep your heart focused on heaven because that's where your true treasure is stored. If you want to honor God later in life when you have been blessed with the opportunity to step back from an earthly profession, retire into Christian service and be a good steward of those years God has given you. Keep in mind that your days, like your money, belong to God.

CHAPTER 16

The Greatest Riches

As we come to the end of our wonderful journey, how can we tie together the many concepts we have discussed up this point, such as stewardship, giving, and saving? Paul might have done that for us when he talked about money in 2 Corinthians 8:15: "As it is written, 'He who gathered much had nothing left over, and he who gathered little had no lack.'" This is a quote from Exodus 16:18 about the manna the Israelites collected each morning during their time in the wilderness.

MANNA AND MONEY

What do manna and money have to do with each other? Quite a bit, actually! The Israelites were to each take "one omer" (Exodus 16:16), which is a tithe: "An omer is *one-tenth* of an ephah" (Exodus 16:36). The term translated "one-tenth" is the Hebrew word also translated "tithe." Manna serves as a fascinating and fitting illustration of money in that it did many of the things for Israel that money does for us. And what Israel was and wasn't supposed to do with manna resembles what we are and aren't supposed to do with money.

Providing and Testing

Exodus 16:4 records that "the LORD said to Moses, 'Behold, I will rain bread from heaven for you. And the people shall go out and gather a certain quota every day, *that I may test them*, whether they will walk in My law or not.'" God sent the manna to provide for the Israelites and test them, just like God uses money to provide for us and test us.

Avoiding Greediness and Wastefulness

The Israelites needed manna like we need money, but they had to avoid being greedy like we must avoid being greedy. The people accused God of "[bringing them] into this wilderness to kill this whole assembly with hunger" (Exodus 16:2). This helps us understand how difficult it was for the people of Israel to take only what they needed. Not surprisingly some didn't listen and couldn't eat all of what they collected. Verses 19-20 record what happened:

> Moses said to them, "Let no one leave any of it over till the morning." But *they did not listen* to Moses. Some left part of it till the morning, and *it bred worms and stank*. And Moses was angry with them (ESV).

They were supposed to avoid wasting the manna, like we're supposed to avoid wasting money. If they kept too much for themselves, versus leaving it for others, there were problems. Similarly, if we keep too much money for ourselves, versus giving it to others, there are problems for us too. The manna began to decay and stink, and, figuratively speaking, money we shouldn't have begins to decay and stink.

Learning to Save

Exodus 16:22-24 tells us what would happen when the Israelites handled the manna correctly:

> On the sixth day they *gathered twice as much* bread, two omers each. And when all the leaders of the congregation came and told Moses, he said to them, "This is what the LORD has commanded: 'Tomorrow is a day of solemn rest, a holy Sabbath to the LORD; bake what you will bake and boil what you will boil, and all that is left over lay aside to be kept till the morning.'" So they laid it aside till the morning, as Moses commanded them, and *it did not stink, and there were no worms in it*.

The manna taught the Israelites to save: They gathered twice as much on the sixth day so they wouldn't have to gather any on the Sabbath. If they handled the manna the right way, striking the balance between saving and hoarding, they had what they needed and there were no problems ("it did not stink, and there were no worms in it"). Similarly, if we handle money the right way, striking the balance between saving and hoarding, we will have what we need and there won't be any problems.

Enforced Differently

We see one important difference between manna and money as we contrast the Old and New Covenants:

- In the wilderness, under the Old Covenant, equality was miraculously enforced. Everyone ended up with the same amount (one omer) regardless of how much they gathered.

- In the church, under the New Covenant, people are cared for not because it is enforced, but because God burdens His people to give (as we discussed in the previous chapters) willingly, sacrificially, and generously.

THE TRUE AND GREATER BREAD FROM HEAVEN

God told Israel to "gather a certain quota *every day*," and Moses said, "This is *the bread which the* LORD *has given you to eat*" (Exodus 16:4, 15). Every day God gave them bread, looking forward to when Jesus would teach us to pray, "Give us *this day* our *daily bread*" (Matthew 6:11). Each day they trusted God to provide, and each day we trust God to provide.

But if we really want to appreciate the manna, we must look beyond the physical to the spiritual. Jesus said, "[The people of Israel] ate the manna in the wilderness, and they are dead...I am the living bread which came down from heaven. If anyone eats of this bread, he will live forever; and the bread that I shall give is My flesh, which I shall give for the life of the world" (John 6:49, 51).

The manna was wonderful, but all it did was give people more years of earthly life. In light of eternity, this is a drop in the bucket. Jesus is the true and greater bread from heaven. He provides eternal life and satisfies better than anything physical, be it food or wealth. David Platt said,

> When we truly come to Christ, our thirst is quenched by the fountain of life and our hunger is filled with the bread of heaven. We discover that Jesus is the supreme source of satisfaction, and we want nothing apart from Him. We realize that He is better than all the pleasures, pursuits, and possessions of this world combined.

As we trust in Christ, He transforms our tastes in such a way that we begin to love the things of God that we once hated, and we begin to hate the things of this world that we once loved.[1]

THE GOSPEL IS FINANCIAL

We have spent so much time discussing finances, let's be clear about the true and greater riches available to us. They also aren't physical. They can't be touched, minted, or printed. The Bible explains the gospel using financial terms; let's consider each term so we can better appreciate what Christ has done for us.

Debt

Jesus told us to pray: "Forgive us our debts" (Matthew 6:12). He was not referring to anything financial, but spiritual: our sin debt against God. Unlike the debt that we can pay off, this is a debt that we can't do anything about no matter how hard we work, how much time we're given, and how wise we are financially. We have this debt whether we're rich, poor, young, or old. In the parable of the unforgiving servant, Matthew 18:23-27 records:

> The kingdom of heaven is like a certain king who wanted to settle accounts with his servants. And when he had begun to settle accounts, one was brought to him who owed him ten thousand talents. But as *he was not able to pay*, his master commanded that he be sold, with his wife and children and all that he had, and that payment be made. The servant therefore fell down before him, saying, "Master, have patience with me, and I will pay you all." Then the master of that servant was moved with compassion, released him, and *forgave him the debt*.

The man had a debt "he was not able to pay." He fell to his knees, begged the master, and he "forgave him the debt":

- The man represents us, and the desperation and fear his debt caused him represents the desperation and fear our sin debt should cause us.

- The master represents the Lord, and the compassion He felt for this man represents the compassion He feels toward sinners who cry out to Him for mercy.

What did the servant do to be forgiven for such a debt? He did nothing more than acknowledge his debt and humble himself. If a parent had a child who acted wickedly, and the child came to the parent humble and broken, wouldn't the parent quickly forgive and embrace the child like the father in the parable of the prodigal son (who represents God) embraced his son? Luke 15:20 says, "When he was still a great way off, his father saw him and had compassion, and ran and fell on his neck and kissed him." This is how our heavenly Father wants to forgive us.

Redeem

To redeem means to "buy back from debt." A redeemer is the one who pays someone else's debt. Jesus is the Redeemer of every believer:

- "[Jesus] gave Himself for us, that He might *redeem us* from every lawless deed and purify for Himself His own special people, zealous for good works" (Titus 2:14).

- "You were not *redeemed* with corruptible things, like silver or gold...but with the precious blood of Christ" (1 Peter 1:18-19).

Ransom

The ransom is the payment the redeemer makes to deliver someone from the consequences of their debt. But we can't redeem ourselves or anyone else because the ransom price is too high:

> No one can redeem the life of another
> or give to God a ransom for them—
> the ransom for a life is costly,
>   no payment is ever enough—
> so that they should live on forever
>   and not see decay...
> Their tombs will remain their houses forever,
>   their dwellings for endless generations,
>   though they had named lands after themselves.
> People, despite their wealth, do not endure;
>   they are like the beasts that perish
> (Psalm 49:7-9, 11-12 NIV).

People might have been rich enough to have locations named after them, but the grave is where they'll remain because no amount of wealth can keep us from death.

> This is the fate of those who trust in themselves,
>> and of their followers, who approve their sayings…
> But God will redeem me from the realm of the dead;
>> he will surely take me to himself (Psalm 49:13, 15 NIV).

They "trust in themselves," but the psalmist trusted in the Lord. We can't redeem anyone, but "God will redeem" through Jesus because He can pay the ransom price:

- "The Son of Man did not come to be served, but to serve, and to give His life as a *ransom for many*" (Matthew 20:28).
- "[Jesus] gave Himself as a *ransom for all*" (1 Timothy 2:6).

Pay

If we owe money, it would be unjust if the debt was never paid. A perfectly just God can't forgive a debt that is unpaid. Jesus paid the debt when He died on the cross and took the punishment that our sins deserve. This allows God to remain just because our sins are punished. The Greek word translated "pay" is *teleo*, the same word used in these passages:

- "Does your Teacher not pay [*teleo*] the temple tax?" (Matthew 17:24).
- "Because of this you also pay [*teleo*] taxes" (Romans 13:6).

Teleo has been found written on papyri receipts for taxes, meaning "paid in full."[2] When Jesus was on the cross, moments before His death, He said, "It is finished [*teleo*]! And bowing His head, He gave up His spirit" (John 19:30). It is as though Jesus said, "I have paid your debt in full so you can be forgiven."

Impute

Impute is an accounting term that refers to moving assets from one side of a ledger to the other:

- "[Blessed is] the man to whom God *imputes righteousness* apart from works" (Romans 4:6).

- "God was in Christ reconciling the world to Himself, not *imputing their trespasses to them*" (2 Corinthians 5:19).

Our unrighteousness is imputed to Christ's account, and His righteousness is imputed to our account. This is classic double imputation: "[God] made Him who knew no sin to be sin for us, that we might become the righteousness of God in Him" (2 Corinthians 5:21).

JESUS'S WORK AND OUR CONDITION

At the beginning of Jesus's public ministry, He returned to His hometown of Nazareth. He visited the synagogue, was given the scroll of the prophet Isaiah, and He read:

> The Spirit of the LORD is upon Me,
> Because *He has anointed Me*
> *To preach the gospel to the poor*;
> He has sent Me to heal the brokenhearted,
> To proclaim liberty to the captives
> And recovery of sight to the blind,
> To set at liberty those who are oppressed (Luke 4:18).

This describes both the beautiful work of the Messiah (preach the gospel to the poor) and the wretched state of unregenerate sinners (brokenhearted, captive, blind, oppressed). Because "[preaching] the gospel to the poor" is listed first, it is tempting to think that is Jesus's most important ministry. But Jesus was anointed to preach the gospel to the poor, and the rest of the verse describes what the gospel does for us:

- We are "brokenhearted" over the consequences of our sins, and Jesus is "near to those who have a broken heart" (Psalm 34:18).

- We are "captives" to sin, but Jesus gives us "liberty." He said, "Truly, truly, I say to you, everyone who practices sin is a slave to sin. So if the Son sets you free, you will be free indeed" (John 8:34, 36 ESV).

- We are "blind" spiritually, but we receive "sight." Jesus said, "Seeing they do not see...but blessed are your eyes, for they see" (Matthew 13:13, 16 ESV).

- We are "oppressed" by the consequences of sin, but the Lord is "a refuge for the oppressed" (Psalm 9:9).

Spiritually Poor

The reason we (1) must be redeemed, (2) need Christ's righteousness imputed to our accounts, (3) have debt, and (4) require a ransom is, simply put, we're poor. If that were not the case, we would pay our debt and we would not need a Redeemer to ransom us. The Greek word translated "poor" is *ptochos*, and it means "reduced to beggary, lowly, afflicted, helpless, powerless, lacking in anything." This is not slight poverty. This is complete poverty, of which Scripture provides a good example:

> At his gate was laid a poor [*ptochos*] man named Lazarus, covered with sores, who desired to be fed with what fell from the rich man's table. Moreover, even the dogs came and licked his sores. The poor [*ptochos*] man died and was carried by the angels to Abraham's side (Luke 16:20-22).

This is poor! I don't know if there's a more pitiful description of an individual in Scripture. The way this beggar looked physically is the way we look spiritually. Isaiah 64:6 says, "All our righteousnesses are like filthy rags." Polluted garments aren't worth much. Learning this is our spiritual condition is discouraging until we remember Jesus was anointed to preach the gospel to the poor.

Recognizing Our Spiritual Poverty

Jesus didn't say He was anointed to preach the gospel to *everyone*. He said to *the poor*. This doesn't mean some are poor and others are rich. Instead, everyone is poor, but only some people recognize it. Jesus taught a parable contrasting two men: one thought he was righteous (spiritually rich), but the other knew he was a sinner (spiritually poor):

> [Jesus] told this parable to some who *trusted in themselves that they were righteous*, and treated others with contempt: "Two men went

up into the temple to pray, one a Pharisee and the other a tax collector. The Pharisee, standing by himself, prayed thus: 'God, I thank you that I am not like other men, extortioners, unjust, adulterers, or even like this tax collector. I fast twice a week; I give tithes of all that I get.' But the tax collector, standing far off, would not even lift up his eyes to heaven, but beat his breast, saying, '*God, be merciful to me, a sinner!*' I tell you, this man went down to his house justified, rather than the other. For everyone who exalts himself will be humbled, but the one who humbles himself will be exalted" (Luke 18:9-14 ESV).

The great paradox is this:

- People who think they are spiritually rich and deserving of heaven are the farthest from it.

- People who know they are spiritually poor and undeserving of heaven obtain it through faith in Christ.

In Matthew 5:3, Jesus said, "Blessed are the poor [*ptochos*] in spirit, for theirs is the kingdom of heaven." How can the poor be blessed, and why would the kingdom of heaven belong to them? They are blessed because they know they are spiritually poor, can't trust their own righteousness, need the gospel, and have nothing with which they could purchase their salvation. The kingdom of heaven belongs to them because they will put their faith in Christ to receive His righteousness and have Him pay their debt. They are the ones of whom God said, "On this one will I look: On *him who is poor and of a contrite spirit*" (Isaiah 66:2).

Jesus made a similar point when He blessed the children who came to Him:

Let the little children come to Me, and do not forbid them; for *of such is the kingdom of God*. Assuredly, I say to you, whoever does not *receive the kingdom of God as a little child* will by no means enter it (Luke 18:16-17).

Children are the premier example of spiritual poverty in that they have done nothing to earn salvation. They receive gifts freely, and salvation is a gift to receive freely: "The gift of God is eternal life in Christ Jesus our Lord" (Romans 6:23). Jonathan Edwards said, "A true Christian is poor in spirit, and *more like a little child*, and more disposed to a universal lowliness of behavior."[3]

In Matthew, Mark, and Luke, the account with the rich young ruler follows Jesus blessing the little children. This presents a fitting contrast because he was the opposite of a little child. It is as though God says, "Be like these children and not like this man." The ruler said, "All [the commandments] I have kept from my youth" (Luke 18:21). Jesus let him walk away because He preaches the gospel to the poor, and this man thought he was as spiritually rich as he was physically rich.

Imagine a conversation between an evangelist and a man like the rich young ruler:

> Evangelist: "Jesus died for your sins!"
>
> Man convinced he's spiritually rich: "What sins? I don't have any!"
>
> Evangelist: "We're all sinners, but God loves you and is willing to give you His Son's righteousness by grace through faith."
>
> Man convinced he's spiritually rich: "No, God loves me because I'm such a good person, and that's also why I don't need Jesus's righteousness!"

In contrast, picture the same conversation with a man who knows he's spiritually poor:

> Evangelist: "Jesus died for your sins!"
>
> Sinner: "Why would He do that for me?"
>
> Evangelist: "Because He loves you and is willing to give you His Son's righteousness by grace through faith."
>
> Sinner: "That's amazing. I'm so thankful He would do this for someone like me."

RICH IN CHRIST

Did you know the Bible speaks of two births and two deaths? The first birth is when we are born physically. The second birth is when we are born spiritually. Jesus told Nicodemus, "Assuredly, I say to you, unless one is *born again*, he cannot see the kingdom of God" (John 3:3, see also John 1:13; 1 Peter 1:23; 1 John 3:9).

The first death is when we die physically, which is experienced by believers and unbelievers alike. The second death is experienced only by unbelievers when they are cast into the lake of fire, which we commonly call hell (Revelation 2:11; 20:6, 14; 21:8). Unbelievers die physically, and then they "die" eternally. But if you experience the second birth, you won't experience the second death: "Blessed and holy is the one who has part in the first resurrection. *Over such the second death has no power*" (Revelation 20:6).

Just as the greatest giving is motivated not by obligation but by worship, so too does the greatest financial stewardship flow not from duty, but from hearts of love and thankfulness.

Proverbs 11:4 says, "Riches do not profit in the day of wrath, but righteousness delivers from death." This refers to the second death, and no amount of earthly wealth can spare us from it. Only righteousness, which we receive from Christ, can deliver us: "You know the grace of our Lord Jesus Christ, that though He was rich, yet for your sakes He became poor, that *you through His poverty might become rich*" (2 Corinthians 8:9). This is another example of double imputation: Our spiritual poverty is imputed to Christ, and His spiritual riches are imputed to us.

I want to conclude with these truths because meditating on them is the best way to be a good financial steward. As we think about what Christ has done for us, how rich we are in Him, and the eternal blessings that await us, how can we not be motivated to apply the principles in the previous chapters? Just as the greatest giving is motivated not by obligation but by worship, so too does the greatest financial stewardship flow not from duty, but from hearts of love and thankfulness.

THE PRAYERS FOR YOU

As I wrote this book, I prayed for everyone who would read it. I will continue to pray for every reader—including you—for years to come. But the greatest encouragement you could possibly receive is knowing that

Jesus is "[making] intercession for [you]" (Romans 8:34). You can be sure His intercession includes the way we handle our finances because it is such an important stewardship. Nobody wants you to be able to manage your finances well more than Jesus Himself. And if you are a Christian, then be greatly encouraged that the power of the gospel is at work in your life enabling you to do so.

Appendix

A t the link below, you will find budget worksheets that you can use for your financial planning. My hope is that these worksheets will enable you to put into practice the principles you have learned in this book.

https://www.scottlapierre.org/book/your-finances-gods-way/budgets/

Notes

ONE OF OUR MOST IMPORTANT STEWARDSHIPS

1. American Psychological Association, *Stress in America: Paying with Our Health*, February 4, 2015, PDF download, https://www.apa.org/news/press/releases/stress/2014/stress-report.pdf.

2. Robert Wood Johnson Foundation, "NPR/RWJF/Harvard School of Public Health Poll Finds Health Most Common Major Stressful Event in Americans' Lives Last Year," July 7, 2014, https://www.rwjf.org /en/library/articles-and-news/2014/07/-new-npr-rwjf-harvard-school-of-public-health-poll-finds-health -.html.

3. Christina Cheddar Berk, "More Couples Arguing About Money, Sneaking Purchases," May 9, 2011, https:// www.cnbc.com/id/42916288.

4. Ramsey Solutions, "Marriage Counselor or Financial Coach: Which One Do You Need?," September 27, 2021, https://www.daveramsey.com/blog/marriage-counselor-or-financial-coach.

5. Sam Paul, "American families barely spend quality time together," *New York Post*, March 20, 2018, https:// nypost.com/2018/03/20/american-families-barely-spend-quality-time-together/.

6. "Visualizing Countries with the Highest Household Wealth," howmuch.net, July 9, 2018, https://how much.net/articles/household-net-financial-wealth-around-the-world.

7. Erik Sherman, "America Is the Richest, and Most Unequal, Country," *Fortune*, September 30, 2015, https:// fortune.com/2015/09/30/america-wealth-inequality/.

8. "The Population of Poverty USA," *Poverty USA*, accessed September 28, 2021, https://povertyusa.org/facts.

9. "What is the current poverty rate in the United States?," *Center for Poverty & Inequality Research*, September 15, 2021, https://poverty.ucdavis.edu/faq/what-current-poverty-rate-united-states.

10. Gautam Nair, "Most Americans vastly underestimate how rich they are compared with the rest of the world. Does it matter?" *The Washington Post*, August 23, 2018, https://www.washingtonpost.com/news/ monkey-cage/wp/2018/08/23/most-americans-vastly-underestimate-how-rich-they-are-compared-with -the-rest-of-the-world-does-it-matter/.

11. Alex Schultze, "Who is in the top 1% of wealthiest people?," *World Innovations Forum*, May 22, 2019, https://wiforum.org/top-wealthiest-people/.

12. "Why Does the Bible Mention Money so Often?" *Wealth with Purpose*, February 19, 2016, https://wealth withpurpose.com/god-money/why-does-the-bible-mention-money-so-often/.

CHAPTER 1: STEWARDSHIP AND FAITHFULNESS

1. John MacArthur, *The MacArthur Bible Commentary* (Nashville, TN: Thomas Nelson, 2005), 1175.

2. William Hendriksen, *The Gospel of Matthew* (Grand Rapids, MI: Baker Book House, 1973), 879.

CHAPTER 2: GOD'S KINDNESS AND SEVERITY

1. All passages cite the ESV: "Blessed are you when others revile you and persecute you and utter all kinds of evil against you falsely on my account. Rejoice and be glad, for your reward is great in heaven, for so they persecuted the prophets who were before you" (Matthew 5:11-12); "If you love those who love you, what reward do you have? Do not even the tax collectors do the same?" (5:46); "Beware of practicing your righteousness

before other people in order to be seen by them, for then you will have no reward from your Father who is in heaven" (6:1); "Thus, when you give to the needy, sound no trumpet before you, as the hypocrites do in the synagogues and in the streets, that they may be praised by others. Truly, I say to you, they have received their reward. But when you give to the needy, do not let your left hand know what your right hand is doing, so that your giving may be in secret. And your Father who sees in secret will reward you. And when you pray, you must not be like the hypocrites. For they love to stand and pray in the synagogues and at the street corners, that they may be seen by others. Truly, I say to you, they have received their reward. But when you pray, go into your room and shut the door and pray to your Father who is in secret. And your Father who sees in secret will reward you" (6:2-6); "When you fast, do not look gloomy like the hypocrites, for they disfigure their faces that their fasting may be seen by others. Truly, I say to you, they have received their reward. But when you fast, anoint your head and wash your face, that your fasting may not be seen by others but by your Father who is in secret. And your Father who sees in secret will reward you" (6:16-18).

CHAPTER 3: MONEY IS THE FOUNDATION OF FAITHFULNESS

1. G.E. Miller, "The U.S. Is the Most Overworked Developed Nation in the World," *20somethingfinance*, January 13, 2020, https://20somethingfinance.com/american-hours-worked-productivity-vacation/.

2. Lydia Saad, "The '40-Hour' Workweek Is Actually Longer—by Seven Hours," *Gallup*, August 29, 2014, https://news.gallup.com/poll/175286/hour-workweek-actually-longer-seven-hours.aspx.

3. Dean Schaber, "Americans Work More Than Anyone," *ABC News*, January 7, 2006, https://abcnews.go.com/US/story?id=93364.

4. Mark Abadi, "11 American work habits other countries avoid at all costs," *Insider*, March 8, 2018, https://www.businessinsider.com/unhealthy-american-work-habits-2017-11.

5. Chris Isidore and Tami Luhby, "Turns out Americans work really hard...but some want to work harder," *CNN Business*, July 9, 2015, https://money.cnn.com/2015/07/09/news/economy/americans-work-bush/index.html.

6. Glassdoor Team, "Average U.S. Employee Only Takes Half of Earned Vacation Time; Glassdoor Employment Confidence Survey," *glassdoor*, April 3, 2014, https://www.glassdoor.com/blog/average-employee-takes-earned-vacation-time-glassdoor-employment-confidence-survey-q1-2014/.

7. Tommy Williams, "How hard do Americans work?," *Shreveport Times*, December 2, 2018, https://www.shreveporttimes.com/story/money/business/2018/12/02/hard-americans-work/38635019/.

CHAPTER 4: THE DANGERS OF LOVING MONEY

1. See also Proverbs 10:19; 13:3; 17:27-28.

2. See also Matthew 15:11; Mark 7:18; Acts 10:15; Romans 14:17; Colossians 2:16-23.

3. Michael Argyle, *The Psychology of Money* (United Kingdom: Routledge, 1998), 153.

4. The KJV renders 1 Timothy 6:10 as "the love of money is the root of all evil," but this is a poor translation because it changes "a root of all kinds of evils" to "root of all evil."

5. Robert Corsi, "The Monkey Trap Is not a Lemmings Myth," October 13, 2011, https://youtu.be/oAyU6wZ_ZUg.

6. J.C. Ryle, *Expository Thoughts on the Gospels* (Grand Rapids, MI: Baker Book House, 1979), 352.

CHAPTER 6: HOW TO AVOID BEING A RICH FOOL

1. John Piper, "Battling the Unbelief of Covetousness," *Desiring God*, October 30, 1988, https://www.desiringgod.org/messages/battling-the-unbelief-of-covetousness.

2. Randy Alcorn, *The Treasure Principle* (Multnomah, OR: Multnomah Books, 2003), 13.

3. J. Stephen Jordan, "Giving," *JStephenJordan.com*, September 25, 2017, https://jstephenjordan.com/2017/09/25/g/.

4. Ralph Earle, *Adam Clarke's Commentary on the Bible* (Cleveland, OH: World Publishing, 1997), 1619.

CHAPTER 7: GIVE WILLINGLY

1. The word *tithe* is a noun meaning "tenth," which is why many Christians think we should give ten percent.

2. The book of Galatians is our Declaration of Independence from the Mosaic law. Galatians 6:2 says, "Bear one another's burdens, and so fulfill the law of Christ" (ESV). The premier book about not being under the Mosaic law still commands us to "fulfill the law of Christ."

3. Leviticus 27:30-32 and Numbers 18:21-32 describe the general tithe given to the Levites. The second tithe is in Deuteronomy 14:22: "You shall tithe all the yield of your seed that comes from the field year by year" (ESV). The third tithe occurred every three years for "the sojourner, the fatherless, and the widow" (Deuteronomy 14:28-29; 26:12 ESV). The three tithes totaled about 23 percent annually.

4. Matthew 5:21-22—"You have heard that it was said to those of old, 'You shall not murder [Exodus 20:13; Deuteronomy 5:17]...But I say to you that whoever is angry with his brother shall be in danger of the judgment."

   Matthew 5:27-28—"You have heard that it was said to those of old, 'You shall not commit adultery' [Exodus 20:14; Deuteronomy 5:18]. But I say to you that whoever looks at a woman to lust for her has already committed adultery with her in his heart."

   Matthew 5:31-32—"Furthermore it has been said, 'Whoever divorces his wife, let him give her a certificate of divorce' [Deuteronomy 24:1]. But I say to you that whoever divorces his wife for any reason except sexual immorality causes her to commit adultery."

   Matthew 5:33-34—"Again you have heard that it was said to those of old, 'You shall not swear falsely, but shall perform your oaths to the Lord' [Leviticus 19:12; Numbers 30:2; Deuteronomy 23:21]...But I say to you, do not swear at all."

   Matthew 5:38-39—"You have heard that it was said, 'An eye for an eye and a tooth for a tooth' [Exodus 21:24; Leviticus 24:20; Deuteronomy 19:21]. But I tell you not to resist an evil person. But whoever slaps you on your right cheek, turn the other to him also."

   Matthew 5:43-44—"You have heard that it was said, 'You shall love your neighbor [Leviticus 19:18] and hate your enemy' [Deuteronomy 23:6]. But I say to you, love your enemies, bless those who curse you, do good to those who hate you, and pray for those who spitefully use you and persecute you."

5. The first and second instances are in Matthew 23:23 and Luke 11:42, when Jesus condemned the religious leaders: "Woe to you, scribes and Pharisees, hypocrites! For you *pay tithe* of mint and anise and cummin, and have neglected the weightier matters of the law: justice and mercy and faith. These you ought to have done, without leaving the others undone" (Matthew 23:23). Jesus said that "the others [should not have been] undone" because the New Covenant hadn't been instituted yet at the Last Supper, when Jesus said, "This cup is the new covenant in My blood, which is shed for you" (Luke 22:20). Because they were still under the Old Covenant, they were still expected to give tithes.

   The third instance of the word *tithe* is in the parable of the pharisee and the tax collector. In Luke 18:12, the Pharisee said, "I fast twice a week; I *give tithes* of all I possess."

   The last place the word *tithe* occurs is in Hebrews 7:5-9, recounting Abraham's encounter with Melchizedek and giving him a tithe. It's simply a record of the account, versus being prescriptive, or commanding us to give a tithe.

6. Warren Wiersbe, *The Bible Exposition Commentary, vol. 2: Ephesians–Revelation* (Colorado Springs, CO: David C. Cook, 1989), 656.

7. Warren W. Wiersbe, *Be Encouraged (2 Corinthians): God Can Turn Your Trials into Triumphs* (Colorado Springs, CO: David C Cook, 2010), 104.

8. Tithing was the national taxation system for the nation of Israel. The parallel for us is paying taxes, which the New Testament commands. Jesus said, "Therefore render to Caesar the things that are Caesar's, and to God the things that are God's" (Matthew 22:21 ESV), and He set an example by paying the temple tax (Matthew 17:24-27). Paul said, "Because of this you also pay taxes, for the authorities are ministers of God, attending

to this very thing. Pay to all what is owed to them: taxes to whom taxes are owed, revenue to whom revenue is owed, respect to whom respect is owed, honor to whom honor is owed" (Romans 13:6-7 esv).

9. David L. Cooper, "The Law of First Mention," *Biblical Research Monthly* (Adelanto, CA: Biblical Research Society, 1947–9), 48.

10. The Old Testament is about Jesus. Luke 24:27 says, "Beginning at Moses and all the Prophets, [Jesus] expounded to them in all the Scriptures the things concerning Himself." In Luke 24:44, Jesus said, "All things must be fulfilled which were written in the Law of Moses and the Prophets and the Psalms concerning Me.'" In John 5:39, 46, Jesus said, "You search the Scriptures, for in them you think you have eternal life; and these are they which testify of Me…For if you believed Moses, you would believe Me; for he wrote about Me." In Hebrews 10:7, Jesus said, "Behold, I have come—in the volume of the book it is written of Me."

Jesus is revealed throughout the Old Testament in types and shadows (Colossians 2:17 and Hebrews 10:1). *Shadows* are a fitting way to describe the types of Christ in the Old Testament because (1) shadows provide an idea of what something looks like without completely revealing the object. The Old Testament does this with Christ. (2) A shadow is evidence that something is casting it, or in the case of Christ, it is Someone. (3) Nobody looks at a shadow and believes it is the real thing. Nobody sees the shadow of a tree or car and thinks it is a tree or car. Shadows have no substance. They are *not* the reality. In Colossians 2:17, Jesus is the substance and in Hebrews 10:1, He is the reality. The sacrifices and offerings are some of the strongest examples.

CHAPTER 8: GIVE SACRIFICIALLY

1. G.L. Morrill, *Life as a Stewardship: Five Bible Studies of Man's Relation to Things* (Louisville, KY: Westminster John Knox, 1924), 19.

2. E. W. Lutzer, *How in This World Can I Be Holy?* (Chicago, IL: Moody Publishers, 1974), 45.

3. Donald S. Whitney, *Spiritual Disciplines for the Christian Life* (Carol Stream, IL: NavPress, 2014), 151.

4. "Church and Religious Charitable Giving Statistics," *Nonprofits Source,* accessed September 28, 2021, https://nonprofitssource.com/online-giving-statistics/church-giving/.

5. Gene Getz, *The Measure of a Man: Twenty Attributes of a Godly Man* (Raleigh, NC: Regal, 2004), 194.

CHAPTER 9: GOD'S GENEROSITY ENCOURAGES GIVING CHEERFULLY

1. John Bunyan, *The Pilgrim's Progress* (Abbotsford, WI: Aneko Press, 2015), 289.

2. John Calvin, Calvin's New Testament Commentaries, vol. 10: *2 Corinthians and Timothy, Titus, & Philemon* (Grand Rapids, MI: Wm. B. Eerdmans-Lightning Source, 1996), 121.

3. Robert Rodenmeyer, as quoted in John Blanchard, comp., *Gathered Gold: A Treasury of Quotations for Christians* (Welwyn, Hertfordshire, England: Evangelical Press, 1984), 113.

4. Charles Haddon Spurgeon, *Devotional Classics of C. H. Spurgeon* (Shallotte, NC: Sovereign Grace Publishers, 2000), 16.

CHAPTER 10: GOOD STEWARDSHIP TOWARD THE POOR

1. See also Leviticus 19:9 and Deuteronomy 24:19.

2. Traditions require wisdom because sometimes Scripture presents them positively, and other times negatively:

   - 1 Corinthians 11:2—"Now I praise you, brethren, that you remember me in all things and keep the traditions just as I delivered them to you."

   - 2 Thessalonians 2:15—"Therefore, brethren, stand fast and hold the traditions which you were taught, whether by word or our epistle."

   These verses make traditions look good, but Colossians 2:8 says, "Beware lest anyone cheat you through philosophy and empty deceit, according to the tradition of men, according to the basic principles of the world, and not according to Christ." In Mark 7, the religious leaders criticized Jesus because His disciples ate with unwashed hands. This wasn't a hygienic handwashing, but a ceremonial one that had no basis in

Scripture. Five times (in verses 3, 5, 8, 9, and 13) their handwashing is called "the tradition of the elders," "the tradition of men," or "your tradition." In Mark 7:6-12, Jesus rebuked them, saying they were hypocrites and their traditions

- "[taught] as doctrines the commandments of men" (verse 7).
- "[laid] aside the commandment of God" (verse 8).
- "[were kept to] reject the commandment of God" (verse 9).
- "[made] the word of God of no effect" (verse 13).

People in the early church could determine which traditions to follow by reading the Scriptures and obeying the teachings from the apostles, such as Paul and Peter. Acts 2:42 says the early church "continued steadfastly in the apostles' teaching and fellowship, in the breaking of bread, and in prayers."

3. 1 Corinthians 4:16; 11:1; Philippians 3:17; 4:9; 1 Thessalonians 1:6; 2 Thessalonians 3:7-9.

4. Jeff Robinson, "How Should Pastors Approach the Salary Question?" *TGC*, September 19, 2018, https://www.thegospelcoalition.org/article/pastors-approach-salary-question/.

5. Thom S. Rainier, "Five Things You Should Know about Pastors' Salaries," *Church Answers*, December 17, 2012, https://thomrainer.com/2012/12/five-things-you-should-know-about-pastors-salaries/.

6. Charles H. Spurgeon, *The Spurgeon Archive*, accessed August 19, 2019, http://archive.spurgeon.org/misc/plowman.php.

7. Isaiah 20:4; 47:3; Nahum 3:5; Micah 1:11; Revelation 3:18 and 16:15.

CHAPTER 11: SPENDING PROBLEMS VERSUS AN INCOME PROBLEM

1. Warren W. Wiersbe, *Be Compassionate (Luke 1-13): Let the World Know That Jesus Cares* (Colorado Springs, CO: David C. Cook, 2010), 163.

2. Patrick Sisson, "Self-storage: How warehouses for personal junk became a $38 billion industry," *Curbed*, March 27, 2018, https://www.curbed.com/2018/3/27/17168088/cheap-storage-warehouse-self-storage-real-estate.

3. Heather Timmons, "America's largest movie theater chains," *The Atlas*, accessed September 28, 2021, https://www.theatlas.com/charts/N1Tu4Izne.

4. "Showtime Is Snacktime," AMC Theatres, accessed September 28, 2021, https://www.amctheatres.com/food-and-drink/order-ahead.

5. Yuichi Shoda, Walter Mischel, Philip K. Peake, "Predicting Adolescent Cognitive and Self-Regulatory Competencies from Preschool Delay of Gratification: Identifying Diagnostic Conditions," *Developmental Psychology* (1990), 26 (6): 978–986. doi:10.1037/0012-1649.26.6.978, archived from the original (PDF) on October 4, 2011.

CHAPTER 12: GOD'S VIEW OF DEBT

1. Rod Rogers, *Pastor Driven Stewardship: 10 Steps to Lead Your Church to Biblical Giving* (Dallas, TX: Brown Books, 2006), 228.

2. Howard Taylor, *The Story of the China Inland Mission* (London: Morgan & Scott, 2008), 238.

3. Michael Farris, *The Homeschooling Father* (Nashville, TN: B & H Publishing Group, 2002), 110.

4. Michael A. Gayed, "COVID-19 Debt: Impact and Consequences," *Seeking Alpha*, August 20, 2020, https://seekingalpha.com/article/4371399-covidminus-19-debt-impact-and-consequences.

5. Alberto Alesina, Carlo A. Favero, and Francesco Giavazzi, "Climbing Out of Debt," *IMF F&D Magazine*, March 2018, vol. 55, no. 1, https://www.imf.org/external/pubs/ft/fandd/2018/03/alesina.htm.

6. Brian Riedl, "Why Government Spending Does Not Stimulate Economic Growth," *The Heritage Foundation*, November 12, 2008, https://www.heritage.org/budget-and-spending/report/why-government-spending-does-not-stimulate-economic-growth.

7. The earliest known attribution of this quote was October 20, 1948, in what appears to be an op-ed piece in *The Daily Oklahoman* under the byline Elmer T. Peterson: "This Is the Hard Core of Freedom," *The*

Daily Oklahoman, 19. The quote has not been found in Tytler's work. It has also been attributed to Alexis de Tocqueville.

8. Jay H. Brown, *Truth in Government: Restoring Pride and Prosperity in America* (San Antonio, TX: Freedom Publishing Company, 1996), 32.

9. The Associated Press, "Standard & Poor's Warns It May Downgrade U.S. Credit Rating," *Fox News*, December 23, 2015, https://www.foxnews.com/politics/standard-poors-warns-it-may-downgrade-u-s-credit-rating.

10. John Harwood, Patti Domm, Allen Wastler, and Kate Kelly, "S&P Downgrades US Credit Rating to AA-Plus," *CNBC.com*, August 6, 2011, https://www.cnbc.com/id/44039103.

11. Shaun Rein, "US Downgrade to Worsen China's Inflation Problem," *CNBC.com*, August 8, 2011, https://www.cnbc.com/id/44053534.

12. Dann Albright, "Average American Household Debt in 2020: Facts and Figures," *The Ascent*, November 18, 2000, https://www.fool.com/the-ascent/research/average-american-household-debt/.

13. Cortney Moore, "Some Americans have more credit card debt than emergency savings," *Fox Business*, February 20, 2020, https://www.foxbusiness.com/money/americans-credit-card-debt-emergency-savings.

14. U.S. News Staff, "Average Credit Card APR," *US News*, September 8, 2021, https://creditcards.usnews.com/articles/average-apr.

15. Kelly Anne Smith, "Americans say their biggest financial regret is not saving for retirement sooner," *Bankrate*, May 29, 2019, https://www.bankrate.com/banking/savings/financial-security-may-2019/.

16. Rick Popely, "Car Depreciation: How Much It Costs You," *CARFAX*, February 3, 2021, https://www.carfax.com/blog/car-depreciation.

17. Ramsey Solutions, "The Truth About Car Payments," *Ramsey*, September 24, 2021, https://www.daveramsey.com/blog/the-truth-about-car-payments/.

18. Jeff Rose, "The #1 Payment Killing Your Wealth," *Forbes*, October 2, 2018, https://www.forbes.com/sites/jrose/2018/10/02/the-one-monthly-payment-killing-your-wealth/.

19. Federal Reserve Bank of New York, *Household Debt and Credit Report*, (Q2 2021), https://www.newyorkfed.org/microeconomics/hhdc.html.

20. Riley Griffin, Suborna Panja, Kristina D'alessio, "As rates and tuition rise, America's student loan debt crisis could get much worse," *Los Angeles Times*, October 18, 2018, https://www.latimes.com/business/la-fi-student-loan-debt-20181018-story.html.

21. The Institute for College Access and Success, *Student Debt and the Class of 2019*, October 2020, PDF download, https://ticas.org/wp-content/uploads/2020/10/classof2019.pdf.

22. Board of Governors of the Federal Reserve System, *Report on the Economic Well-Being of US Households in 2016 to May 2017*, June 14, 2017, https://www.federalreserve.gov/publications/2017-economic-well-being-of-us-households-in-2016-education-debt-loans.htm.

23. Abigail Johnson Hess, "College grads expect to pay off student debt in 6 years—this is how long it will actually take," *CNBC*, May 23, 2019, https://www.cnbc.com/2019/05/23/cengage-how-long-it-takes-college-grads-to-pay-off-student-debt.html.

24. Ramsey Solutions, "Overcoming the Student Loan Crisis," October 12, 2021, https://www.ramseysolutions.com/debt/student-loan-crisis.

25. Ramsey Solutions, "The State of Personal Finance 2021 Q1," September 24, 2021, https://www.ramseysolutions.com/debt/state-of-personal-finance-2021-q1-research.

26. Maryalene LaPonsie, "25 Best Jobs That Don't Require a College Degree," *US News and World*, January 28, 2021, https://money.usnews.com/money/careers/slideshow/25-best-jobs-that-dont-require-a-college-degree.

27. Rebecca Lake, "Rule of Thumb: How Much Should You Spend on Rent?," *The Balance*, August 9, 2021, https://www.thebalance.com/what-percentage-of-your-income-should-go-to-rent-4688840.

28. Dave Ramsey, *The Total Money Makeover* (Nashville, TN: Thomas Nelson, 2013), 187.

29. Frank James, "Nearly One in Four U.S. Homes with Mortgages 'Underwater'," NPR, November 24, 2009, https://www.npr.org/sections/thetwo-way/2009/11/one_in_four_us_homes_underwate.html.

30. Stan Humphries, "Negative Equity Down by Almost Half Since 2012 Peak, But There's Still a Ways to Go," *Zillow*, December 16, 2014, https://www.zillow.com/research/negative-equity-2014-q3-8532/.

31. Lisa Prevost, "A Decline in Problem Mortgages," *The New York Times*, January 2, 2015, https://www.nytimes.com/2015/01/04/realestate/a-decline-in-problem-mortgages.html.

32. Marilyn Geewax, "You Be The Judge: Is The Housing Market Really Improving?," *NPR*, March 21, 2013, https://www.npr.org/2013/03/21/174873797/you-be-the-judge-is-the-housing-market-really-improving.

33. NPR News, "A Decade Out From The Mortgage Crisis, Former Homeowners Still Grasp For Stability," *KTOO*, May 22, 2016, https://www.ktoo.org/2016/05/22/decade-mortgage-crisis-former-homeowners-still-grasp-stability/.

34. Irina Ivanova, "Nearly 19 million Americans could lose their homes when eviction limits expire Dec. 31," *CBS News*, November 27, 2020, https://www.cbsnews.com/news/eviction-19-million-americans-risk-moratorium-coronavirus/.

CHAPTER 13: AVOIDING AND ELIMINATING DEBT

1. Rod Rogers, *Pastor Driven Stewardship: 10 Steps to Lead Your Church to Biblical Giving* (Dallas, TX: Brown Books, 2006), 230-231.

2. Charles H. Spurgeon, *The Promises of God* (Wheaton, IL: Crossway, 2019), 24.

CHAPTER 14: SAVING THE RIGHT AND WRONG WAY

1. "New Years Resolution Poll 2020-2021," *YouGov*, December 12, 2020, PDF download, https://docs.cdn.yougov.com/2v6sawx0rr/US_New_Years_Resolutions_2020.pdf.

2. Harrison Monarth, "You've Already Abandoned Your New Year's Resolution. Here's a Better Path to Reach Your Goals," *Entrepreneur*, January 14, 2019, https://www.entrepreneur.com/article/326096.

3. David Guzik, "2 Timothy 3—Perilous Times and Precious Truth," *Enduring Word*, accessed September 29, 2021, https://enduringword.com/bible-commentary/2-timothy-3/.

4. Christina Cheddar Berk, "More Couples Arguing About Money, Sneaking Purchases," *CNBC*, May 9, 2011, https://www.cnbc.com/id/42916288.

5. Kathleen Elkins, "Here's how much money Americans have in their savings accounts," *CNBC*, September 13, 2017, https://www.cnbc.com/2017/09/13/how-much-americans-at-have-in-their-savings-accounts.html.

6. "'Getting Paid In America' Survey Results," *National Payroll Week*, October 2018, PDF download, https://www.nationalpayrollweek.com/wp-content/uploads/2018/10/2018GettingPaidInAmericaSurveyResults.pdf.

7. Kelly Anne Smith, "Americans say their biggest financial regret is not saving for retirement sooner," *Bankrate*, May 29, 2019, https://www.bankrate.com/banking/savings/financial-security-may-2019/.

8. Paul Katzeff, "Americans Confess Their Biggest Financial Regrets," *Investor's Business Daily*, September 25, 2019, https://www.investors.com/etfs-and-funds/personal-finance/financial-mistakes-americans-learn-from-biggest-financial-regrets/.

9. Ramsey Solutions, "Return on Investment: The 12% Reality," *Ramsey*, September 27, 2021, https://www.daveramsey.com/blog/the-12-reality/.

10. See also Proverbs 16:11; 20:10, 23. The book itself opens with a stern warning against obtaining money illegally (Proverbs 1:10-19). These schemes lead to prison or even death. Amos 8:5 condemned cheating others: "Offer wheat for sale, that we may make the ephah small and the shekel great and deal deceitfully with false balances" (ESV). They skimped on what was owed, overcharged, and accomplished this with dishonest scales.

11. Multiple variations of this story have appeared over the last several decades, and this is one such variation.

CHAPTER 15: RETIRING WELL

1. Tristin Hopper, "In 1905, a Canadian hero said old people were useless—and sparked an Internet-sized public shaming," *National Post*, September 22, 2016, https://nationalpost.com/news/canada/in-1905-a-canadian-hero-said-old-people-were-useless-and-sparked-an-internet-sized-public-shaming.

2. William Osler, *The Principles and Practice of Medicine* (New York: Appleton and Company, 1899), 109.

3. John Piper, *Rethinking Retirement: Finishing Life for the Glory of Christ* (Wheaton, IL: Crossway, 2009), 6.

CHAPTER 16: THE GREATEST RICHES

1. David Platt, *Follow Me: A Call to Die. A Call to Live* (Carol Stream, IL: Tyndale, 2013), 110.

2. John MacArthur, *The MacArthur Bible Commentary* (Nashville, TN: Thomas Nelson, 2005), 1421.

3. Jonathan Edwards, *Religious Affections* (New Haven, CT: Yale University Press, 1959), 339 (emphasis added).

About the Author

Scott is the senior pastor of Woodland Christian Church in Woodland, Washington, and a conference speaker. He holds an MA in Biblical Studies from Liberty University. Scott and his wife, Katie, grew up together in northern California, and God has blessed them with nine children, with the ninth on the way when the above photograph was taken. You can contact Pastor Scott or learn more about him at the following:

- Website: www.scottlapierre.org
- Facebook: @ScottLaPierreMinistries
- YouTube: @ScottLaPierre
- Twitter: @PastorWCC
- Instagram: @PastorWCC

Subscribe to Pastor Scott's newsletter (www.scottlapierre.org/subscribe) and receive:

- Free gifts and resources such as videos of his conference messages and guest preaching
- Updates on his ministry, including his upcoming books, and invitations to the book launch teams
- Insights into his life and family

Would you like to invite Scott to a speaking event?

Pastor Scott is a frequent speaker at churches, conferences, and retreat centers. He speaks on a variety of topics that build up believers and serve as an outreach to share Christ with your community.

For more information, including sample messages and endorsements, please visit: www.scottlapierre.org/conferences-and-speaking.

If you would like to contact Scott for a speaking engagement, please do so here: www.scottlapierre.org/contact/.

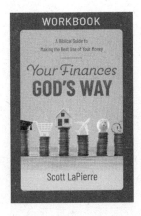

YOUR FINANCES GOD'S WAY WORKBOOK

Move beyond your financial fears by applying a practical plan to spending, saving, and paying off debt. This companion workbook to *Your Finances God's Way* gives you opportunity not only to further explore the Bible's financial wisdom and strategies, but also to do more in-depth personal money management.

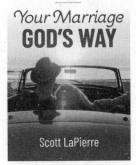

YOUR MARRIAGE GOD'S WAY

With *Your Marriage God's Way*, you'll learn what the Bible reveals about God's original design for the unbreakable commitment between a man and a woman, and how you can have a healthy and joyful relationship centered on Christ.

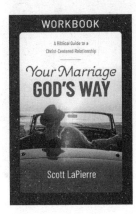

YOUR MARRIAGE GOD'S WAY WORKBOOK

This interactive companion to *Your Marriage God's Way* invites you to work together with your spouse to take a closer look at the biblical principles for a healthy, Christ-centered marriage relationship and make them an active part of your own union.

To learn more about Harvest House books and
to read sample chapters, visit our website:

www.HarvestHousePublishers.com

HARVEST HOUSE PUBLISHERS
EUGENE, OREGON